SON OF

A Maya

TECÚN UMÁN

ndian Tells His Life Story

James D. Sexton
EDITOR

THE UNIVERSITY OF ARIZONA PRESS
Tucson, Arizona

About the Editor ...

JAMES D. SEXTON has worked with Ignacio Bizarro Ujpán since his first field trip to Guatemala as part of an anthropological team in 1970. His most recent work focuses on development and modernization in fourteen towns surrounding Lake Atitlán in the department of Sololá. Since 1973 Sexton has taught anthropology at Northern Arizona University. He holds a Ph.D. in cultural anthropology from the University of California at Los Angeles and is author of a monograph and several articles on highland Guatemala.

Second printing 1985

THE UNIVERSITY OF ARIZONA PRESS

Copyright © 1981
The Arizona Board of Regents
All Rights Reserved
Manufactured in the U.S.A.
This book was set in 10/12 V-I-P Caledonia

Library of Congress Cataloging in Publication Data

Bizarro Ujpán, Ignacio.
    Son of Tecún Umán.

    Includes index.
    1. Bizarro Ujpán, Ignacio.   2. Tzutuhil Indians
—Social conditions.   3. Indians of Central America
—Guatemala—Social conditions.   4. Tzutuhil Indians
—Biography.   I. Sexton, James D.   II. Title.
F1465.2.T9B59   972.81'004970924 [B]   81-11702

ISBN 0-8165-0736-8   AACR2
ISBN 0-8165-0751-1(pbk.)

❧ Contents

Background of the Story

☙Background of the Story

This is the life story of a Tzutuhil Maya Indian who resides on the shores of Lake Atitlán in the department of Sololá, Republic of Guatemala. For the sake of anonymity, we shall call him Ignacio Bizarro Ujpán, and his town we shall name San José la Laguna. Ignacio's story is based on his autobiography, written in 1972, and a five-year diary he kept from 1972–1977. Ignacio is bilingual, fluent in both Tzutuhil Maya, a branch of Quiché Maya, and in Spanish, the national language of Guatemala.

Tecún Umán, a national hero in Guatemala, was the ancient Quiché warrior prince who was killed in hand-to-hand combat with Don Pedro de Alvarado, who conquered Guatemala in the early 1500s. Tecún Umán and his warriors, who battled the Spaniards as they marched into the Guatemalan highlands from Mexico, have given Ignacio and other Mayans a heritage of which they are proud.

More than anything else this is a book about Ignacio's life,[1] his people, his town, and his country. It gives the reader some understanding of what it means to be a Joseño, or person of San José, and of the nature of the problems that Ignacio and thousands of others like him face on a day-to-day basis as inhabitants of Central America.

Ignacio wrote in longhand most of his life's story in Spanish; the rest I tape-recorded. With Ignacio's consent, I have assigned pseudonyms to nearly everyone whose name appears in the text. And with the exception of Panajachel and Sololá, I have changed the names of the towns surrounding the lake along with the villages, hills, rivers, and place names. All the proper names, however, are names that can be found in Guatemala.

I met Ignacio in 1970 when I began my first anthropological

3

fieldwork in San José as part of a team of researchers studying the towns surrounding Lake Atitlán. Ignacio lived across a rocky, unpaved street from the house where I lived. When I asked him to be my research assistant, he agreed. Two years later, toward the end of my third season in Guatemala, I decided to approach Ignacio about writing his autobiography and keeping a diary. I asked him to write his own life history including what was happening in his town and in his family, with his friends, his religious activities, his work, and even his dreams.

By the fall of 1974, Ignacio had given me the first Spanish draft of his story and diary to date, and by the summer of 1975 I had completed the first English version of his story. In successive trips to Guatemala I asked Ignacio to amplify certain events in his autobiography and diary that he had only touched on in his first draft. The questions that I used to solicit more specific details have been included in italics throughout the text, and I have indicated when a whole episode has been inserted that Ignacio had originally omitted. In this manner the reader can better discern how much and what kind of information Ignacio volunteered and how much of it is material I solicited from my own perspective.

As I edited the story, one type of information I considered redundant was Ignacio's description in successive years of the routine events of holidays such as Christmas and All Saints' Day. Other kinds of information that I judged as trivial included repetition regarding the kinds of meals he ate each day, the saying of his nightly prayers, his daily work routine, how well he slept, and common illnesses like colds and headaches.[2]

What contributes to the uniqueness of this account is that at age 31 Ignacio wrote an autobiography and began keeping a diary in which he recorded life for eight years in a community that has neither a literate nor historical tradition. Ignacio was able to document beliefs and behavior that I would have had limited access to even if I were living in San José the year around. He was able to attend, for example, the celebration of the unauthorized brotherhood, Maximón, and record the immediate response of those who were banned from the church by the priest because of their participation.[3]

As of the writing of this introduction (March 1981), Ignacio was continuing to keep his diary. The last entries published here, however, were written in February 1977, when he and the people of San José celebrated a mass in memory of thousands of their comrades who perished in the February 4, 1976, earthquake. Because this was the last event in a group of several pages that Ignacio had sent me, it made a natural ending.

✎ The Land and People

Of the seven countries that make up Middle America (Costa Rica, El Salvador, Guatemala, Honduras, Mexico, Nicaragua, and Panama), Guatemala is fourth in size with 42,044 square miles, but it is second in population, estimated in 1979 at 6,849,000 of which 54 percent were Maya Indians, 42 percent Ladinos, and 4 percent whites, mostly Spanish and German (Lane 1981:540). In a 1959– 1962 census (which has not been repeated recently) Guatemala was compared with the other Middle American countries with respect to the number and percent of Amerinds, or native Americans. The results were that Guatemala had a more absolute number of Indians than any other Middle American country with the exception of Mexico, but it had the largest percentage of Indians— 53.6 percent of the total population (Ruddle and Barrows (1974:102).

A special tabulation of the 1950 census (which was not repeated in subsequent years) shows that, of the three major groups of Quiché-Maya-speaking Indians living in Guatemala, Ignacio's group, the Tzutuhil, is the smallest, accounting for only 1.9 percent of the total Indian-speaking population, and 18,761 individuals. Of the other two groups, the Quiché is the largest with 33.6 percent of the population and 339,232 individuals, followed by the Cakchiquel with 16.6 percent and 167,352 individuals (Whetten 1961:56).[4]

The ancestors of the Quiché, Cakchiquel, and Tzutuhil Maya elite were a Nonoalca-Pipil-Chichimec mixture of warlike groups who migrated from Mexico into the highlands of Guatemala along the river routes during the early postclassic period (A.D. 1000– 1200). They competed with earlier Mexican immigrants, the Pipi-Nicarao, who had established commercial relationships with the original inhabitants, the Pokomam and Mam. Eventually, the more recent Mexican (Indian) migrants extended their influence over the entire central highlands (De Borhegyi 1965), and became warring rivals over political and economic dominance of the region.

The lords and leaders settled in three major areas—the Cakchiquel at Iximché, the Quiché at Utatlán, and the Tzutuhil at

Atitlán. Gradually these hilltop settlements developed urban characteristics, but rather than becoming urban centers like Teotihuacán or Tenochtitlán in Mexico that permanently housed large numbers of residents, they were more like European castles and fortress towns. In peacetime, they were used as temporary quarters for festivals and market activities. During war they served as strongholds for the warrior classes and as a refuge for the outlying populations and satellite villages. Each royal fortress was protected by natural geographical features—Iximché and Utatlán by deep ravines and Atitlán by Lake Atitlán and the volcano Nimajuyú (now called San Pedro by some) which reaches 9,908 feet in elevation (De Borhegyi 1965; Aguirre 1972).

Stone and plaster (burnt limestone) buildings housed the king and his royal officials and their families. The commoners lived in scattered hamlets of huts made of mud, cane, and straw. They supported the lords with tribute such as beans, corn, and squash from the surrounding fields.

Because of their expansionist policy and an interest in the rich cacao lands of the Pacific slopes, Mexicans from Tenochtitlán (Aztecs) founded a colony of Pipils at a coastal region called Soconusco. Traveling Mexican merchants traded not only with these Pipils but also with the Tzutuhils, Cakchiquels, and Quichés. From Mexico they brought copper, cloth, and wooden products, and they exchanged these for cacao, coastal cotton, and iridescent feathers of the quetzal bird found in the Guatemalan highlands. In an attempt to control the trade with Mexico, the Tzutuhils, Cakchiquels, Quichés, and Pipils formed and broke alliances frequently with one another (De Borhegyi 1965; Miles 1965).

If the Spaniards had not arrived in the early 1500s, it is conceivable that the Aztecs might have conquered the Maya of the Guatemalan highlands. Their influence was marked by the tribute the Pipils of Soconusco were paying to Mexico well before the arrival of the Spaniards (Miles 1965) and also by Montezuma's network of communication with the Pipils and the Cakchiquels.

In any case, Pedro de Alvarado, Cortez' handsome and daring lieutenant, entered Guatemala in 1524 with 570 soldiers and 300 Indian allies from Mexico. With superior weaponry and tactics, he broke the violent resistance of the Quichés by killing Tecún Umán, the warrior prince, in a fierce battle near Quezaltenango. Like the Aztecs, the Cakchiquels mistook the Spaniards for returning gods, and the conquerors marched into Iximché without resistance. The Cakchiquels then joined ranks with the Spaniards, and they con-

quered Atitlán (Muñoz and Ward 1940; Recinos et al 1953; Díaz in Mackie 1972).

The Spaniards replaced the Indian nobility at the top of the social hierarchy in the Guatemalan highlands and throughout Middle America. A plural society composed of different ethnic elements in a single social structure was created. This structure was based on ethnic differences that placed the Spaniards in the upper levels and the Indians in the lower ones.

By the time Guatemala and the rest of Middle America broke away from Spain in 1821, culture, class and race had become the criteria used to define an Indian from a non-Indian.

Whereas the Indian wore native dress and spoke an Indian dialect as his mother tongue, the Spaniard wore Western clothing and spoke Spanish as his first language. While the Indian had the role of the rural peasant or farm hand, the Ladino was the administrator. The Indian was thought to have Mongoloid genes, the Ladino was believed to be more Caucasoid. Although these characteristics were clearly marked shortly after the conquest, by the time of independence they were becoming blurred.

Class and occupation are also important variables today, and it is an exception to find people identified as Indians enjoying middle class positions and jobs. Indians are usually found in the towns working as artisans or farming nearby fields or both. In some towns Indians hold service occupations catering to tourism. In ethnically mixed towns the Indian clearly occupies an inferior social position. Even the term indio (Indian) carries a negative connotation, and it is not used in polite or official language. Instead, the words natural (native) or indígena (indigene) are preferred. In contrast the term Ladino has no negative connotations.

Since many Indians speak Spanish and adopt Ladino material culture, the best description of an Indian is one who identifies himself or herself and is identified by others as being Indian. In any case, in the urban centers such as Guatemala City, the upper stratum of society is mostly of European descent. Spanish emigrants tend to own grocery stores, bars, and money lending businesses. Many large plantation owners, especially those growing coffee, are of German descent.

Lake Atitlán

Few have described the majestic beauty of Lake Atitlán more graphically than John Lloyd Stevens who passed through the area

*during his bold explorations in the mid-1800s with his companion,
the artist Frederick Catherwood:*

> *...I have forborne attempting to give any idea of the magnifi-
> cent scenery amid which we were traveling, but here fore-
> bearance would be a sin. From a height of three or four
> thousand feet we looked down upon a surface shining like a
> sheet of molten silver, enclosed by rocks and mountains of
> every form, some barren, and some covered with verdure,
> rising five hundred to five thousand feet in height. Opposite,
> down on the border of the lake, and apparently inaccessible
> by land, was the town of Santiago Atitlán ... situated between
> two immense volcanoes eight or ten thousand feet high.
> Farther on was another volcano, and farther still another,
> more lofty than all, with its summit buried in the clouds ...
> We both agreed that it was the most magnificent spectacle we
> ever saw. (Stephens 1969:157–158)*

*Despite some unpleasant signs of encroaching development, his
description is as fitting today as it was then. Lake Atitlán is
60 miles west of Guatemala City in the midwestern highlands
of the Guatemalan Republic. Lying 5,100 feet above sea level in
a basin about 10 miles wide and 20 miles long (McBryde 1933:33),
the fresh water lake spans approximately 11 miles from east to
west and 6 miles from north to south, reaching a maximal depth of
1,112 feet (Serrano 1974:14).*

*In the department of Sololá there are 19 municipios (political
and geographical subdivisions of departments, the 22 major di-
visions of the republic), and each municipio has its own cabecera
(main town) and often aldeas (villages). Although the Indian populations in all the towns share a general Mayan heritage, there is
considerable cultural variation both between and within towns
(Sexton and Woods 1977). The Indian inhabitants of the towns still
speak one of the three Maya-Quiché dialects—Quiché, Cakchiquel or Tzutuhil—as their mother tongue, and, while these three
dialects are similar and mutually intelligible, there are some lexi-
cal items peculiar to each community (Nash 1969). All of the communities share such Maya-derived cultural patterns as kinds of
indigenous dress, but the colors, styles, and patterns vary from
town to town. As Manning Nash (1969) notes, Guatemalan highland towns differ more in the way traits are combined and emphasized than in the presence or absence of certain traits.*

*Individual towns in the lake region are known for their spe-
cialized economic pursuits—San Jorge for rope making, Santa*

Apolonia for fishing, San Luis for trading, San Martín for cash cropping—and their participation in a system of economic exchange that involves rotating market days in each town. But most of the inhabitants in the towns also engage in subsistence horticulture, growing such staples as indigenous corn, beans, squash and tomatoes and diffused crops such as onions, potatoes, and carrots. Many families have their own coffee, avocado and lemon trees. Surplus produce usually is sold for small amounts of cash.

Since the 1920s paved highways have contributed to opening up the towns to tourism and to easing the transport of coffee from local fincas *(farms). Financial opportunities from these enterprises have attracted increasing numbers of Ladinos to the area. In the more underdeveloped towns like San José, however, the few resident Ladinos tend to be the municipal secretaries, government nurses and medics, and school teachers and their families. The percentage of resident Ladinos varies in the urban sectors, ranging from .2 percent in Santa Rosa la Laguna to 42 percent in Panajachel (Dirección General de Estadísticas 1973).*

The influx of Ladinos, tourists, and emigrants has allowed some Indians to become independent shopkeepers and merchants. Also, it has created a number of service occupations in hotels and restaurants and in chalets *(vacation homes). In some towns these new jobs have replaced farming as the primary occupation, although employees often continue to work the land as well. The degree to which a town is developed determines the extent to which its inhabitants are involved in nonagricultural pursuits.*

San José la Laguna

Territory and Population. According to Gerardo Aguirre *(1972), who examined the history of several Tzutuhil towns through parochial records, the Tzutuhils were living in the area of San José before it was established as a municipality. They contributed to Don Pedro de Alvarado's* encomienda *(a system of the Spanish Crown that allowed conquerors and colonists to demand tribute and labor from Indians while supposedly providing them with religious instruction and military protection but without gaining jurisdictional and land rights that would make them feudal lords, though some* encomenderos *acted like lords). Based on census information of an early* encomendero *and a subsequent* corregidor *(royal magistrate), San José became a* cabecera *with its own mayors and councilmen by the early 1600s.*

In the early 1600s there were about 100 adults living in San José. By the mid-1970s the number increased considerably, but San José's total population was still relatively small with less than 4,500 total individuals living on less than 54 square kilometers of land. The urban and rural populations are about equally divided, but the urban population is over 90 percent Tzutuhil Maya whereas the rural population is nearly 100 percent Quiché Maya who live in three aldeas; Pachichaj, Tzarayá, and Patzilín. Although San José is not as densely populated as some other lakeside towns and its rate of percent natural increase is somewhat lower (Sexton and Woods 1981), there is still a severe land shortage. The fertility of the once volcanically rich land has been weakened by continual use and the lack of natural and commercial fertilizers, which are expensive to the farmers. Much of the good land that Joseños owned was lost to their enterprising neighbors of a town called San Martín who gained title to it during the mandamientos *(forced labor sponsored by the national government) of the early 1900s that required* Joseños *to migrate to work on the coastal plantations. Consequently,* Joseños *are often forced to rent land that once belonged to them from* Martineros *(people of San Martín), when* Martineros *are not farming it themselves. Otherwise,* Joseños *migrate to the coast to grow corn or to work as wage laborers on the cotton plantations. Some fertile land is worked on the steep slopes of mountains and volcanoes, but this is somewhat hazardous because of the possibility of heavy rains washing away the crops and topsoil and because of the danger of falling from the cliffs.*

Businesses. *There is no weekly market in San José, and for that reason* Joseños *usually walk to neighboring towns of San Martín or Santa Ana to purchase necessities. On Tuesdays, Fridays and Sundays they may take a public launch to Panajachel, shopping in the stores or the Friday market of Sololá or the Sunday market of Panajachel. Occasionally they will travel by bus or truck to Guatemala City and buy goods there.*

Small items such as cokes, beer, rum, wine, pastries, and canned juice may be purchased in seven little shops scattered throughout San José. Since the arrival of electricity in 1972, two of the shops now have refrigerators for keeping drinks cold. In addition six bars specialize in alcoholic beverages. One baker makes regular and sweet bread; two candle factories produce small and large candles.

A poultry farm does a rather brisk business in eggs and chickens. Two small meat shops and one small pork shop operate out of homes, but an outsider would only be able to recognize them by the red flags waving above the windows that signal the availability of meat. One family has a few milk cows providing dairy products, and another family has an inconspicuous comedor (small restaurant) near the Catholic Church.

Unlike more developed towns around the lake such as Panajachel and San Luis, San José does not have any hotels or boarding houses. Also there is no resident doctor or pharmacy, but there is a public eye and health clinic manned by a nurse or medic. There is no resident priest or missionary.

San José has one coffee plantation, but not many Joseños are working in this enterprise. Most Joseños have their own trees that produce coffee for home consumption and the market. A few families make rope from maguey.

Transportation, Housing, and Communication. San José differs from towns such as San Carlos and San Diego because it does not have a paved road linking it directly to urban centers. A medium-sized passenger bus Reina Martinera (Queen of San Martín) provides transportation from San José to Guatemala City and other towns via San Martín, San Luis and San Diego, but the road is unpaved and rocky until it passes San Diego. Consequently, the trip is bumpy, slow and tiring. In part, poor transportation and inadequate municipal facilities account for the absence of tourists and part-time residents who build vacation chalets.

The only newspapers readily available in San José are received at the mayor's office. Centroamérica arrives every other day and the Oficial every fifteen days. There is no library in San José, and the teachers report that schools do not receive newspapers, magazines or books.

Communication by electronic media is becoming more evident in San José. About half the families have portable radios; two families have purchased televisions; and three have radiolas (large, cabinet radios with record players). Occasionally, motion pictures are shown in the Catholic Church by the priest from San Martín.

House styles range from the traditional cane or adobe walls with straw roofs and dirt floors to plastered walls with sheet metal roofs and cement floors. Spanish tile is still a popular roofing material. Houses are usually one-room structures with corner *kitchens which consist of three stones on the floor for cooking with firewood from the surrounding hills. In some homes the kitchen is a separate room, and it has a raised cooking hearth. Thus, the roofs are often caked with black smoke from the wood fires, but the smoke helps keep the insects away.*

Furnishings are meager with a simple dining table and wooden chairs either adult or child size. Beds may be wooden or iron with straw mattresses or mats. Large mats may partition a room and help keep out the cold from the sleeping quarters. Since 1972, several homes have received electrical lighting, but only the mayor's office has a telephone. None of the houses has indoor toilet facilities.

***The School.** The primary school in San José began offering a first-grade education in 1939. In 1940 a second grade was added; in 1952 a third grade; in 1960 a fourth grade; in 1964, when a new building was constructed, a fifth grade; and in 1967 a sixth grade. By 1969 there were 197 students, 107 boys and 90 girls, and it was necessary to continue to use the older, adobe school house due to lack of space. In 1972 the total number of students had increased by only 5 although the proportion of boys (125) to girls (77) differed. During 1972 a general health clinic was established in one of the two rooms of the older school building. By 1976 enrollment increased sharply to 130 boys and 129 girls, and a nearby house was converted into an extra classroom. Seven teachers instruct in seven classrooms—two rooms of Castellanización (a grade for learning basic Spanish); two rooms for the first grade; one room for the second grade; one room for the fourth and fifth grades combined; and one room for the fifth and sixth grades combined.*

Primary schooling is mandatory for children ages 7 to 14. The academic year begins in January and lasts through early October. Until June 1975, the daily schedule of classes was from 8:00 A.M. to 12:00 noon and from 2:00 P.M. until 4:00 P.M., Monday through Friday, and from 8:00 A.M. to 12:00 noon on Saturday. To better accommodate parents who needed students to work in the fields, the weekday schedule was changed from 7:30 A.M. to 1:00 P.M. and on July 3, 1976, the half-day on Saturday was discontinued.

Students must buy their own pencils, pens and notebooks which average about $1.08 per year. To some families this sum may be more than nominal, but as of the 1970s fewer students were dropping out of elementary school because of excessive expenses or loss of time they could spend in the fields.

The primary school, which is designed to prepare the student for secondary school, plans curricula around the following subject areas: Spanish language; mathematics; social studies; science; agriculture; industrial arts and home economics; aesthetic education, including plastic arts and music; and health and safety, including theory and physical education.

Formal education is strongly associated with exposure to electronic and printed media (nonformal education) and with acculturation to Ladino culture. But this does not necessarily imply identification as Ladino (Sexton 1979a, 1979b).

Municipal and Government Employees. *In the recent past civil cargos (burdens or offices) were ranked and intertwined with the religious cargos of the brotherhoods. Before the 1944 Revolution, service in the civil-religious cargos was mandatory even though it might be expensive in money and time lost from work. Today, one may only be forced to serve in the civil offices, and these are usually the lower ranking ones such as alguacil (constable, policeman). The higher offices such as mayor and síndico (syndic) are elected. Because serving in the higher offices brings pride and prestige, there are usually candidates running for these offices under the banner of one of the four political parties of the Guatemalan Republic.*

There is a trend now for national government officials such as postmen to replace local civil officers such as alguaciles. But in San José, which is less developed in this regard than towns like Panajachel and San Diego, fewer of the functions of the traditional hierarchy of civil offices have been replaced by salaried national officials. Unlike the mayors in the larger towns, the mayor of San José only began receiving a salary from the town treasury in 1976, and then the amount was just $30 per month. The only other paid public officials are the town secretary-treasurer, who is selected by the current, elected tribunal, (in 1976, $90 per month), the nurses (in 1971, $60 per month for the eye clinic and $70 per month for the general health clinic); and the school teachers (a base of $100 per month that rose to $160 per month in 1976).

Religion. *The ancestors of the present Tzutuhils were under the influence of Mexican Indians. They identified their god with Quetzalcoatl, the Aztec god; they called a class of priests and the coastal Pipil "Yaqui," or sacrificers; and they believed that local lords of mountains and day lords were capable of interceding with celestial gods like the sun, moon, and stars (Miles 1965:286–87). But* *there was a solid foundation in the midwestern highlands that was more Mayan than Mexican (Recinos and Goetz 1953). That is, much of the religion was concerned with curing, divination, witchcraft, and gods of various types and functions. There were* dueños *(owners or patrons or gods) of land, hills, mountains, water, rain, wind, and other natural phenomena. Both the ancestors and the gods were consulted in sacred caves. Prevalent was a belief in each person's having an animal form* (nagual), *and important persons might have more than one form that could be used on different occasions.*

Among the ancient Tzutuhils, rituals were both private and public. Private rituals involved the offering of incense, turkeys, blood, flowers, and liquor to the gods. Public rituals might add an occasional human to the long list of sacrificial items of food and precious metals and stones, but human sacrifices apparently played a minor role compared with the practices of the Mexicans in Tenochtitlán. During public ceremonies, the images of gods were richly dressed and paraded through the towns to the accompaniment of trumpets and drums, usually ending at the ritual ball courts. Dance dramas celebrated historical events such as a victory in war or the reenactment of local myths (Miles 1975; Thompson 1970).

In San José almost all of the elements of native religion mentioned above survive with the exception of human sacrifice and parading the images of gods. The blending of native religion and the early Catholicism introduced by the Spanish friars is most obvious in the cofradías *(brotherhoods with the major function of sponsoring the saints). In San José there are three official, active* cofradías: *San Juan Bautista, established in the 1600s (Aguirre1972), Virgen Concepción; and Santo Domingo Guzmán. There is also one relatively inactive* cofradía, *San José.*

Each cofradía *has an* alcalde *(head), and the more active cofradías also have a* juez *(vice-head) and a first* mayordomo *(a liason between the* juez *and the secondary* mayordomos *who are the rank and file members of the religious brotherhoods). The* cofradía *San Juan Bautista is the most important with five secondary* mayordomos. *Santo Domingo Guzmán and Virgen Concepción have only four secondary* mayordomos, *but they have three* texeles *(low-ranking female members).*

In 1976 an unofficial cofradía *of Maximón, also known variously as San Simón, Judas of Iscariot, and Don Pedro de Alvarado, was established by three brothers who are shamans. The emer-*

gence of the cofradía Maximón coincides with the attempt of the priest from San Martín to play down Maximón's influence, which acts as an obstacle to the acceptance of orthodox Catholicism. Catholic Action, the movement to revitalize the Catholic church along the lines of Roman Catholicism, does not favor the custom in San José of making an image of Judas on Wednesday of Holy Week. The image, made of banana leaves stuffed in old clothes and a large sombrero with the face of an ancient wooden mask that has a cigar between its lips (max in the Mam dialect means tobacco), is placed in the window of the church as a reminder that Judas is an enemy of the church. But many Joseños fear rather than scorn the image of the disciple who betrayed Christ. Some even warn their children not to venture into the streets after dark during Holy Week lest Maximón, who may be roaming around in the guise of a man, capture and persecute them. Since the new cofradía has been established with its own images of Maximón, the three brothers sponsor a fiesta on the third of May, the Day of Santa Cruz, with fireworks, chirimía (wind instrument similar to an oboe), and lots of alcoholic drinks.

Most Joseños claim to be members of Catholic Action, or reformed Catholicism, rather than folk Catholicism (in 1972, 153 families compared to 42 families), but the distinction between Catholic Action and folk Catholicism is blurrred. In addition to purging folk Catholicism of pagan elements, reform-minded Catholics envision that a "cleansing" of church practices will help counter the pull of Protestantism (Sexton 1978), which has gained a toehold since 1938.

Of the 227 families living in San José in 1972, 32 were Protestant and 195 were Catholic. Two sects of Protestantism are represented—the Assembly of God and Central American churches. Martineros helped Joseños build the first Central American Church in 1939, and it now claims 27 families as members. In 1960 Joseños built their own larger Central American Church. The Assembly of God did not gain any converts until 1970, but by 1972 five families were members even though they still do not have their own church and worship in one another's homes or in the churches of San Martín or San Jorge.

World View. Compared with more developed towns on the lake, San José is sometimes significantly different in world view. For example, compared with Panajacheleños (people of Panajachel), Joseños have lower occupational aspirations, are more

*fatalistic, have higher civil office aspirations, accept more tra-
ditional beliefs, and are more inclined to delay their gratification.
In addition, although there is no significant difference between
Panajacheleños and Joseños with respect to literacy and political knowledge, Panajacheleños have more formal education and
are more exposed to mass media and travel. Thus, in many re-
spects Joseños tend to have a more traditional world view than
Panajacheleños.*

*The kinds of traditional beliefs that may still be accepted by
Joseños include the belief that it is important to perform costumbres (rituals) before and after harvesting to honor dueños of
the land; asking permission from the dueña of the lake to travel
and to fish; the belief that certain days of the week are unlucky;
the belief that humans, especially shamans, can change into animal forms; the belief that drowning victims are the result of the
water goddess's wanting more souls as servants; and the belief that shamans can divine and witches can send misfortune
and death. Many of these beliefs and similar ones seem to be
vestiges of an ancient Mayan world view (Tax 1941; Mendleson
1967; Hinshaw 1975).*

The Family. *Since ancient Mexican groups intermarried with
ancient Mayan groups during alliances, it is not surprising that
Quichés, Cakchiquels, and Tzutuhils modified kinship terms with
Mexican (or Nahua) words and that Mexican lineage personal
names were found among the Maya. The family was the basic
social and economic unit. For those who could afford it, plural
marriages occurred with patriarchs having more than one wife. A
common household, therefore, might consist of the adult male
head, his wives, unmarried daughters, and both married and unmarried sons (Miles 1965).*

*With the arrival of the Spaniards in the 1500s, the structure
of the Indian family changed little with the exception that plural
marriages were less common, probably due as much to inability to
afford them as condemnation by the church. A great many couples
continued to live juntos (together) without official sanction from
the church or state.*

*A significant introduction was the compadrazgo, or god-
parenthood, system. Its diffusion was the result of the early
Catholicizing efforts of the priests (Ravicz 1967). This new institution increased the range of social, economic, and political ties
in addition to providing added means of social harmony since*

godparents were sometimes called upon to settle family disputes or help in child rearing problems.

Today in San José the tendency is toward nuclear units (the married couple and their children). The comparative wealth of the parents of the newly united couple determines largely whether the couple lives with the parents of the groom or the parents of the bride. When a newly married couple lives in the sitio *(homesite) of one set of parents, they usually have their own cooking hearth (kitchen), and in such cases may be considered independent family units. As soon as a couple can afford it, they establish their own home. Despite some exceptions, there is a tendency toward the couple's living in or near the groom's family. Inheritance tends to go to both female and male children. While there are traces of polygamous unions, monogamy is the norm.*

In some cases, traditional and formal procedures of parents' negotiating the marriage proposal and arrangements are still followed, but males and females may have more to say in the choice of a spouse than before. The young man may petition the parents of his prospective bride with gifts of food, drink, or clothing in several appropriately spaced visits. If a couple is not willing to wait or if parents disapprove, they have the alternative of elopement. But with the spread of Protestantism and reformed Catholicism, elopement is being discouraged. Elopement may be an attractive alternative, however, if one set of parents is Catholic and the other is Protestant and they do not consent to the proposed, religiously mixed marriage. Nevertheless, Protestantism and reformed Catholicism are influencing a trend toward church supervision of marriage. A church marriage usually follows a civil marriage.

Today in San José couples are known to rely on the courts to settle marital disputes. Husbands may be fined for beating their wives, and wives may be fined for adultery. Serious problems may lead a young woman to return to her parents' household. Such separations may end in divorce. However, both divorced men and women remarry.

❧ Major Themes

Ignacio's account is important because a number of significant themes emerge from it that help us better understand a different people in a different situation. These themes include: (1)

family and community solidarity of hardworking, decent people taking pride in special aspects of their culture; (2) grinding poverty (3) reliance on drink during moods of elation but more often during periods of frustration in order to blot out certain aspects of hopelessness; (4) constantly recurring illness that may be serious, but is often minor, seeming to me to be almost psychosomatically induced as a means of getting a brief respite from grueling manual labor; and (5) sensitivity to agents and institutions who are actively and inactively promoting change at the individual and community level. For further discussion of these major themes see the Appendix.

With a compelling narrative flow, Ignacio provides us with an insider's account of his people, town, and country in uncommonly rich, candid detail. His is a rare account which offers penetrating insight into the human condition of countless peasants in Latin America. We are indeed fortunate to have such a remarkably articulate spokesman as Ignacio Bizarro Ujpán.

J.D.S.

Autobiography

❧Autobiography

In 1947, when I was six years old, my aunt María and her husband Martín, who adopted me, decided to move to Panajachel because Señor Martín got a job at the Hotel Casa Contenta. I, too, left San José with my foster parents.

When I arrived in Panajachel, I did not know a single word of Spanish [the national language of Guatemala], I only knew Tzutuhil Maya, [the native tongue of San José]. But little by little I became friends with the sons of the landlord from whom we rented a house in Panajachel. They taught me some words in Spanish. Gradually, I gained some confidence in speaking this new language.

The landlord's sons treated me well. They gave me toys of cups and balls. Occasionally they even gave me sweet bread and caramels. On the twenty-fifth of December, during Christmas, one of my little Ladino [Hispanic] friends gave me a package of fire-crackers. But I was unaware that fireworks are dangerous. I grasped a piece of burning firewood, lit the package, and it exploded in my right eye, knocking me unconscious!

I was not cognizant of their taking me to a pharmacy for medication. Twenty days I was sick suffering from this accident. Two months after the mishap I was hit with a fever which lasted fifty days. Only this time my foster parents did not give me medicine from a pharmacy. Instead, they doctored me with a drink of chocolate and butter in water.

I recovered slowly, but when they took me back to San José with them, I was still a bit sick. Although I was sick when I lived in Panajachel, I at least learned a little Spanish.

In 1948, on the twenty-fifth of March, my foster parents let me go to school, the National Mixed [coeducational] and Urban School

21

of Rodolfo Juan García of San José la Laguna, to study Spanish with an Indian teacher from San Martín la Laguna named José Jorge Martínez Coj.

But the teacher did not teach us anything in Spanish. Not a word! Instead, he gave us classes in the Tzutuhil dialect. When the school officials examined us in the middle of October, none of my classmates passed the grade *Castellanización* [which is designed to teach Indian children basic Spanish]. Because of my exposure to Spanish in Panajachel, I was the only one who passed.

When the academic year ended, I was ordered by my foster parents to herd animals in the fields to earn my daily keep. I would leave the house at six in the morning and return at two in the afternoon. Such were my days in November and December of 1948.

When school began again in March, I began struggling to attend the first grade. Because I was poor, I had to leave early every morning to fetch water from the lake for the people to earn my daily sustenance. When we were tested on October 15, I got a certificate of eighty percent, or grade "B." After the examinations, I went back to pasturing animals in the fields until the latter part of February 1950.

At this time I was able to attend school again. By now I had gained a little knowledge of letters. In this era, there were no teachers for each grade. I continued in the same grade with the same teacher. He taught me the same things as the year before. That is, I repeated the same lessons that I had learned in 1949. Nevertheless, I continued to go to school, although I could only attend three days a week. The other three days I searched for firewood to sell in order to buy some of the little things I needed for my upkeep. This is how I spent 1950.

In February 1951, the second and third grades were established at the school in San José. I returned to school, but I still had the same teacher. I concentrated on learning to read and write Spanish, and when we were tested in October, I came out first among all the students in the second grade.

When the school year ended, I dedicated myself to cultivating vegetables in the fields. By selling these, I made my *centavos* [little money] for buying food and clothing. This is how it was when I was ten years old.

In 1952, I returned to school in the third grade. [This time I had a new] Indian teacher named Diego Pedro Ujcom Ovalle. But I had a problem. It was absolutely necessary for me to be excused from school two days a week because I had to work. Frankly, my uncle gave me food, but I had to buy my notebooks. Although I did not go to school every day, I earned a certificate of one hundred percent—a grade of "A"—at the end of the school year.

~ I Discover That I Am an Adopted Child

When I was about eleven years of age [1952], I discovered that I was not living with my real parents. My grandmother, Isabel Soto, told me this because she resented my aunt, María, and her husband, Martín, whipping me a lot. If I was not busy doing something worthwhile, they would whip me.

Because I was small, I did not pay much mind to the spankings. But my grandmother Isabel worried about me. One day she declared, "Ignacio, you should understand the reason they whip you a lot is that María is not your real mother and Martín is not your real father. This is why they are always striking you."

"Who, then, is my real mother?" I implored.

"Your real mother is Elena Bizarro Soto," she explained.

"And who is my real father?" I queried.

"Your father," she replied, "is Jesús Ujpán García."

I had always known my real mother, but I had known her as an aunt or someone not close to me in kin. It was not until then that I found out Elena was not my aunt, but my mother, and that María was not my mother, but my aunt. And my Uncle Jesús was not my uncle, but my father, while my father was really not my father, but my uncle.

When I learned all of these things, I thought deeply about those with whom I was living, and I considered not living anymore with my adopted parents who were really my aunt and uncle. Unfortunately, by now my blood mother, Elena, had married a man other than my blood father, Jesús. Finally, I concluded that it would be better to continue living with my aunt, my adopted mother. It was true that they whipped me often, but I did not believe it was because they resented giving me food and other provisions. Perhaps I was just disobedient and they wished to correct my behavior.

Thanks to God and his good heart, my Aunt María gave me sustenance when I was just a baby, and thanks to the good heart of Señor Martín Coj for all the struggling he did for me. He sent me to school, though not every day. Because of these noble persons, I learned to read and write. They also taught me to appreciate the value of work in the fields. Today I work in the fields to sustain my own family. And although I live in poverty, I am improving my condition little by little. If I had gone to live with my real father, Jesús, I would not have improved myself at all. Life with him would not have allowed me to develop a sound mind.

I am an only child by my mother and father. I have brothers and sisters, but they are of second degree [half brothers and sisters].

We are nine brothers and sisters by the same father [Jesús] but not the same mother [wife of Jesús]. My half brothers and sisters [by Jesús] include Josefa Ujpán Sánchez, who is the daughter of Josefa Sánchez Bizarro; Geraldo Ujpán Sánchez and Marta Juana Ujpán Sánchez, who are children of Josefa Sánchez Martínez; and Juan Pedro Ujpán Celado, who is son of Juanita Celado Coj. None of these four half brothers and sisters live with our father. The other four brothers are Santos Diego, who was murdered with a machete on November 30, 1972; Mateo Ujpán and Jaime Sánchez Ujpán; and Juan Ujpán Sánchez. All four of these are children of Isabel Sánchez Bizarro. At first this Señora Isabel Sánchez Bizarro was a sister-in-law of my father Jesús because the second woman that my father had after my own mother was named Josefa Sánchez Bizarro, and she is the sister of Isabel, who later became Martín's wife.

When I was older, my real mother, Elena Bizarro, told me that when I was born, she was only 16 years old. Since I am now [1972] 30 years old, she is about 46. I was told that when I was an infant, my mother Elena went to live with another man because my real father, Jesús, left to join the army. My mother abandoned me when she took off with another man, and that is why my Aunt María took me to live with her as an adopted son.

Do you have half brothers and sisters by your mother Elena too?

Eventually, my mother Elena had three more children. They are Julia, Catarina, and Jorge. Thus, I have altogether eleven half brothers and sisters, but no whole ones. I am the only child by my real mother and my real father. He is about 50 years old. My father, I feel badly about him. He once was a rich man who owned a lot of land. When his parents died, they left him a lot of land, which he squandered little by little. When my mother gave birth to me, he was away in the army. According to what I am told, when he returned from the army, he took up with many different women. I suppose that during his lifetime, he has lived with about ten women, including the one he has now. First, he lived with my mother, Elena, before going away to the army. Then he lived with a second woman after his tenure in the army, and later he had other women. He did not live with all of these women at the same time. He just had many different women during his life who more or less were wives.

The reason that my mother, his first woman, went away to live with another man in Patzilín [a village district of San José] was that she was left truly without means of support when my father, Jesús, joined the army. She needed clothing and food. Because my father was gone when I was born, I don't use the same first surname. Instead, I go by my mother's last name—Bizarro.

My father says that he could not bear the army for even a year. He only lasted about nine months because he could not stand such a life. He deserted. Because he squandered all his land, he no longer works as a farmer. Rather, he is now just a day laborer. He does not have anymore land to farm because he sold it all. Earlier, he was a big farmer with a lot of land by San José's standards. He had about 600 *cuerdas* [about 107 acres] of land, which is a lot of land here!

Like my mother, my father was born in San José. But his father was a *Martinero* [inhabitant of neighboring San Martín la Laguna].

My mother is Catholic Action [reformed or Roman Catholic], but my father does not have a [Christian] religion now. He is a shaman, but I don't know how many clients he has. He never goes to the Catholic Church, only to caves in the hills. He takes patrons from Santa Rosa and Sololá to break the spells that sorcerers cast on them. They say that my father is also a sorcerer.

ᕕᐛ All Saint's Day, Socialists, and Reflections

In 1975 Ignacio added the following account to his original autobiography.

In 1953 when I was about twelve years old, I went with my Aunt María and Uncle Martín to a farm in Suchitepéquez called

Bajavista. It was November 1, All Saints' Day. Like my real father, Jesús, my adoptive father, Martín, is a shaman. He took us with him to Bajavista to perform ceremonies for his deceased relatives interred there.

We arrived at the farm about 1:00 P.M., but we didn't reach the cemetery until about 3:00 P.M. When we arrived, he began to perform the rituals with flowers, candles, and incense. He called the names of the dead whom he had known as a young boy.

There were a lot of people at the graveyard. On this farm, only a shaman had the right to perform ceremonies for all other people. When the people living there saw that Señor Martín was a shaman, they began to ask him to do them the favor of making ceremonies for their own dead. They wanted him to do this because it helps the spirit of the dead person because the spirit does not know where it is. So to help the spirit feel satisfied and happy for a little while, they have a shaman perform a ritual for it. It is said that the spirit always stays in the graveyard. According to the beliefs of the people, if the shaman is not used, the spirit becomes sad and will cry because it does not have protection.

Some believe that if a shaman did not perform a ceremony for the deceased spirit's protection, those who are still alive would get sick or would suffer much poverty or their children would die because they didn't help the dead spirit.

Well, Señor Martín told the people in the cemetery that he would with much pleasure perform ceremonies for their dead. He did all kinds of ceremonies—burning candles, drinking a lot of guaro [plain distilled liquor], aguardiente [sugarcane liquor], and lots of beer. Many people gathered to watch Señor Martín make the ceremonies, leaving one tomb and going to another. They gave their centavos and lots of guaro to him.

Señor Martín finished the ceremonies about 10:00 P.M., but he wanted to stay another day to make more the next day, All Souls' Day. He got up about 5:00 A.M., but he was still drunk from the previous day. He left again for the cemetery to perform more rituals for the people and to make more money. Around midday he finished these additional ceremonies, but by this time he was quite drunk. More or less he had earned about $15 to $20.

At 2:00 P.M. we headed back to San José. With us came a nephew of Señor Martín named Geraldo Pérez to protect him from having an accident on the road because the day was the Day of the Dead. After walking to an aldea [district of a municipality, usually a village] of San José called Pachichaj, we were still 12 kilometers away from home. Señor Martín went into a bar to drink more tragos [cups or glassfuls of liquor], getting even drunker. We were pretty far from home.

We struggled to make it home safely with Señor Martín, but between Patzilín and San José, about 4 kilometers from home, he went out of his mind from so much alcohol. He started beating Aunt María, Geraldo and myself with a stick. He struck us as one would strike a dog. It was late at night and dark; we could neither escape nor defend ourselves. I was just a small boy, so I let Aunt María, Geraldo, and myself be hit. He struck us all!

When we finally arrived home about 2:00 A.M., my aunt was crying loudly because the blows she had received hurt her very much. The boy Geraldo departed, and Aunt María and I went to sleep. Señor Martín left for a bar and continued drinking.

When dawn came, the señor was still drunk. He readied himself and set out for Patzilín to perform more ceremonies for the dead. It was the third of November, and this time we did not accompany him. He was crazy with drink, and he carried a shotgun to defend himself from his political enemies because during this time Señor Martín belonged to the Socialist party.

But it happened that when Señor Martín arrived in Patzilín he continued to drink instead of doing ceremonies for the dead. He fell into the hands of his enemies who were worse than he was. They captured him, took away his shotgun, tied him up with a lasso, and took him before the military commissioner, Ricardo Puc.

With his arms tied behind his back, his enemies marched him back to San José. At 10:00 P.M. when Señor Martín was escorted into San José, he had bruises on his back and all over his body.

Because he had been carrying a shotgun, he was taken as a captive back to San José as a criminal suspect. Besides the blows they had given him, they took away his rifle, threw him in jail, and fined him $30.

But he only spent six days in jail for carrying a weapon. He was insolent, but he had friends. He had contacts in the Socialist party when Jacobo Arbenz Guzmán was President.[5] Señor Martín sent a telegram to the party informing them that he was being held prisoner in San José. A deputy of the party arrived from Guatemala City and paid his fine. This representative was named Marino Cruz Aguilar, but I don't know if he is still alive.

It is true, *"El que mal hace mal espera"* [he who commits evil will meet evil]. Señor Martín beat us with a stick while we were on the road for no reason, but within 24 hours he received the same punishment from his own enemies. He went to Patzilín with the intent of making more money, but he lost money instead.

How many people believe that a spirit will send misfortune if ceremonies are not performed for them during All Souls' Day?

In San José, most people do not believe this anymore. For every 100 people perhaps there is one who still believes this. Maybe 10 to 15 families still believe this will happen. But in 1953, when I was a small boy, almost all of San José believed it.

Why did some people dislike the Socialists during this time?

This was a time when the liberals were in control of the government of Guatemala. The anti-liberals considered the liberals to be Communists. Half of the town of San José had adopted the Socialist party because the Socialists had promised them land, jobs, and other things that Joseños did not have. Although no land had been confiscated from the wealthy, there was a rumor that this was about to happen.

When did the Socialists lose power?

In the following year of 1954, the socialist government collapsed at the hand of Colonel Carlos Castillo Armas. In some parts of Guatemala many [alleged] Communists were shot. Since the anti-Socialists kept a list of all the Socialists, the latter in San José were extremely frightened for their lives. For this reason, Señor Martín, a well-known Socialist, was afraid to leave the confines of San José for three years afterwards.

You told me that you and your uncle traveled to other towns to do ceremonies.

That was my uncle Señor Martín. With regard to the subject of ceremonies, he was famous. He claimed that a man of his profession was not a spiritualist but a spiritual center. He called all of the owners [gods] of the hills, like the god of the Hill of Chuitinamit and all of the neighboring hills as well. He says the hills have spirits, and they come to talk to him.

The spirits of volcanoes too?

Those too. First one voice comes to him and then another. Each is distinct in tone and pitch. This all happens in darkness. Many voices come to him while there is no light in the room.

Many patients came to see him. When there were sick people in San Jorge, he performed ceremonies for them. He also went to Santa Ana to perform rituals. I went with him twice, once to Santa Ana and once to San Jorge. But I did not like to go with him because he drank too much. I wasn't very old and I felt weak, as if I could not be left alone. I could not go home alone either. If he slept in San Jorge, I had to sleep there with him. If he slept in Santa Ana, I had to sleep there with him. I did not have enough nerve to leave him and go home alone. I was just a youngster, and he told me that spirits were lurking all around. I was afraid to travel without anyone to protect me.

And this is how it was in those times. The people coming to visit my uncle brought him flowers, bread, bottles of beer, *aguardiente* and money. He was earning good pay being a shaman, but he squandered it on drink and women.

What was good pay?

Everybody brought him about $5 each. If four people came in one night—that was $20 for him. I suppose for me and us poor Indians, $10 or $15 is good money. And he earned this amount of money with little bother. But he wasted his money on alcohol and women.

He is still alive, but he claims he is not the same as a spiritualist. He calls himself a Shaman of the Center, but I don't understand this center. Maybe he is a spiritualist because he talks to the spirits of the deceased, but he also performs ceremonies with candles and incense and *guaro*.

Is he a sorcerer?

I am positive that he isn't a sorcerer because he told me that he doesn't know anything about witchcraft. Some people say that he performs black magic, but he told me that he does not. These people believe that he is a sorcerer because humans are gullible and cowardly. When they see something they are unfamiliar with, it scares them, like seeing a *gringo*. And that is how things are—to see a shaman, one thinks he is going to die. Thus, the people said that he was a sorcerer.

When were the people here afraid of gringos? *How many years ago?*

Even some ten years ago this fear existed. And I remember when you first were here in San José in 1970. *Gringos* came before

that but only to visit, to walk through the streets. But remember
when we visited the people here? Many were afraid. Do you remember one man Señor Juan Gómez asked us, "Is it true *gringos*
eat people?" I remember him asking us that.

Yes, I remember.

He really did say that! Then people were more afraid.

Did the people who were afraid go to a shaman for protection?

No they didn't go to shamans. What they did was not leave the
house to walk around in the morning or afternoons. This was a
perilous time to them because they thought *espiritados* [persons
possessed by foreign spirits] could capture and carry them away in
the darkness, especially from 4–5:00 A.M. and 6–7:00 P.M. when
there is no sunlight.

But after you got to know the people, as soon as they knew
that *gringos* didn't kill or hit people, everything was all right. And
that is how it was. When people met shamans, they were afraid of
them. If they saw a drunk shaman, they did not bother him. They
could die that way! They go to a shaman when a child falls sick or
when they have a bad dream. When one has a bad dream, he says,
"I'm going to a shaman to see what the dream is telling me." Or
many people go to a shaman to see if they can obtain some good
luck or a good harvest. This is the reason that there are shamans.

I began to think a lot about what had happened to my adoptive
father, my uncle [after he was jailed in 1953 for carrying a shotgun].
The kind of life he led seemed to be a bad road to follow. I began to
suspect that what he was doing was unimportant because he was
not producing any fruit for the improvement of life. It is true that he
had money because he worked alone and did not share his earnings
with anyone. But he spent the money he earned on women and
drink, and he fought a lot. I began to suspect that shamans were
fakes because I kept witnessing that there was really nothing to
them. Little by little I was beginning not to believe in them.

❧ My Last Year in School

In the year of 1953, the Ministry of Education ordered that no
child could leave school until the age of 14. But at this time I was

only 12. I was obliged to continue in school, but again in the third grade because there still was no fourth, fifth or sixth grades in the school in San José. After spending two years in the third grade, I left school for good in 1954. I was only 13 years old, but I was too poor to leave San Josè to continue my education elsewhere.

❧ First Communion, But Church Interests Wane

In February of 1955, I went to register for the Christian doctrine of the Catholic church to receive first communion. In May of the same year, Father Rodríquez asked all of us who wanted communion what we had learned. I demonstrated that I had learned the Christian doctrine by memory—seventy-two religious questions in all. On June 24, the day of the main town fiesta, I received the bread of the heavens for the first time. After receiving the sacred communion the priest congratulated us with an embrace and a gift of a religious canticle.

In 1956 I was very happy with my religious life. I went to church four days a week—Tuesday, Thursday, Saturday, and Sunday. However, as time passed, I began to devote more time to fishing on the banks of Lake Atitlán and less time to attending church. Finally, I quit going to church on Sundays because I had to work very much and I was very poor. I would not be finished until 8:00 P.M.

And this is how it was for me during this time.

❧ Witnessing Nagualism

Ignacio added this episode to his autobiography in 1975 after I asked whether he knew of any cases of nagualism, or humans changing into animal form.

When I was 16 years old, in 1957, I was commuting to Santo Tomás la Unión to sell onions, tomatoes, and chickpeas with friends from my town, San José. We could only do this during the months of January, February, and March because it was necessary to cross the Nahualate River with the cargo on our backs in order to reach Santo Tomás. In April, May, and June one cannot go to Santo Tomás by this route because during these months the rainy season begins and the water level in the river rises too high for crossing. So we *Joseños* are able to negotiate this trip to this beautiful town in the department [state] of Suchitepéquez only three months of the year.

One day during the time when passage is possible, we left San José on a Saturday in order to be able to sell on Sunday. My traveling companions were Jorge Sánchez Choror, Miguel Gonzáles Mendoza, and Juan Ujpán Ovalle, the latter now deceased.

We arrived in Santo Tomás on a Saturday, but I do not remember the exact day, only that it was in February before Holy Week.

It is the custom of us travelers to sleep on the porch of someone's house when we do not have money for a room in an inn. My companions and I bedded down on the porch of a house, and later three more men from Santo Tomás Chichicastenango came to join us.

What happened is that I witnessed a very strange thing in this place. At 11:30 P.M. I woke up suddenly and saw a little black cat walk over to one of the strangers from Chichicastenango whose mouth was agape. The cat, not a large one just small, crammed itself down the mouth of the man. In less than two minutes after swallowing the cat the man moved his body. Now I could not sleep at all. I was too scared!

In vain I tried to arouse my friends, but they only continued to sleep soundly. I kept thinking about the belief of my people in San José that each person has a *nagual* [spirit] and that only evil persons such as sorcerers and thieves are able to change themselves into animal forms while they are sleeping. I was so upset I could not get back to sleep. I was afraid that something would happen to me if I did. I have seen this happen only once in my life, but watching that man from Chichicastenango swallow a cat while he slept convinced me that the belief in nagualism is true.

Are you sure you were not dreaming?

There was a light shining from the roof, and the man was very close to me. I knew I was not dreaming.

❧ My First Love

By the time I was 16, I began running around with chums, and I quit going to church. I was living a sad life because I was not in accordance with God's wishes.

At this time I met a girl named Lucía Méndez, and I fell in love with her. This young girl accepted me, and we performed the ritual of engagement. We bought bread and chocolate for friends and relatives. We spent about $50 on this custom.

But the girl's parents are Catholic, and they wanted me to marry their daughter [in a church]. Their wishes resulted in our going to the parish in San Martín la Laguna because in the Catholic church, all who marry must ask for permission to do so.

When we arrived in San Martín, the priest asked me, "Is it true that you want the young lady with all your heart?"

"Yes, father, with all my heart I want Señorita Lucía Méndez for my wife."

Then the priest asked, "How old are you?"

"Sixteen years old," I answered.

Then he asked the señorita in this fashion, "Do you want Ignacio Bizarro for your husband?"

"Yes, father, I do," she replied.

"How old are you?" he asked her.

"Fourteen years old," she answered.

Then the father became very rude with me because the ecclesiastical law does not permit women of only fourteen years of age to get married. The father said these angry words to me, "No Ignacio, you do not have the right to marry Señorita Lucía Méndez, nor she to marry you."

He told me that we should wait two more years—more time! He also would not give me permission to live together with her [as common law man and wife].

Lucía and I returned to San José very dejected and embarrassed in front of the townspeople because almost the entire population of our town knew we had been prohibited from getting married by the father.

A month later we separated. It was a very great hurt for me. I was very depressed. For the first time in my life I got drunk. This all happened in the year of 1957.

❧ A Second Affair

In 1958 when I was 17 years old, I fell in love again. This time it was with a señorita named Julia Méndez, who lived in Patzilín. Once a week I went to this *aldea* to convince this girl to marry me. Finally, after two months of courting she agreed, and we arranged an engagement. This was after performing the proper customs. The girl's mother stipulated a time when she would surrender her daughter. We did all of this in view of two witnesses as is the custom. The day was the twentieth of October.

In the month of October I was required to buy *cortes generalizados* [wraparound skirts of a general design], two blouses, a shawl and other things. When the noted day arrived, we went to Patzilín to fetch Señorita Julia Méndez. I was very pleased to carry with us more liquor, beer, soft drinks and other gifts.

We returned to San José about midnight accompanied by two witnesses, as was the custom of the town. The bride and groom both have a witness. If the couple begin to break apart, the witnesses are obliged to negotiate with them to bring them back together—to save the marriage.

For six months we were very happy. We had no strife. We were impoverished, but our love was great. Then one day we quarreled over a simple matter. She simply did not prepare lunch when I needed it. I got mad and slapped her in the face. She ran to the police. Consequently I had to present myself to the señor judge who applied the law to me, sentencing me to five days in jail or a fine of $2.50.

I obtained the money for the fine, and I did not spend any time in jail. But after this happened, I separated from my woman, and she returned to her *aldea*.

I remained in my house, but I was sad because now I had no one to prepare my meals. I thought it over somewhat remorsefully, but it was too late. Our separation was on April 29, 1959.

❧ My Third Love Affair

In October of the same year, I fell in love with a pretty señorita named Josefa Ramos of the same town San José. Although she was hardly 14 years of age, she fell in love with me too. Our relationship was very great. With her parents' knowledge, she moved in with me on December 27. I did not perform the custom of asking her parents to let her live with me because they had a lot of affection for me, and it was unnecessary.

Thus, we began to live together. We were very happy at first. It was true that my woman did not know how to cook, but I surmised that this was because of her young age.

Then they named me *alguacil* [runner and policeman] of the municipality for a year. I began performing this gratuitous but mandatory service on February 5, 1960. It meant that I had to look for work during the night to earn sustenance because the truth is that I did not have enough money to support us while serving this *cargo*.

We were poor but happy until one day I was ordered to make a citation by the *alcaldía* [tribunal]. As I was carrying out my instructions, I began to chat with a young girl who was standing on the corner. When my wife saw me talking to her, she got jealous. Her suspicions continued until we quarreled.

The result was sad for me. On November 20, we separated. We did not go to the justice of the peace because her parents still liked me. Because she felt offended, she would not see me anymore.

I soon was overcome with a great sense of depression. I began to drink heavily. Pondering over my behavior, I decided my life was not very upright. Because I had separated from three women, I could only walk the streets of San José in shame.

On Christmas day my soccer team played a game in San Jorge la Laguna. When it was over, we began to drink. When we got back to San José, I continued drinking with my first cousin Ignacio Mendoza. Like me, he had separated from his woman. We were in the same situation. Two Ignacios in the same disgrace. Only by drinking could we find solace.

Then I declared that I was going to join the National Army. As we talked about the advantages of the army, my cousin Ignacio also became interested in joining. Finally, we took off for the city of Mazatenango to enlist.

When we arrived in the Fourth Military Zone of Mazatenango, we asked the guard whether there were any vacancies. He quickly invited us into the barracks, but once inside they would not let us leave.

They made us wait until December 28 for a doctor to examine us. By God's grace we passed the physical examination. On January 1, 1961, they gave me papers certifying that I was a private in the artillery.

ℵ My Life in the Military

The first week of training covered military regulations and responsibilities. They taught me the soldier's regulations, sentinel's orders, and fifteen articles of the military code. I paid careful attention to everything the instructors said, and after eight days I knew it all, including such things as how to show military courtesy to officers, who can approach a guard at night, and the obligations of soldiers on guard duty.

What was your rank, and how much did you earn?

I was a private earning $10 a month. Because I was quick to learn these things, in the second week of training they advanced me to a higher group of soldiers who had been in training longer. During this early period, I hardly suffered. It was my intelligence that kept me out of trouble.

After a month we went out for field practice. I acted as munitions soldier of the 81 millimeter mortar. We made good grades on this practice. The señor officer, the commandant of the Fourth Military Zone, commended us.

What kind of field training did you have? Was it difficult? How long did it last?

In the first month we had a lot of individual training to keep us alert and in shape. This included instruction in self-defense, hand-to-hand combat, and plenty of physical exercises. We were taught land navigation in the jungles of Mazatenango. We would leave the barracks at 7:00 P.M. with our backpacks, some sandwiches, and a canteen of water. When one is in training one looks not for a highway but the steepest and most difficult terrain to cross. Some of the places were really rough, and we suffered. It was not that we were lazy. Rather, when one is not accustomed to such exertion, it is hard. We went over gorges with ropes, we crossed rivers at night, and sometimes we traveled (marching and double-timing) 20 to 30 kilometers in one night. After leaving early in the evening we sometimes would not get back to the barracks until 5–6:00 P.M. the following day.

On nights when it rained, they would take us out for training. We wore ponchos, but the army ponchos aren't worth anything. We got soaked! But all of this happens to a soldier when he is just beginning his stay in the military. After two or three months have passed, one suffers less. It was not until the second month that we began our field artillery training.

Did they teach Spanish classes?

After the basic military classes, they taught me things in general education—cultural things and Spanish, how to express a word properly. When I left school in San José, I could speak a little Spanish, but in the army I learned a lot. I learned how to speak well and to be able to say all of the things I wanted to say. This was an improvement from my limited fluency in San José.

How long did the classes last?

For three months I had a half-hour of instruction in Spanish for five days a week—Monday through Friday.

Were the Spanish classes mainly for Indians, or did Ladinos attend also?

These classes were for the many people, both Indians and Ladinos, who go into the army not knowing Spanish well or not knowing it at all. They teach verb conjugations and composition, and even the Ladino has to go to class to do well in it.

There are three courses. The first is for those who are completely illiterate. A teacher says, "This is such and such." The students have notebooks like children who cannot read and write, who are in the first year of school. Little by little the instructors teach them how to read and write and speak. For those who do not know any Spanish, there are two hours of instruction daily.

After three months have passed they have advanced literacy training. At this time they are also taught about artillery— armaments, the machine gun, and mortars—in another class. Within six months the soldiers are speaking Spanish well. They are examined, and if they pass the army gives them a diploma signed by the defense minister saying that the soldier can read and write. It is not the same as a grade school diploma because it just says, "Alphabetization of the Army." However, it shows that the soldier with hard work has learned something in the army—it shows that he learned to read, write and to speak Spanish. I didn't get one of these because it is for those who asked to be certified.

Do you think this kind of training is important?

Yes. For example, when I joined up, I had a friend from San Carlosito near Mazatenango. He is named Leandro Pérez Larios. When I first joined, I could read and write a little, but he couldn't at all! He could not even write a single letter! In six months he was writing letters to his mother and father. This is why I think the military schools are worthwhile.

On this first of April they ordered me to Tiquisate to be a rearguard for the paymaster of the Agricultural Company. I did not want to leave Mazatenango, but I had to muster the courage to go.

In Tiquisate seven other soldiers and I were provided with room and board by the Agricultural Company, but the Guatemalan government paid our salaries. I spent five months guarding the paymaster when he was paying the workers for the jobs they completed. At about 1:00 P.M. a car came to pick me up to ride with the paymaster. I was always ready for an emergency with my Mehiser 45 millimeter submachine gun, the same kind that the roving military police use.

What was the Agricultural Company?

The Agricultural Company [at that time the United Fruit Company, now known as the United Brands Company] is an incorporation of banana agriculturalists whose bananas are sent to the United States. This company belongs to the gringos. It is a big company with many farms like Petén, Antigua, San Marcos, Sololá, Totonicapán, Esquipul, Lorqueta, Victoria, Esquipulas, Esquipulitas, Alotenango, Alotenanguito, la Vera Paz, Tecpán, Cobán, Pacaya, Ixtepeque, Ipala, Moyuta, Tolimán, Xebacu, Ticanlu, Talo Blanco, Primavera, Lebón, La Ceba, and La Noria. I can't remember them all because there are many. The company is huge! It had a lot of land—hundreds of *caballerías* [land measures of about 33½ acres each]—and that's big!

A worker in this company earned a lot of money. Some earned $30 to $40 per week. And they were paid by the week. Because there were many farms, someone was paid everyday. A lot of money went out to the workers. It astonished me to pay them so much!

Nowadays there aren't anymore companies in Tiquisate like the Agricultural Company because at that company the workers earned good money. They say that the company exists at Puerto Barrios in the East, but I'm not sure of this because I am not acquainted with that area. But they told me when the company left Tiquisate, it moved there. They moved in 1964 when there weren't anymore bananas on their land. In the 1950s they started growing a lot of cotton around Tiquisate, and the Agricultural Company allowed another company take over the land. Cotton is still grown in this area.[6]

By God's grace we never had any trouble in Tiquisate on the farms. I had been there from April to September. On the sixth of

September my replacement arrived, and I was ordered back to Mazatenango. I was anxious to return because in Tiquisate there was nothing to do for self-improvement. There were no classes or anything. I was just there protecting the paymaster of the Agricultural Company with a submachine gun.

On September 15, we received orders from the commandant of Mazatenango to organize a parade in honor of our homeland because it was Independence Day. My companions and I put on a good show for the people, something that the university students could never do. After the parade was over, the señor officer of the artillery company gave everyone in the unit a hug, commending us for a job well done.

On October 2, some other soldiers and I were sent to a place called Brazitos to keep an eye on the public order. This only lasted for 20 days because on October 28 the entire personnel of the Fourth Military Zone of Mazatenango were ordered to the city of Retalhuleu, arriving under the cover of night. Also, the next day personnel from the Fifth Military Zone of the City of Quezaltenango arrived at night.

On November 1, the General Manuel Lisandro Barillas Brigade was organized. This command was given its name by the order of the Ministry of National Defense with Colonel Enrique Peralta, an infantry colonel, commanding. This is when they promoted me to private first class. Later on January 2, I was promoted to corporal as a squad leader in the Third Platoon of the Second Company of the First Infantry Battalion in the Barillas Brigade at Retalhuleu.

How much did you earn as private and a corporal?

As a private first class I earned $12 a month, and as a corporal I made $15 a month. As a corporal I had eight men under me—two private first class soldiers and six regular privates. In Retalhuleu none of us in the army was paid for 90 days because we were in a state of siege [similar to martial law].

Why?

The students from the University of San Carlos went on strike, and we were expecting to be attacked. We were expecting a war and there would have been a big riot had they attacked. The barracks at Retalhuleu are very much enclosed. On one side passes the railroad tracks and on the other the highway. The barracks are locked in between. They could not attack from the road and neither could they attack from the railroad. They could only attack from one direction, and we were ready and waiting with our machine guns, 50 calibers and mortars. We went two days without any food. All of us troops were ready for battle, but thank God nothing happened.

Why were there problems with the students?

Imagine, I did not know the cause of the disturbance. Not just any soldier can know what the higher-ups know, can they? All we knew was that the students had made a strike and this was the reason there was supposed to be a war. We waited, but nothing happened.[7]

We suffered a lot through this turmoil. We received no pay the first month, none the second. Not until the end of the third month did we receive any money, and then it was not much—just our meager $10 to $15 a month.

Why did you prefer the barracks at Mazatenango?

We were very discouraged when we first arrived at Retalhuleu. Unlike Mazatenango, the barracks in Retalhuleu are not right in town. One could not easily take leave to visit the bars and other places because they were too far away. From the barracks one cannot even see houses—only trees and other barracks. But the quarters turned out not to be too far away from town—about five kilometers—and a bus passing on the highway toward town stops at the guard station. In addition to the barracks being outside town, the climate in that area is really unpleasant. It's very, very hot! Here in San José by comparison, it is not at all hot! It's cold! But there at this time [July], God, if one is training it's rough!

In January 1962 a soccer team was formed. I played the position of goalkeeper and got many privileges in the army because of it. I was an Indian, but they took me along with Ladinos to form a team. I became a famous player because I always won the points. I was an Indian and a good runner. Whenever I took a shot, it was a sure thing for the ball to go in and score. The officers appreciated my ability to play, and they always made it possible for me to be on the field. They always said, "Let Bizarro play!" Sometimes I would be tired and would not want to play, but they would say, "Go play!" So everyday I got to practice, and because of this I stayed in shape and remained a good player.

Our soccer uniforms cost $86 total, and we bought them at a store named Monblanc in Mazatenango. Even the guys who were not on the team would chip in about 25 cents to help defray the expense. Our uniforms represented our team which was called the Tigers of the Second Company of the First Battalion of Special Training.

We won many games. For instance, we beat the First Company because we were in better shape. Also, we defeated the Heavy Arms, Military Police, and Command and Services companies. These latter fellows had been the champions of the whole army.

After the games, the player who made the goals had the right to have a good time. Sometimes they would be given a beer in the officers' tent, or they would be given a one-night pass to go out on the town. To me such rewards were important because they showed the officers were pleased with my performance. When the game was over, they would say, "Take a leave home." But my house was far away, and I didn't have money for passage. So I didn't go.

Didn't the soldiers occasionally visit prostitutes?

You see, when I was in the army, I didn't see women who were prostitutes. I made use of women ... I made use of them because I am a man, right? But not prostitutes.

Where did you meet them, in bars, at the movies?

In the park because there are pretty women there. And one falls in love with them, right? I became enamored with a beautiful señorita. She told me that she loved me, and I even fooled myself into believing that I would make her my wife. But I did not take her home with me because when my tour of duty was up, I went back to my house in San José [with Josefa].

What do the soldiers do for entertainment?

The free time a soldier has in the military varies. If one stands guard duty from 12 noon one day until 12 noon the next, 24 hours, he might get 6 hours off to go walking around or to have a few drinks or get drunk or do whatever he wants. For regular passes, one must wait to see who is next on the alphabetical list. That is, one must wait to see whose turn it is to be off on a Thursday or a Friday. But every day there is always someone who gets a pass. The only exception is when there is a disturbance and the soldiers are on alert or in a state of siege. When it is peaceful, some 15 to 20 men get passes each day because there are enough left to man the barracks. But it is possible to go for two weeks without any time off.

In addition to soccer games and drinking, soldiers do a lot of things for amusement like building human pyramids. Sometimes 100 men would form a human tower in the shape of an Egyptian pyramid that would be eight levels high.

In May we took an examination. When the results came out on June 1, I was promoted to sergeant, making $20 a month. I think I would have made sergeant faster had I not been given many assignments away from the barracks. Note that I am not a Ladino, but the officers took me places with them because of the knowledge I had. For example, once they took me to Tahuexco to work as an engineer on a stretch of highway. The captains and colonels had confidence in me and requested that I go with them on missions. Had I not been away from the quarters so much, I would have advanced to sergeant within five or six months because it was easy for me to learn whatever they told me. Unfortunately, when it was time for promotions, I often was not there and lost out.

When I finally made sergeant, I assumed many responsibilities because I was in charge of a platoon of soldiers—three squads with 29 men in all. I was confident of my men, and they respected me. I did not mistreat any of them as some sergeants mistreated their own men.

In what ways were soldiers punished?

There were many ways to punish the soldiers for breaking the rules. One might have to do as many as 600 *pírricos* [jumping, deep-knee bends] with full 81 millimeter shells in one's arms. Oh, was this exhausting! It was really painful! Also, one might have to put on five overcoats—five of them! Then he would have to run. For a person all bundled up and running on the coast, it was very hot! Another punishment was to make a soldier take off his shoes and go barefoot on the air strip in the field. Without shoes, oh, how hot it is! Yet another thing they might do was to fill a soldier's backpack with stones weighing as much as 150 pounds. Then they would make him run. Depending on what the sergeant said, he would have to run once or twice around the camp. Some might fall down because of the weight and the heat. But falling down could be worse. For instance, a soldier named Oliverio de Juarachac from Santo Domingo collapsed. He was hit in the ribs until all his skin was gone—just bones were left! He spent two months in the military hospital recuperating.

But I never behaved badly toward my men. I thought to myself, "I'm going to be here in the army now, but later I'm going to be on the outside with them as a civilian. When we are out together, I won't get along with them if I am mean to them now." Mainly I did not punish them because I did not like doing this.

And so it was from June until July.

Were you ever punished as a private?

Yes. In Tiquisate it was difficult for me to adjust to the hot climate. Once I was punished for wasting water at a hydrant. I was ordered to do 300 *pírricos* very rapidly with my hands behind my head.

Once in Retalhuleu, I was punished for not obeying instructions. It was Palm Sunday. A buddy of mine wanted to go to San Antonio Suchitepéquez, but he did not have a cent. I had about $60 so I lent my friend some money, and I went with him. After arriving, we went to a *comedor* [small eating place] to drink alcohol. We foolishly allowed the hours of our leave to pass by while we were there. We did not leave until 6:00 P.M., and we did not return back to camp until 11:00 P.M. which was past curfew. The military police threw us in a *calabozo* [jail-like cell]. They made us stay there all night.

Did they fine you?

No. We did not have to pay any fines as punishment. One only had to pay for something that he lost such as clothing, shoes, or cartridges that belonged to the army.

When my tour of duty expired on August 1, I decided not to stay in the military. Sometimes I wonder why I didn't remain. Colonel Calderón promised to promote me to staff sergeant if I would re-enlist. In six months he said he would send me to the Military Academy to become an officer. But now it is too late to think about such things. The opportunity has passed.

My superiors cried when it was time for me to leave. Even though I was anxious to go home, I was feeling quite sad about leaving! Maybe it had been good luck that they had helped me a lot in the army.

A military band of 30 men and many pieces accompanied us to the guard station as we were leaving. The commanding officer sent us off with some final advice. "You are leaving the military," he said. "Now, don't go looking for fights or drinking in bars. Show that here you were good soldiers and learned self-discipline. Don't go taking things like a thief. Take only with the permission of the owners. Respect others and their property." He gave us a lot of advice as we were leaving.

You wrote that you learned a lot about other people and places in the army. What kinds of people and what kinds of places different from San José?

I found out that people who live on the [southern] coast have different customs than the people of my home town. On fiestas they don't go to church. Instead, they only try to have a good time drinking, and they enjoy their drinking more. In San José, ladies do not dance during fiestas, but they do on the coast. First women will begin to dance, and then men will follow. All the young people—15 to 20 year-olds—dance during the fiestas. In San José (although times are changing) they do not. Only men dance, and they dance when they are drunk. At the coast, in contrast, everyone dances.

Also, during the fiestas on the coast, there is nothing happening during the day—only at night. Unlike San José, during the day there is no trace of a fiesta—it is calm! The parties on the coast begin at 6:00 P.M. and continue throughout the night until 5:00 A.M. There are dances and entertainment—many different kinds—but it all takes place at night! I have also noticed that San Luis is more like San José la Laguna than it is like the towns on the coast. In San José and San Luis the fiestas are during the day. Not so on the coast. They are at night!

Also, I found out about some strange people in the barracks. For example, one guy wanted me to learn how to become a sorcerer, but I refused. He had a book which cost $38. It told all about how to take possession of other people. Since this guy slept next to my bunk, he bothered me. But I didn't read much of his book. I know that it explained how to bewitch someone. It told how to use orations to put a rat or a snake in someone's stomach to make him sick, or to put a beetle in someone's head to make him go crazy. The book had in it a picture of Satan with his sword and spear. It was a horrible book! The man was from San Andrés Villa Seca in the state of Retalhuleu.

There are also certain differences between the people of my home town San José and the towns of the coast. I have relatives in San José, but they never came to visit me while I was in the army. Other families from other towns came to see their relatives while they were in the military, bringing them presents such as packages of fruit. These people have different customs than those of *Joseños*. In San José if one joins the military, his relatives do not go to visit him while he is in the barracks.

From the guardhouse at Retalhuleu, I hitched a ride on a bus headed for Mazatenango. I wanted to say good-bye to my cousin Ignacio because he was stationed there. He had reenlisted for six more months of service.

After chatting with my cousin Ignacio, I left Mazatenango for Chicacoa by truck in order to catch a bus from there to San Martín. When I arrived in Chicacoa, I couldn't find a bus, so I rented a room in an inn to spend the night. That evening I went for a stroll, and I ran into two of my friends from San José. Imagine, I was really surprised! I invited them to have a beer. We fell asleep around 12 midnight after drinking a few beers.

Because there wasn't any transportation to San Martín we got up in three hours at 3:00 A.M. and started walking toward Lake Atitlán. We reached San Luis after walking seven hours. When we arrived two *Joseño* comrades spotted me. They invited me to lunch and drinks. Then I caught a canoe headed for San José.

I arrived home about 3:00 P.M. Having been away so long, I just dropped off my bags and went for a stroll through the streets of the town with friends.

Many of the townspeople gave me hugs when they saw me. Others congratulated me for having successfully completed my military service. I celebrated my homecoming by drinking cups of liquor with my friends. I certainly was pleased to have arrived home safely and without bother. The next day I went to church and thanked God for having guided me through my military service.

On August 12, I went to a party in Santa Ana la Laguna. There were several games and other amusements. There was a *zarabanda* [dance] in which the women asked 10 cents to dance each number. I didn't want to dance. I'm not exactly sure why, but I felt bashful. Perhaps I was afraid one of the drunks would hit me and I would hit him back, and someone would end up in jail. In any case, I realized that my life-style had changed after my military experience. I thought that dancing is not useful for a man. It just isn't, and I don't like it. After the army I now had more self-respect and a little more culture—I was not the same as I was before I had joined.

ᔣ Reunion with Josefa Ramos

On September 8, Josefa and I were very much surprised to meet again. I had been away for a long time, and we chatted about how it had been before I left. We made up and started a new era together. She still loved me, and I still loved her.

She declared, however, that if I wanted her I would have to move into her father's house to live. I figured it would be better to live in her father's house than not at all. But I would have to ask her father to forgive my former rude behavior.

On September 10, I arrived at her father's house to ask for reconciliation for all the faults I had committed while I had been living with his daughter.

"Well, all right," he said, "but the same thing had better not happen again. What has happened has happened."

"Then you have forgiven me," I answered. "That's good."

"You can come here." That is all that he mentioned about the past. Thus, I moved in with my woman at her parents' house. The truth is that I had nowhere else to go. Her parents accepted me without bringing up the past anymore. And I was soon earning enough to pay for our upkeep.

Before long her father said that it would be better for us to marry rather than just live together. I had thought a lot about having a wife. We would be poor but happy.

On November 2, we were married by the state at the justice of the peace. On the next day we received the sacred sacrament of marriage in the holy Catholic Church. From that day we have lived happily—impoverished but without quarreling.

ᔣ Our First Two Children Die of the Measles

On July 23, 1963, my wife gave birth to a beautiful baby boy. We named him Juan Martín (after my adoptive father). We were delighted to have a new baby, but we were stricken with tragedy. A month after he was born, he came down with an attack of the measles. He was gravely sick with a high fever, and little red spots broke out all over him. There was no doctor in San José, and we did not know how to treat the illness. It was a pity that the poor infant died on August 25 for lack of medication.

My wife and I were so grieved at the loss of our first child that we left to work on the southern coast to try to overcome our depression and sadness. But after six months, because we could no longer endure the extreme heat, we returned to San José to live in the same house where our baby had died.

In February 1964, we argued with my wife's parents. I began to think that to be living in a house with so much friction was too unpleasant to bear. For this reason, I thought it better to rent a place and live by ourselves. I found an unoccupied house, and the owner allowed us to move into it. The landlord was very compassionate—he did not charge us any rent for 11 months.

In this house my wife gave birth to a baby girl whom we named Ana María. Even though I had to struggle to support my family as a day laborer, my wife and I were proud to have a baby.

Despite my poverty, the town elders named me a *mayordomo* [low ranking member] of the *cofradía* [religious brotherhoods sponsoring Catholic saints] San Juan Bautista. This meant I had to come up with money for my share of the *cofradía*'s expenses. This was in January of 1965.[8]

In May of the same year our little girl, Ana María, died. This caused my wife and me much grief. Because we were unable to bear the memories of our little girl in our house, we went to work on the coast again.

Why did she die?

Like our first son, she took sick with the measles. She died within a month of becoming ill.

After three months of our picking cotton on the coast, my wife and I came back to San José. The elders reminded me to continue with my service as *mayordomo* of the *cofradía* of San Juan.

I struggled for a better life. I earned money, but I would drink it away with friends. They would invite me to drink. We would exchange drinks, and after they left, I would continue drinking. Finally, I realized my life was bad so I tried to avoid drinking altogether.

❧ Community Responsibilities and the Dance of the Conquerors

In 1966, they named me the secretary of the Committee of the Silver Anniversary of Father Alonso Orellana to be celebrated in Sololá on December 21. He had come to Central America from Colombia 25 years ago. The president was Señor Jaime Mendosa

Sánchez, the vice-president was Ignacio Sánchez Hernández, the treasurer was Francisco Mendoza Rodríquez.

The four of us struggled to raise money to sponsor the fiesta. Each person in the town gave his *centavos*, and we managed to collect about $140. This was to be a celebration of all of the Catholics in the department of Sololá, the capital of the province, and people in other towns were raising money, too.

Were there any personal costs to you?

Because everyone participating in the activities was asked to wear the traditional *traje* [dress] on the day of the festivities, I had to rent a suit of traditional *Joseño* clothing. My wife wore her own *traje* of *Joseñas*.[9]

On the day of the fiesta we took the launch to Panajachel and arrived about 7:00 A.M. But by the time we reached Panajachel, everyone else had already left for Sololá, leaving my wife and me without transportation. I don't know from where the good priest Ignacio Pérez of Spain was coming, but when he passed us he stopped.

"Where are you going?" he asked.

"We are going to the celebration in Sololá," I answered, "but we are waiting for a bus because there apparently wasn't enough room in the truck for us, and they left without us."

"Well, come with me in my car. I'm going there myself."

He took my wife and me with him to Sololá, and when we arrived all of the people were waiting for us. There were many other Indians from all over Sololá—San José, San Jorge, San Martín, San Benito, San Diego, and San Luis. All the representatives of each town were wearing the colorful *trajes* of their towns. It was very pretty!

First a mass was celebrated in the general school of Sololá. Then we walked down to the site where the construction of a new church was beginning because the old one was deteriorating. Father Alonso blessed the first stone of the Cathedral of Sololá which was to be completed within 15 to 25 years from that day, which was December 21, 1965.

On Christmas day we four committee members invited Reverend Father Ignacio Epelde (of Spain) who was in San Jorge to a party. Father Ignacio told us that the children of San José should be instructed in Catholic catechism so they could receive their first communion in February. We made a list of about 96 boys and girls. Then we began teaching the Catholic doctrine.

Unfortunately, I was unable to witness the children receiving first communion on February 20, the day of Tecún Umán, a national hero in Guatemala. I needed money so much that I had to go to the coast to pick cotton in the middle of January.

When I returned from the coast, my three fellow committeemen told me what had happened. They raised some money to take to the priest in San Martín.

On March 19, we walked to San Martín to the priest to inactivate our committee. We had a few cups of whiskey before he invited us to lunch. When we returned to San José, we continued drinking. Afterwards, I didn't feel very well because I had a tremendous hangover.

In April they named me secretary of the committee for the main fiesta of San Juan. I didn't want to accept this responsibility because of my extreme poverty. Thus the tribunal released me of this duty.

In May 1966, the same year, however, I agreed to be a dancer for the fiesta of San Juan, which began on June 24. I committed myself to dance *El Baile la Conquista* [the Dance of the Conquest of Guatemala by the Spaniard Alvarado]. We dancers had to rent our own costumes either in San Cristóbal Totonicapán or Santa Cruz del Quiché, where the better uniforms can be rented, or in Sololá, where the cheaper suits are available.

Unfortunately, not until four days before the dancing was to begin, did I manage to raise the necessary $15 with which to rent a suit in Sololá. By this time everyone else already had rented an outfit.

On June 21, a day before the dancing was to begin, all of us dancers went with a shaman to Cujil Cavern [a sacred cavern in the hills behind San José] to burn candles and incense to insure safety and good luck while dancing. The shaman was Gregorio Sánchez Tuc, a *Joseño*, who was about 75 years old.

How many of you went, and what did you do?

Including the shaman, drummer, and flutist, there were 25 of us. We carried with us yellow candles for the dead, *pom* [myrrh] incense, sugar, cigars, *guaro* and *aguardiente*. These were all things that would please the gods and spirits, whom we were asking for protection against falling down and injuring our heads or breaking an arm or a leg.

Before [an old wooden] cross, burning candles, and a stone image, the shaman prayed to the god of the hills and the god of the world. The sugar and incense that he burned was a cake [offering] for the gods. The shaman drank and smoke cigars. The rest of us smoked, but only cigarettes. The cigars and cigarettes were not for the gods of the hills but for us because it was cold and because we were supposed to be happy during the fiesta. The *guaro* and *aguardiente* were for the shaman and for the cross, which he sprinkled for the god of the world. And that is the way it was.

After all the *costumbres* [ceremonies] the shaman was so inebriated he was unable to walk. Because of this we arrived home at 5:00 A.M. It took a long time to get back, and when we arrived home the manager of the dance, Señor Martín, my adoptive father, was very rude because it had taken us so long—almost a whole night. But this was the fault of the shaman. When he was performing the *costumbres* in the cave, he called all of the dead he had known since he was a small child. He called the spirits of all the oldest people, who are now dead, to present the *costumbres* to them. This is what happened.

After eating breakfast we went to dress as dancers, but before beginning to dance we went with the shaman to the Catholic Church to entrust our souls to God. Then we danced all day, June 23.

On June 24, I remember well that I was broke. By the grace of God, I had planted a field of onions that was ready for harvesting. Early in the morning Juan Chavajay Toch, from San Martín la Laguna, arrived and asked to buy the onions. Since I didn't have a cent, I was delighted to sell him the whole lot for $12. During a fiesta is a bad time to be without money, especially if one is obliged to be a dancer. My wife and I had been buying a few little things to eat, but they were not really nutritious. Thanks to my sale, we were relieved because we could now buy necessities.

After making the sale, I hurried back to join the dancers around 9:30 A.M. Señor Martín called to my attention that I had arrived late on the very day of San Juan itself.

In the afternoon, all of my dancing companions got very drunk. But I didn't drink much. Such was the afternoon until we went home to our houses.

In the evening, my wife and I spent a little while in the Town Hall. I remember well that we drank beer and ate tamales with some friends.

On June 25, all of us conquest dancers were summoned to dance for the *cofradía* of San Juan Bautista. At that time the head of the brotherhood was Señor Domingo Cholotio Gómez. Señor Diego Sánchez Hernández gave several drinks to the dancers, members of the *cofradía*, and to the most important people of the town. They also gave us dancers lunch. Because we had drunk so much liquor, we ate quietly. And so the day went.

On June 26, Señor Martín told us all to go dance at Señor José Mendoza's place. Everyone went there except me because I was too tired. This was easy for him to do because at that time he owned a bar.

Why did he lose the bar?

He lost the bar because his three sons would come home from the fields tired and help themselves. Little by little the tavern went broke. As soon as their father ran out of money, the sons moved to Guatemala City to work in a clothing factory. They left their father in San José with nothing. But they still have their little amusements from their earnings at the factory.

All of the dancers got quite drunk. But I was unable to complete the celebration as a dancer because I did not have enough money to spend.

I was asleep at 2:00 A.M. when tragic news arrived. One of my dance companions Felipe Bizarro Ramos had his eye poked out in a fight. I don't know all of the details because I was not there. Apparently Felipe had entered a bar where Jorge Coc L. was drinking. Jorge was not a dancer, and I don't know what Felipe might have done to cause Jorge to strike him in the eye. Because only the two of them were inside when it happened, there were no witnesses. Felipe came out screaming that his eye had been poked out. Jorge left for his house. When the police arrived, they were unable to determine the culprit because no one saw him. Jorge claimed that he was innocent, that he did nothing but go home and go to sleep.

We took Felipe to the hospital in Sololá across the lake at dawn when the launch arrived. He stayed a few days, and when he returned, he was totally blind in one eye. I began to think about the ceremony that Señor Gregorio had performed for our protection. Obviously, since Felipe lost his eye, the ceremony had not worked. Since then I have no confidence in shamans or witches. They are liars who are in business only to take money from others because they do not wish to do any real work.

❧ A Futile Attempt to Obtain Work on the Coast

In December 1966 I left as part of a crew of 125 to pick cotton on the Laguna Farm in the Champerico region. Unfortunately, the trip turned out badly for us. When we arrived at the farm, the administrators told us they did not have anything for us to do because the number of workers they needed had been filled. Those who had money for passage took a bus back to San José. Those who didn't went to look for work at other farms.

My two friends—Felipe, who had lost an eye, and Geraldo— and I did not have any money for the fare back to San José. In vain we remained on the Laguna Farm hoping they would give us work. They didn't.

We had no choice but to head back toward San José, which was some 196 kilometers away. We started walking about 2:00 A.M. without food or money. By 9:00 A.M. we reached a farm called Los Angeles. At this place we were able to get only a few cents worth of tortillas.

We didn't know the right route, but we immediately started to walk again. We were fortunate to meet a man on the road who knew the right direction to San José, and he pointed out the way. At 6:00 P.M. we arrived at a town called Tierras del Pueblo. In that town my friend Geraldo managed to sell his machete for 80 cents.

With this money we were able to buy passage to Mazatenango. There a relative of mine, Benito Bizarro García, was working as an attendant in the Suchitepéquez hospital. He lent me a dollar. With this money we paid for passage to San Antonio Suchitepéquez. There we bought a few tortillas and rented a room in an inn named Los Cerritos.

It was a Sunday night, and we were sleeping in a bar. In the middle of the night some hoodlums tried to rob us, but we had no money for them to take. After they left, we could not sleep peacefully.

At 5:00 A.M. we each had a cup of coffee and a piece of bread, and we headed out walking again for San José, which was still 40 kilometers away. We walked through many farms— San Ignacio, El Marne, California, Brazil, La Abundancia, Colima, Esperanza, La Paz, and Filadelfia. Finally, we reached one named Los Horizontes.

Lucky for us, my Uncle Huberto Bizarro Mendosa, who owns a *marimba* [band], was playing there to celebrate the fiesta of Santa Lucía, which is celebrated on December 13. My friend Felipe walked over by the *marimba* because they were passing out tortillas near them. I didn't walk over with him because I felt too ashamed of our predicament. Felipe managed to get some tortillas, and he shared them with Geraldo and me.

Then we began walking toward San José again. At 5:00 P.M. we arrived at a village outside San José named Pachichaj. This meant we were still 15 kilometers from home. A friend of mine who lives in this village gave us food when I asked him. At last Felipe, Geraldo and I were able to eat. We were given plenty of meat with tortillas and coffee!

At 7:00 P.M. we passed through another village on the outskirts of San José called Patzilín. There I found some more friends. I told them about our unpleasant ordeal. They had sympathy for us, and gave us two bottles of wine which we drank in the half-hour we chatted with them.

Because Geraldo walked more swiftly than we, he already had left us behind. Finally, Felipe and I arrived in San José at 10:00 P.M. I got some change from my house to buy a couple of drinks to ward off our weariness.

Thus went the trip to the Laguna Farm. We had set out to gain, but instead we lost!

What was the value of the machete that Geraldo sold for 80 cents?

It was worth at least $3.

❧ Working on the Esquipulas and Caoba Farms

Two days after Christmas in 1966, I returned to the coast to pick cotton at a farm named Esquipulas. This time I went with a contractor Señor Oscar Arnulfo Cabrera. For thirty days I picked cotton, but the work was not very good. I returned home without much money—only $35.

Nevertheless, I needed work, and at the end of January 1967, I went to the Caoba Farm as part of a work crew for Señor Oscar. On this farm many guys from the West (Mazatenango, Tacaná, Itzapa) turned out to be my friends. Every Sunday we would go swimming in the Pacific Ocean, and afterwards to the bars to drink.

Unfortunately, all of this drinking gave me a disease of the mouth, and soon I could neither drink nor eat. My mouth became so infected that I had to go to Tiquisate to a pharmacy to buy medicine. The whole month passed with my having an infection. I hardly earned any money because of it!

After the work was finished at the Caoba Farm, I went to the Totonicapán Farm for 25 days more of cotton picking. I earned $40, and with this money I was able to go home again to San José. However, the infection had still not gone away, and I had to go to a doctor in Sololá for treatment.

The medicine that the doctor gave me brought the first relief from my discomfort in two months. The illness depressed me, making me feel badly about my condition of poverty. I had to work to support my wife and myself. But I was very poor, and I had to work for others. This is to say, I was, sadly, a *jornalero* [day laborer].

You wrote that the people cortar *[literally cut] cotton. What is it exactly that they do?*

Cortar means to take the cotton from the plant with one's hands. The cotton is about to burst white, and so they take hold of the plant and gather it by hand and put it in a big sack. Then the people can see the different capabilities of the hands. There are hands that are smoother and gather cotton faster.

Are the workers paid by the pound?

The farm pays them a penny a pound. How much a person makes depends on his ability. When the crop was good—and it was not always the same—I picked between 150 to 170 pounds daily. But the amount varied. Some days I only picked 140 pounds because of fatigue or having to travel a long distance to get to the ripe fields. In addition to paying the workers one cent per pound, the owner of the farm supplies the meals, but they are always beans three times a day.

Don't they have machines for picking cotton now?

No, only by hand. Someone told me that there was a farm that sent for a cotton-picking machine, but he said that it didn't work out.

Why not?

Because there are parts of the cotton field that are not ready for harvest at the same time. Some bolls are not ready. But the machine came along and took everything. It took all the green cotton and the stems, and so it is a loss of crops. That's why they don't use machines, only hands.

❧ My Son, José, Is Born

On October 30, 1967, my wife gave birth to a son whom we named José Juan Bizarro Ramos. Within a month he came down with a disease like pneumonia that is very serious. We were afraid he would die as our first two babies, so we went to Señor Augustín Pop's pharmacy in San Martín for medicine. It cost $8 for five days of treatment. Fortunately, our little baby boy recovered.

Before he reached the age of five months, however, little José was stricken again with the same illness. But I had no money. My Aunt María said it would be better to take José to a shaman in San Martín named Eduardo Tuc Sumosa. I was reluctant, but eventually my wife and my mother, Elena, convinced me to go.

Eduardo, the señor shaman, told us that our baby had ailments of the world and that he could not help him. He suggested we take him to a doctor. We didn't get back to San José until around midnight.

I tried to borrow money from friends to take José to a doctor in Sololá, but they did not have any more either. In desperation I went back to San Martín to speak with Father Rodríquez. I told him of my grief, and without asking him twice, he lent me $10.

With this money we took José to Dr. Archila in Sololá. This man only charged me $3 for both the examination and the medicine. By the time we arrived home, the baby was already looking better, and my wife and I were relieved.

With this problem solved, I went to the coast to work as a traveling salesman with a friend. He lent me enough money to start my own business of selling vegetables such as tomatoes, onions, avocados, and oranges. In a little while I had made enough money to pay back Father Jorge H. But he had forgotten about the loan. Instead of collecting interest, he gave me $2.

Little by little, I was paying off my debts when bad luck struck again in June 1968. Little José was only eight months old when he caught the whooping cough. Again we went to the pharmacy to purchase medicine and injections. But these did not bring him relief.

Finally, José was cured not by medicine from the pharmacy but by a natural medicine. We gave him water boiled with mango leaves to drink. We also bathed him in the same kind of mixture. Because many children were dying at that time with the whooping cough, we were quite worried about José. We well remembered the death of our little daughter, Ana María, who along with some 50 other children had died in a measles epidemic in one month because San José had no doctor. We thanked God that little José recovered.

❧ I Am Accused of Murdering my Adoptive Mother

*Ignacio first included this entire episode without any
dialogue. When I asked him to explain the nature of his adoptive mother's wound, he retold on tape the entire story, including the dialogue.*

On November 15, 1968, fifteen of us workers from San José
went to pick cotton on the Caoba Farm. Four of my family went
with me—my mother-in-law, my aunt María, my uncle José, and my
sister-in-law Esmeralda. The rest were friends.

We arrived in Tiquisate and assembled with workers from El
Salvador, another country. In total 35 persons comprised our crew.
The foreman assigned me as overseer in charge of the crew.

The picking was good, and we worked contentedly the whole
month. The people from El Salvador became our good friends.
They told us that one can earn good money in their country but that
these are dangerous times there. Once in a while their countrymen
were killing one another, so they preferred to come to Guatemala to
work. One of the El Salvadoreños gave me a card game and a photograph of the champion soccer team there. I still have these gifts in
my house.

On a Saturday at the end of the month they paid us, and we set
out for home by bus. In Chicacoa we stopped to spend the night.
There was a fiesta going on, but I did not go out to stroll because I
felt somewhat sick.

Sunday about noon we arrived in San José. My Aunt María
sent me to buy meat to celebrate our homecoming. When lunch was
ready about 3:00 P.M., they called my wife and me to come eat with
them. Then Aunt María sent for a bottle of liquor. Everyone took
some but me. I was still a bit sick. I am not sure whether it was a
little malaria or I was just tired. But I did not feel like drinking.
About six in the afternoon, I went to bed. Aunt María, my grandma,
and my uncles continued drinking.

Then Aunt María, my adoptive mother, came to my bed and
said, "Come, Ignacio, have a cup of liquor!"

"I don't want to," I told her, "I feel bad." Then I took a pill.

"Have a drink!" she insisted.

"Well, no!"

Then she left to continue drinking with the rest of my family.

About 10:00 P.M. Aunt María returned to where I was trying to
sleep. She had with her a five-cent candle and matches. She lit the

candle and began to say her prayers. She had been drinking, it is true, but not too much. Her mind was still clear.

"Ignacio," she said, though I was trying to sleep, "have a cup of liquor with me!"

"No! I don't want to!"

"Ignacio, only a cup."

"No, I'm not going to drink!"

"Why not?"

"Because I am sick, and it would be dangerous to drink after taking a pill. If I have a cup of liquor, it can kill me."

"Ah, man, drink a cup!"

"No!"

"Then you don't want to drink?"

"No, I don't want to drink, thanks."

"Sleep then!"

"Good," I said.

She took her candle and matches and went to the room in our house where she slept and laid down on her bed.

I went back to sleep.

About 2:00 A.M. my aunt went banging on the door of the house of my sister, whose husband is a medic. Blood was gushing from my aunt's temple!

"Open the door," she pleaded, "I'm hurt!"

"Go to sleep," my sister answered, "don't bother us now. We are sleeping."

"Please, open your door. Roberto must help me!"

But my sister didn't want to open the door. She must have thought Aunt María was just drunk.

Then my aunt went to my grandmas's little house about 25 meters away.

"Open the door," she shouted, "I'm dying!"

"And what happened to you?" my grandmother implored.

"I fell off my bed and hit my head on the corner of the chest," she moaned.

Then Aunt María collapsed at my grandmother's door and died.

My grandma got up, my sister got out of bed, and my mother, Elena, came running over. The ruckus they were making awoke me, but only after my aunt was already dead.

"Look! Your Aunt María died!"

"What happened to her?" I gasped. "I don't know what happened because I was sleeping!"

"She is dead!"

When I went over to examine her, she was indeed dead. I was scared because I did not know why she had died. As I looked at her lying there, I felt cold, cold, cold!

My brother-in-law Roberto went with me to report the death to the police. I very well remember that we got to the courthouse about 3:00 A.M. The commissioner, municipal policemen, and constables accompanied me to inspect the corpse. A large crowd of neighbors had gathered, and my grandma was wailing.

The justice of peace, Nicolás María Mendosa, arrived about 4:00 A.M. together with the town secretary to draw up the certificate of death. Before the secretary had finished writing up the certificate, Señor Martín, who had separated from his wife, María, arrived with my Uncle Bonifacio, the older brother of the deceased.

These two men astonished me when they claimed I had killed my own aunt and adoptive mother. Yet, the notion that I was a murderer spread throughout the town. The rumor was that I killed her because I was drunk.

Señor Martín's cruel words, "You are the murderer!" bothered me very much.

I had not been drinking—not even a cup! I built my defense around this fact. God must have been telling me not to drink because I had nothing—not even one beer!

My grandma vouched for me that I had not drunk anything. She reported that Aunt María told her that she had injured her head between her ear and eye (her temple) when she fell from her bed and hit her head on the chest.

I confessed before God and the people of San José that it was not I who had killed her. Finally, the justice of the peace, who had taken me captive and was going to send me as a prisoner to Sololá, set me free.

We took the body to the cemetery to be buried. For three days members of my family and I drank a lot of liquor in grief. But people continued to talk about us. They claimed that I had killed my aunt. It was just slander.

All of this happened on December 10, 1968.

❧ Rejection of the Cargo Comisario [Commissioner]

In January 1969, they tried to name me commissioner of the municipality, but because I was so poor I did not accept the post. Instead, I went to work for two months on the Tolimán Tiquisate Farm.

On March 8, four days after I returned from working in the cotton fields, my wife gave birth to a little baby girl whom we named María, after my late aunt.

During this month I labored at planting corn though I only had three *cuerdas* of land. Also I planted onions on a *cuerda* of land that I rented. I only planted this much land because it is expensive to buy fertilizer. I paid for the seed corn and the fertilizer that I used by working as a laborer for the man who owned the land. During the months of April and May, I would water my onions early in the morning and then spend the rest of the day working for Señor Bonifacio, a very good person.

In June I harvested and sold the onions, but only for $90. With this money, I bought more fertilizer and a few clothes for my wife and myself. That was all the money I had to spend because life in San José is very difficult. Sometimes it seems that it isn't worth working. The sale of the onions, however, did enable us to enjoy somewhat the fiesta of June 24.

❧ San José Disputes with San Martín over Water Rights

When I lived in San José in 1970, a Joseño *told me that San José had fought with San Martín over the water supply the previous year. You did not mention this in your autobiography originally. Can you explain what happened?*

Yes, I remember it well. From August to September of the year of 1969 there were heavy rains. The rain caused a landslide that in turn caused the main water tank from the source of the Kaimbal River to tumble down. With the collapse of the tank there was no potable water for either San José or San Martín. [San José and San Martín are two kilometers apart, and they get their water from the same source, which is in San José's municipal jurisdiction.]

Most of the *Martineros* have water faucets in their homes now, and it is a burden to carry drinking water from the lake. The water that *Martineros* use really belongs to the *Joseños;* the river from which the water flows is situated on San José's land. When the tank fell down, San José wanted to punish San Martín by not allowing them to repair it.

Friction between *Joseños* and *Martineros* goes back to the period of the *mandamientos* [orders for forced labor to coastal farms] during the presidency of Manuel Estrada Cabrera [1898–1920]. Well, I really only know what the old people tell me. They say that it was mainly the years of 1930 to 1936 [which places it during the vagrancy laws of President Jorge Ubico].

Because the *Martineros* were literate and rich, they were able to avoid the *mandamientos*. Perhaps they were able to become wiser by studying with the fathers in San Martín or they were more interested in going to school. Nevertheless, the poor *Joseños* were affected by the orders to go to the coast to work. To raise money for corn and beans they needed, they had to sell their land to *Martineros*. The *Martineros* paid them pesos during this period because that was the kind of money we had then, not *quetzales* [equivalent to U.S. dollars]. Although I am not sure of the exact amount, *Martineros* paid *Joseños* about $10 to $15 for each parcel of land, which was cheap. Because the poor little *Joseños* did not know how to read and write, the *Martineros* cheated them. That is, if a *Joseño* sold a *Martinero* one plot of land, and the *Joseño* actually had two plots, the *Martinero* bought one and stole the other. The *Martinero* would write on the deed that he bought two plots instead of one, and because the *Joseño* could not read, he was swindled.

One old man, Señor Juan Ujpán Coj, who is still alive, told me that during this period that only eight families managed to stay in San José.[10] It was almost as if San José did not exist. They say that the *Martineros* even wanted to take out the image of San Juan Bautista to carry to their church in San Martín. Thus, the remaining few families carefully guarded the image of the saint from the *Martineros*.

Little by little, the *Joseños* returned from the coast, but they had no land. They had to go to the *Martineros* to ask for work. Since *Joseños* were poor, the *Martineros* mistreated them. The *Joseños* did not have anything because *Martineros* had bought everything. But eventually San José began to recover.

Now, there are certainly changes. This is because *Joseños* go to the coast to plant their corn. They bring their harvest home to San José, and thus they do not have to go to San Martín to buy corn. They plant their own beans. Because they pick cotton on the coast, *Joseños* earn their money in December, January, and February. Now, they no longer have to work for *Martineros*. For these reasons *Martineros* are looking now upon *Joseños* as equals, with the same worth as themselves. But before, this was not the case. They had to go to a rich *Martinero* to ask for work to sustain their families. Today, if a *Joseño* needs money, he goes to a farm where he can work at a regular price, or he goes to the coast to plant a patch of corn. Many *Joseños* are progressing. They are buying the land back from the *Martineros*. Now *Martineros* are coming to San José to ask for work or to buy corn from them. Really, what I am saying is that not long ago the *Martineros* wanted to act like kings toward *Joseños*. They can no longer do so. San José is still poor and *Martineros* still own land here, but San José is moving up. *Joseños* are able to work independently. Their work experience on the coast is making them more wise, and what they earn on the coast they are not spending in San Martín but in San José.

Thus, you can see why there could be problems between *Joseños* and *Martineros* over water in 1969. But there is more to the history of this problem. Actually, *Joseños* believed *Martineros* were abusing their privilege of using water from San José. That is, when potable water came to San José on February 15, 1960, a decree of the state government of Sololá stated that San José could have 60 faucets and San Martín could have 100 since San Martín had more people living in it than San José.

San Martín built the water tank and installed the pipe, but San José provided the water. (*Martineros* installed the water facilities in San José as well as their own town.) What has resulted is that the *Martineros*, in the nine years since piped water began, have installed more than 400 faucets [about 300 more than they were allowed originally]. They have so many that the water pressure is low in San Martín, and the *Martineros* are always having pressure problems because they have too many faucets. In San José, there is usually enough pressure.

Because the tank that serves both San José and San Martín is in the municipal district of San José, the problem of San José's not allowing San Martín to repair the tank was appealed to San José's *principales* [town elders who are important political figures]. San José said, "You [San Martín] may have our permission again to use the water but San Martín must pay a very high tax—$60 a month."

San Martín had not been paying a water tax before, and it did not want to agree to such a tax. The case was taken to the state court of Sololá to be settled. But since the case could not be settled in the state court, it went to Guatemala City to the Ministry of Public Works and the Ministry of Government.

When *Martineros* began to see they had a weak case against *Joseños*, they became insulting and aggressive. San José was still in conformance with the 1960 decree because it only had 38 faucets, while San Martín had 400.

Rumor arrived that *Martineros* were angry and were talking about killing *Joseños*. When *Joseños* discovered their reported intentions, they arose against *Martineros* with the same ill feelings. San José publically stated at the border between San José and San Martín, "If one *Joseño* dies, we are going to kill 10 or 20 *Martineros* because the people of San José are in their own town and are in the right. Therefore, if one *Martinero* kills a *Joseño*, know that 10 or 20 *Martineros* are going to die!"

It was true that some people were sincerely concerned over the need for water while others just were interested more in criminal acts. *Martineros* certainly had to go to San José because they had to take the harvest from the land they owned there. But they only would come to San José in groups of three or four persons. One person would not come alone because he was afraid of losing his life.

Once a man came brandishing a machete in San José. But San José gave notice, "If one *Joseño* dies, we are going to the boundary and wait for *Martineros* and kill them." Then *Martineros* calmed down and did not do anything until this conflict was settled.

Unlike *Martineros*, who needed to come to San José, *Joseños* did not need to go to San Martín because they had no land there. Since San José does not have its own market, *Joseños* usually went to San Martín to buy necessities. But during the dispute, *Joseños* opted to climb the mountain to Santa Ana for their market needs. Thus, the situation was less threatening to *Joseños* than *Martineros*.

The conflict sharpened when someone cut down ten coffee trees belonging to Señor Alfonso García Sumosa, a rich *Martinero*. He thought the guilty person was Señor Bernardo Coj Mendosa, the syndic of San José. Then Señor Alfonso tried to find witnesses to prove that Señor Bernardo had cut down his coffee trees, but he could not.

Then four members of the national police arrived in San José to capture Señor Bernardo. Señor Alfonso must have paid the national policemen to punish Señor Bernardo because they struck him several times with their billy clubs, tied his hands behind his back with a rope, and marched him off to jail in San Martín. In jail they would not give him food or bedding.

The next day they took him to jail in Sololá. He was lucky since he only spent one day in jail there. The police in Sololá could not hold him because he had an alibi. When the coffee trees were cut down, he had been in the Town Hall carrying out his duties as syndic.

In February 1970, by order of the Ministry of Justice of the Government, the governor of the department of Sololá arrived in San José to execute an affidavit of reconciliation between the two towns. In effect, San Martín obtained the right to repair the tank and use the water. But in order to do this San Martín had to construct five large *pilas* [water basins] in the streets of San José.

By March the water was running again in San José and in San Martín. During the six months of conflict, the poor women of the two towns suffered the most. They had to carry water laboriously from the lake to prepare food for their families and to do the washing. And without running water, this was a real hardship.

By the grace of God, the peace has been permanent. Since the end of the conflict, there has been peace and goodwill between the towns.

ᕐᐧ Organizing Cotton Picking Crews

After the November 1969 harvest season, in which I harvested only 400 pounds of seed corn, a cotton picking contractor named Adrián Sánchez García came to consult with me from San Martín la Laguna. He was looking for *cuadrillas* [work crews]; he asked me to be his assistant. He promised that if I would talk to people in the streets and go from house to house to organize crews that he would pay me a regular price for my assistance.

We agreed, and I organized about 60 people to go to pick cotton on the Pacalle Farm. We gave the crew their customary $3 advancement to buy the little things they would need for the trip such as sugar.

At the farm I met Señor Adrián, who was coming from San Martín with his crew. I had my own crew from San José. He stayed with the crews on the Pacalle Farm, and he took me to Tiquisate to work with another crew.

The work was bearable, and we finished at the end of the month. The farm paid me as part of the crew, but I also expected to receive half of the ten percent that the farm paid Adrián for contracting the crew. We agreed, for example, that if the crew earned $1000, and he received $100, I would get $50.

We left the farm after payday, and we headed back to Lake Atitlán. When we arrived in San José, Adrián urged, "Ignacio, leave your things in San José and come with us to San Martín."

"Thanks," I replied, "but my wife does not like me to go to San Martín. She doesn't like it because I will go to San Martín and drink. That upsets her." Then I went to my house and stayed there.

The next day I went to try to get my percentage from Adrián in San Martín. I arrived at his house, but when he answered the door, I found out that he no longer had any money. He had gone drinking with 10 or 15 of his chums, and he squandered all of the money on *guaro*.

Then, he pleaded, "I want you to keep working for me, to help me organize more crews to work on the farms."

"Why should I keep working with you if you are not going to pay me my share? I work because I need to support my family and myself. My work is not a gift to someone else!"

"No," he said, "I'm going to pay you for this. I will pay you for everything."

"No," I answered, "it will be better for me not to work with you anymore. I don't feel like it. But if you want me to work as a regular cotton picker, I will be happy to work for another month. You promised to pay me a salary apart from what I earned picking cotton. I must work to support my family, but I will not give my time free to someone else."

He never did pay me. He was a thief because I gave up my time looking for people to form a crew, and he promised to pay a regular salary for this. But I didn't receive anything for doing it—not a thing!

Later I found out that Señor Adrián had made an enemy of another contractor, Señor Pedro Castro Puac. Señor Adrian also had made false promises to Señor Pedro. They quarreled, and now they are enemies.

One day Pedro Castro came to me and asked, "Why aren't you working with Adrián?"

"No, because he was dishonest with me."

"How?"

"Because he did not pay me."

"Look, it is better that you don't work for him anymore. It would be better for you to come to work for me instead."

"All right," I said. "I will work for you."

Well, for me, Pedro Castro was not a thief. I went with him all over Guatemala to form work crews. We took crews to many farms—Caoba, San Juan las Bordas Jurisdición de Tiquisate, and Escuintla. We worked well together and he paid me a regular percentage of the amount the administrators paid him for bringing crews to them [half of the ten percent]. We worked together from March until May of 1970.

In June and July I worked with Jim Sexton in San José. I had already left for the coast to work on my patch of corn so I did not see him off. He left many going-away gifts with my sister the night before he left. I did not think we would see him again.

ᴙ Felipe Fights with a Shaman: A Dire Prophesy

On August 8, 1970, the secretary of San José, Señor Florencio Mogollón Telle, who is a Ladino *compadre* [ritual co-parent] of my son José, was preparing to move away from San José to another town. He had not been getting along with the *alcalde* [mayor], and he decided to leave. My friend Felipe, who had lost an eye, and I went to say good-bye to the secretary, who was also Felipe's *padrino* [godfather].

When we arrived at Señor Florencio's house, several friends of his had gathered and were drinking *tragos* at his farewell party. Because it was his last night in San José, we drank a lot of *aguardiente*.

When we ran out of liquor, Felipe and I went to a nearby bar to buy more. As we entered the bar, we noticed a shaman named Agustín Sumosa from San Benito la Laguna. He was with two *Joseños*, Candelaria Coché Méndez and Carlos Bizarro Yojcom. Without doubt they were buying *aguardiente* for ceremonies.

Felipe began to argue with the shaman. I don't really know why or how it started. Perhaps Felipe was harboring disillusionment with all shamans since he had lost an eye despite the ceremony performed by Señor Gregorio Sánchez Tuc for protection of all of us dancers during the fiesta of San Juan. In any case, Felipe and the shaman from San Benito began to fight violently. One of Felipe's blows broke the collarbone of the poor shaman, and he cried out in pain. He had reason to cry because the blow was a severe one. The two *Joseños* for whom he was going to perform a ceremony of some kind began to cry too, since they pitied their hapless friend.

Señor Agustín, the injured shaman, groaned to his enemy Felipe:

Today you struck me for the first time, but you will never strike me again because it is certain that you are going to die. To the justice of the peace of San José, I will not go. Instead, I am going to take my case to *El Dueño del Mundo* [God of the World]. For sure you are going to die [because I am going to perform a ceremony that will put a death curse on you].

These words the shaman uttered to Felipe. Although inebriated, we were somewhat surprised at his prophesy, but we both doubted the power of sorcerers after our experience in the Cujil Cavern.

Señor Agustín Sumosa remained bedridden for eight days in the house of Carlos Yojcom. Other friends from San José came to visit with this man, and they performed healing ceremonies to help him recover. They protected him and gave him a lot of food and tragos.

∿ Pedro Castro Puac Quits Contracting

In September 1970, I continued working with Pedro Castro. But it happened that Castro got himself deep in debt with the owners of the farm. At the end of the month, when the workers would be paid, they would withhold the debt. Sometimes the money lenders would collect as much as $300 to $400. When this happened I did not earn my percentage either. I really don't think it was Castro's fault. Finally, I told the owners that I was not going to continue organizing crews for them because I felt I was just working for them for nothing.

Pedro Castro Puac decided that he did not want to work contracting crews anymore. On Christmas day we gave him a farewell party. We reminisced about the hard times we shared in the short time we had been working together. We had traveled all over to find workers—Santa Cruz del Quiché, San Pablo Jocopilas, Samayac, Jutiapa, Retalhuleu, Sacatepéquez, and many other places. Sometimes we endured hunger because we would be unable to obtain food after arriving in a town. Although we had plenty of money we might not find a *comedor* open. Despite such hardships, we had pleasant memories, and we parted as good friends.

∿ Meeting Old Army Buddies and an Invitation by a Spaniard to Dinner

In January 1971, I went with my friend Felipe to pick cotton on a farm called Los Alamos. The picking was good, and the lodging was very agreeable, but the place was extremely hot.

One Sunday we were craving something else to eat besides the beans and tortillas they were giving us three times a day on the farm. So we went to San Antonio Suchitepéquez to get something different. Suddenly we chanced upon two of my former army buddies from Mazatenango with whom I had been stationed in Retalhuleu in 1962. It had been nine years since we had seen one another. I had no money on myself, but they invited us to a restaurant to have some drinks.

We got carried away with our conversation about all the things that had happened over the years. Drink after drink, the time began to slip by. Before we realized it, the bus that ran to the Los Alamos Farm had already left. Because it was too far to walk, Felipe and I kept on drinking with our friends the rest of the night. We did not leave for the farm until the following day. Thus we lost two day's work. We didn't really mind, because we worked on the farm two months.

At the end of the month on Saturday we were paid. The route home required us to walk to the Siaquacán River. There the countryside is quite beautiful. One has to travel by canoe across the river which is about 300 to 400 meters wide. The river is clean and immense. There are different people in different *trajes* going to and from Tiquisate, Escuintla and Suchitepéquez.

We paddled down the river by canoe to Pacaya where we waited for a bus. We flagged one down and took it to Cocales. In this town, we met some friends and had a few drinks with them. Then we caught another bus to Chipo, but we slept all of the way there. When we arrived in this town, we were still in the mood to drink so we went into a little bar.

As we were drinking, a stranger who was sitting beside us spoke to me. "What's your name? Where are you from?"

"My name is Ignacio Bizarro and my friend's name is Felipe Bizarro, though he is not kin to me. We are from San José la Laguna in the department of Sololá. What's your name?"

"I am called Pedro Avascal. I am from Spain. Would you like a drink?"

"Thank you."

"I am the owner of the farm next to this bar. Would you like to come to my house to visit?"

I was a little startled that a farm owner would invite two poor men like Felipe and me to his house. And I was a little apprehensive that he might be planning to murder us. But the liquor gave me courage even though I felt it incredible that we poor souls could walk together with a farm owner. I agreed to go visit his house, and Felipe came with us.

When we reached his farm, we saw that it was beautiful. It had a church, a school, and other buildings. The house was nearby, and we went inside. I was still afraid that he might be planning to harm us, but, on the contrary, he treated us very well. He gave us many drinks of whiskey and beer. Around midnight we ate dinner. We had *Pica Pica* [sardines], with French bread, not tortillas! We stuffed ourselves! And we continued drinking because this man had a lot of liquor in his refrigerator.

In our chatting, the Spaniard told us that he did not have a partner nor did he have a wife and children. He lived alone in his big house. I could not help but wonder who would inherit all of his property.

We left his house early in the morning. Indeed, this had been an unforgettable experience for me. I had been eating and drinking with a Spaniard!

ᔪ During Holy Week I Am Gravely Ill

I arrived home Sunday after being away two months. I was feeling somewhat hung over from having drunk so much liquor.

A few days later Felipe came over to my house to discuss going to the coast to plant corn. We decided to leave, but when the day approached for departure, I was still too sick to go. Felipe went alone, and I stayed at home in bed. I was gravely ill with three diseases—a disease of the liver, a disease of the heart, and a mild case of malaria.

All of the money I had made on the coast was spent on medicine because I was sick for three months (March, April, and May). I even had to sell all of my little possessions to make ends meet. When Holy Week came, which is celebrated a lot in Guatemala, I remained in bed. On that day I really thought I was going to die! I surely suffered from my diseases.

When the patron fiesta came to San José in June, my wife and I were pathetic. We were broke because of my illness, and we had no corn nor any land planted. We were very sad!

ᔪ The Anthropologists Return to Lake Atitlán and I Get a Strange Cigar

About July 20, 1971, I don't remember the date precisely, but I remember the day well, I received a telegram from Panjachel from my friend Jim D. Sexton. I was surprised because I really doubted that I would ever see him again. The telegram said that Señor Jim wanted me to come to Panajachel.

On Friday, I caught the 4:30 A.M. launch to Panajachel. Don Jaime was waiting at the pier when I arrived. He invited me to breakfast at his house, and he explained that he would like me to help him and Dr. Woods construct and demonstrate the use of a new interview schedule. It would be used by the students in various towns on the lake.

In the evening, Don Jaime took me to eat dinner in a small restaurant named Comedor Ramírez. We had a tasty meal of beefsteak, vegetables, and beer. I spent the night at Don Jaime's house.

Saturday morning, the next day, all of the students gathered in Don Jaime's house. They told me that they had been out in their towns working on the interview schedule [pre-testing]. When Dr. Woods arrived we spent the entire morning going over the questions. At the same time, we demonstrated the proper way to conduct an interview with the people. We finished in the afternoon, and Don Jaime and I went again to eat lunch at Comedor Ramírez.

Late in the afternoon I went with Don Jaime to the house of Dr. Woods where all the students had gone for a fiesta. [There was a fire in the fireplace, a portable stereo played tapes from the United States, and we had plenty of tamales and beer.] That evening Dr. Woods gave me a handful of U.S. cigars.

Don Jaime and I left the party about 2:00 A.M. I told him that I had enjoyed the fiesta very much.

Sunday morning I was very content because Señor Jaime paid me well. I went to the market in Panajachel to buy a few things for my house in San José. At 3:45 P.M. I waved good-bye to Don Jaime, and boarded the launch headed back to San José.

I arrived about 5:30 P.M., and I told my wife of my good fortune at having spent the weekend in Panajachel with the anthropologists. That evening I went for a stroll, and I met some friends. We went to a bar to drink.

While we were drinking, I took out one of the cigars that Dr. Woods had given me. I lit it and began to puff. But then my friends began leaving quickly, one by one. And the owner of the bar, Señor Jorge Criado, became very frightened. Later, I found out that my friends and Señor Jorge thought I had lit up a cigar of marijuana. Of course, this was not the case. I was just smoking an ordinary cigar. That night turned out to be really curious for me because my friends and the bartender had been terrified because they were unfamiliar with the strong smell of the kinds of cigars that gringos smoke.[11]

∾ My Friend Felipe Is Killed

On August 13, 1971, my friend Felipe and another friend came to my house to congratulate me because it was my birthday. They had been drinking, and it was about 4:00 A.M. when they came by to offer me some drinks for my birthday.

About 5:30 A.M. my unforgettable North American friend Don Jaime arrived at my house to give me a book *Los Pueblos del Lago de Atitlán* [*The Towns of Lake Atitlán*]. It is a book about the Indian towns surrounding Lake Atitlán. My friend said that he could not stay because he was going to San Martín to take a canoe to San Luis and then a launch to Panajachel.

The next day my friend Felipe left for the southern coast to harvest and bring back corn he had planted in March. I never saw him again alive. On August 27, two weeks later, he was struck and killed by a car driven by a gringo who was employed by the Tawson Granary Company.

I was not there when the accident happened so I did not see it. When they brought Felipe back to San José, he was already dead. He was survived by a family who was grieved by his death. Felipe had been a very good person to them, and they suffered immensely.

Felipe was killed nearly one year from the date he had broken the collarbone of Señor Agustín Sumosa, the shaman who had promised to bewitch him. As the shaman prophesied, it was certain that Felipe was going to die soon, but God only knows whether Felipe's death was caused by *El Dueño del Mundo* or if it was just an accident. Yes, it is true that there are those in San José who believe the death of my good friend, Felipe, was caused by the shaman. My own thoughts are that only God and the spirit of Felipe know whether he was bewitched or whether it was just his destiny.

Do you know of any other reported cases of witchcraft like this?

In my town, San José, the belief exists that sorcerers are able to end the life of a person. They say that Felipe's life ending abruptly is an example. But I have been told of other similar cases of witchcraft.

My father-in-law told me about a case in 1958. This was when Señor Daniel Morales of San José argued with Señor Pablo Ajcac of San Martín over a parcel of land in a place called in *lengua* [native tongue] Ixtahuacán [Nahuatl], which means place of flatland. Señor Pablo lost the land to Señor Daniel because the latter could not produce a legitimate land title.

In April Señor Morales planted the land, but in July he fell ill, and on August 9, he died. My wife's father said that two minutes before Señor Morales died he vomited stones that were two inches in diameter and like wood. He threw up about a pound of these splinters. My father-in-law said the deceased had been bewitched.

After his telling me this story, I went to verify it with Señor Daniel Morales' widow. She told me the same thing—that her husband's death was not a death at the hands of God, but that it was an unnatural death and that he had been bewitched by the sorcerer Pablo Ajcac for the parcel of land they had argued over.

There is also the case of Señor Pascual Canajay and his brother-in-law, Ricardo Ramos. Pascual's mother sold a piece of land to Señor Samuel Pérez of Santa Bárbara. But when Señores Pascual and Ricardo found out about the sale, they did not want to part with the land. They argued that Ricardo's mother did not have the right to sell the land because the title was held by Ricardo's father.

The dispute over the parcel of land went to the justice of the peace in San José and finally to the state court in Sololá. The suit began in 1966, and it lasted in the civil courts for three years when it was finally settled. The judge ruled that Señor Samuel Pérez could not gain title to the land, but it turned out that Señor Samuel did not lose his money because in the interim he had sold it to another person—a señor from Totonicapán who was living in Santa Ana. This señor bought the land under deception because he was not aware of the court battle ensuing. The name of the deceived buyer is Sacaria Sicay.

When Señor Sacaria went to plant the land, Señor Pascual and Señor Ricardo met him in the field and told him that the land was not Señor Samuel's to sell, that in fact it belonged to Pascual's wife, Ricardo de Catarina. Then Señor Sacaria was sued by Ricardo and his sister, Catarina. The case also went to the state court in Sololá where it was settled two years later against Señor Sacaria Sicay, the defendant. He lost his money, and he felt he had been swindled.

But it turned out that Señor Pascual died in the middle of 1972, and in 1973 Ricardo Ramos died of the same illness. Their testicles had swollen very large, and they died suffering from this illness. Their wives, Señoras Catarina Ramos and Josefa Canajay, told me that when they died worms wiggled out of their testicles. Both of these women told me crying, "Yes, witchcraft exists."[12]

❧ A Ceremony for Felipe's Spirit

You said, but not in your autobiography originally, that a ceremony was performed for Felipe by a shaman. Can you explain what happened?

Because there is a custom in my town that when a person dies a ceremony must be performed for his spirit, nine days after Felipe's death his family gathered at the cemetery about 5:00 A.M. They took with them candles, flowers, incense, and a wreath as gifts to Felipe's spirit to make him happy. They stuck a cross into the ground over the tomb since Felipe's spirit is supposed to be there. All of this was done to placate the spirit and allow him to forget his house and family. If these things were not done, it is believed that the spirit would come at night to haunt its family.

After planting Felipe's cross over his grave, Felipe's family and I marched solemnly back to his wife's house. As is the custom, we were given bread, breakfast and drinks. Then Felipe's widow stated that in order to pacify Felipe's spirit it would be necessary to place a cross over the spot where the accident took place and to have a ceremony performed by a shaman there. Everyone else agreed that this should be done.

They sent me to fetch a shaman, Ruben Flores Tziac, to do the ceremony. He is a *Joseño* who is about 42 years old and who studied to be a clergyman in the Protestant church, but they did not give him a diploma because he did not have enough money to finish his training in the Biblical Institute. Later, he became a shaman. Señor Ruben said, "With much pleasure I will perform the ceremony and all that is necessary for the deceased."

He told me that he would need yellow candles, the color for death, valued at 5 and 10 cents each [about five and ten inches long, respectively], incense, five-eights of a quart of *aguardiente*, three beers, flowers, a white silk handkerchief, and a cross to place in the ground where the accident took place. Felipe's widow bought all of these things that I reported would be needed.

Because Felipe's widow asked me to please go with the shaman to the distant crossroads San Pedrera and Río Bravo where

Felipe had fallen, I set out with the shaman toward the Pacific Ocean. We left early Wednesday morning, but we did not reach Santa Río Bravo until about 5:00 P.M. because it is about 125 kilometers away. We asked permission of the owner of the property, Señor Rosario Sumoza Ixtamer, to perform the ceremony, and he gave it to us. Then we cleaned the place where Felipe had fallen because the belief is that the spirit of the deceased comes to that place.

After preparing the spot where Felipe died, we went back and slept on the porch of Señor Rosario's house until 1:00 A.M.

"Let's go," Señor Ruben, the shaman, commanded as he nudged me awake.

"Fine," I mumbled, and got up and ready to go.

Where the body had fallen, Señor Ruben used everything we had brought with us. He placed the candles in the shape of a cross, dug a little hole in the dirt and stuck in it the wooden cross that bore the name of the deceased and the date of the accident. He lit all of the candles and sprinkled them with *aguardiente*. Then he said a prayer to the dead and asked *El Dueño del Mundo* to surrender the spirit of the fallen Felipe. He spread out the white handkerchief and placed flowers over it. At 4:00 A.M. Señor Ruben and I began to drink a lot of *tragos*, and I began to relax and get high and content with the shaman because I was soon half drunk with him. At 5:00 A.M. Señor Ruben tied the flowers up with the silk handkerchief, telling me that with these flowers came Felipe's spirit.

With the bundle of flowers, we set out walking to Patulul. We arrived by 9:00 A.M., and we had breakfast and drank more *tragos* there. The shaman put the flowers bundled in the handkerchief inside his shirt, explaining that otherwise Felipe's spirit might slip out and fly away back to the place of the accident.

By truck we traveled back to San José with Felipe's spirit inside Señor Ruben's shirt, arriving home about midnight. The shaman marched to the gate of the cemetery and arranged the flowers that he carried in the handkerchief, telling me that this signified that Felipe's spirit was now with his body in his grave.

Upon returning to the widow's house, the relatives of the deceased filled us up with more *tragos*.

"Would you like to speak with Felipe's spirit?" the shaman asked them.

"Yes," was the answer.

Señor Ruben concentrated very hard to entice the spirits of the world and Felipe's spirit. Then the señor shaman said that Felipe's spirit had arrived in his own body and asked if anyone wanted to talk with him. In the mouth of Señor Ruben, Felipe's spirit affirmed that he was now content to be with his body in the cemetery in San José.

But I never heard Felipe's own voice. Instead it was only Señor Ruben's voice that I heard, although this was supposed to be Felipe's spirit talking. I felt that the whole ceremony that Señor Ruben had performed was a fake. He just made a lot of money from Felipe's widow. In addition to the cost of all the things used in the ceremony and the passage to the coast, Señor Ruben was paid $10 for his services. Because the poor widow paid me $3 to accompany the shaman to the place of the accident, altogether she spent about $25 for the ceremonies.

❧ Cheated by Another Contractor

On November 15, 1971, Señor Eduardo Hernández, a contractor, talked me into organizing a crew to pick cotton on the Pangola Farm. We organized 125 workers (a crew of 62 for me and another of 63 for Eduardo). But when it was time to advance the workers their customary $2 to $5, Eduardo did not have any money. When I saw that Eduardo was unable to get a loan, it upset me, and I suspected that Eduardo's credit had run out among his lenders.

Finally, I decided to ask Father Juan González to lend me $100 for 15 days. The father knows and trusts me, and he lent me the money with a promissory note.

As I returned from the parish in San Martín with the money needed to make the trip, Eduardo was waiting for me in a street of San José. He was pleased that I had the money, but we were not able to give money to all of the 125 workers who were waiting at my house. We only had money enough for 57 persons, so I went as a regular cotton picker too, although still as Eduardo's assistant.

The work was satisfactory. The workers earned from $35 to $55 each, and I made $42. When we were paid, the $100 that I had borrowed from Father Juan was included. I saw the field boss give this sum to Eduardo, but it actually was neither his nor mine but the father's who lent it to me.

Unfortunately, when Eduardo got his hands on the $100, he did not want to turn it over to me so that I could return it to Father Juan. Eduardo finally handed the money over to me only after considerable persuasion and not until we arrived in Cocales.

Upon arriving in San Martín, I discovered that Father Juan had been ordered to the Church of Santa Teresa in Guatemala City during the month that I had been working on the farm. I had to catch a bus to Guatemala City to return his money. I didn't arrive in Guatemala until 2:00 A.M.

Staying up all night, I finally found the good father, and he was very pleased that I was returning his money. We chatted awhile, and then he gave me a book entitled *Misal Romano Diario* [*Daily Roman Missal*].

When I reached San José, I found Eduardo quite drunk. He told me that he had spent all of the money and that he could not pay me my percentage.

After Christmas, on December 27, I went back to the coast with Eduardo, but only as member of a crew. I did not help him raise money to finance the trip. What Eduardo did was to talk another assistant Alberto Munroy into borrowing $200 from one of the owners of a truck.

Can you explain how this works?

The owners are usually Indians in San Martín. They advance money for passage to the contractor, and they use their own truck to take the crew to the coast. When the farm owners pay the contractor for the crew passage within eight days of arrival, the owner of the truck gets the money back. But they also have made $2 each for each way. Thus, for a crew of 100 workers, they make $400 less expenses for the truck such as gasoline. They don't charge the contractor interest, but they still make money. It's a good business for them!

❧ A New Baby but Illness Strikes Again

On February 10, 1972, about two weeks after I returned from the coast, my wife, Josefa, gave birth to a beautiful baby boy whom we named Ramón S. Antonio. Shortly thereafter, while my wife was still bedridden with infant Ramón, my other two little children, José and María, came down with a severe case of the measles.

By the grace of God I had a little money to spend because I had just returned from working on the coast. I spent some $60 without hesitation because the measles are dangerous. We well remembered little Juan Martín and little Ana María dying with this horrible disease.

We were terribly worried that little José and María might die also, but just when we were the most desperate by the grace of God two doctors, Señor Antonio Gómez Velásquez and Señor Mendoza, arrived to check on the people of San José.

I had spent all of my money on medicine, and I did not have any to pay the doctors. Fortunately, they only charged me 25 cents for their services, and they gave my two children injections and left pills for them to take without charging me anything. My prayers had been answered because gradually my two children began to recuperate.

How often do doctors visit San José?

They say that doctors are supposed to visit remote towns such as San José and San Martín every eight days. But sometimes they are only able to come once or twice a month. In any case, these doctors came when I needed them most. Indeed, it was they who saved the lives of my two children!

Only twenty days after my having been encouraged by the recovery of my children from the measles, my wife's breast suddenly became infected. Since her breasts swelled up, she could not nurse our infant Ramón. I did not have any money to buy formula milk so my wife's sister Catalina Cristina Ramos, who was nursing her own nine-month old baby, began to nurse Ramón.

Because it was necessary for the doctor to operate on my wife's breast to cure the infection, my sister-in-law gave Ramón milk for 15 days until my wife improved. After my wife recovered, only one breast was normal, and now she feeds Ramón [who was three years old in 1975] with only one breast.

By now I was desperate for money. I asked a *Joseño*, Señor Franco Coj Vásquez, for work because I needed money for necessities at home. He offered me work on the coast, and I replied that all he had to do was advance me $10.

The next day I left with the Señor for the San José del Carmen Farm. He paid me $2.50 for each *cuerda* that I cleaned. It took me two days for each *cuerda*, and in all I worked about eight days. Señor Franco gave me money for passage home, but to save the $2 bus ticket, I walked. It took me 15 hours to walk from San José del Carmen to San José.

When I returned it was Holy Week in the end of March. We were poor, but, by the grace of God, my children had been saved from dying, and the infection in my wife's breast had been cured.

Subsistence Farming with My Family on the Farm San José Del Carmen

On April 5, 1972, I returned to the same farm San José del Carmen. But this time I went to work for myself, and I took my family along, except my little daughter María, who stayed with my wife's mother.

When we arrived at the farm, I went to ask the administrator for land to rent for planting corn. He said that he would pay for the lease on the land if I would plant livestock pasture (or grass for cattle) for him in return.

I began to work the next day, but since we only had $3 for expenses such as food, I had to work some of the days as a day laborer. In all I planted nine *cuerdas* of corn. We stayed 35 days on the farm until after I had finished the second cleaning of the field.

On May 10, we got up at 2:00 A.M. and set out walking back to San José. I carried all of our kitchen utensils and clothing on my back. Most of the time I also carried José because he was too small to walk very much. By the time we reached San Luis at noon, we were exhausted. We had walked all of the way. In San Luis we boarded a large canoe to San Martín, and from there we walked to San José. It had been a long, tiring trip.

Eight days later I returned for 20 days more on the coast to clean the cornfield again. Once more, I planted pasture for the cows to pay for renting the land.

I returned to San José on June 5, during the patron fiesta of the town. For us the fiesta was not a happy time for we had no money to celebrate. For the next two weeks I worked as a *jornalero* whenever I could find work. Usually, one can earn 50 cents a day as a *jornalero*, but during the harvest season, there is more work, and it is possible to make as much as 75 cents a day. Of course, I had to work at something to support my family.

I began to think that nine *cuerdas* of corn would be more than my family needed, and on June 21, I went to offer three *cuerdas* to my father-in-law. He agreed to buy them at $15 a *cuerda* so he paid me $45. I used this money to buy necessities for my family. During this period, my family and I suffered a lot because of our extreme poverty!

❧ The Anthropologists Return to Lake Atitlán

In July 1972, the anthropologists returned. I agreed to work again with them. I would first work mainly with Ruben (Tito) Paredes, a Peruvian student. He is a very good person. He brought his wife, Chona, to live with him in San José.

This is when I also agreed to write my autobiography and keep a diary for my friend Don Jaime. But I would not begin until the work with Tito was complete.

Diary (1972–1977)

ᑫᕉ Working with Tito, the Peruvian Student
AUGUST 5–6, 1972

Around 2:00 P.M., after working all day in the corn fields, I went with Tito, my Peruvian friend, to interview *Joseño* families. We asked about their beliefs, how they make a living, their present condition, and many other things. About 6:00 P.M. we quit.

I ate dinner with my wife and two little children, José and María. Although we are quite poor, we ate our beans and tortillas contentedly because we are happy and in good health.

After dinner, I took a stroll through the streets of San José to find out what had happened in our town during the day. The evening was peaceful. I returned home about 9:00 P.M., thanked God for giving me this day and asked him for his blessings tomorrow. I fell asleep quickly.

After sleeping soundly I got up about 6:00 A.M. and thanked God for a good night's sleep. Immediately I went to bathe at the edge of Lake Atitlán.

Around 9:00 A.M. Tito arrived, and we set out looking for families on the list to be interviewed. We interviewed three families before noon.

During noontime, I practiced with other members of the Blue and White Sports Club. I played the position of goalkeeper on our soccer team. I got back to my house just in time to catch a snack before Tito arrived again.

This afternoon, however, we were unlucky. We gave up trying to get interviews about 4:00 P.M. We did not get a single interview. Tito went back to his house, and I took off to San Jorge la Laguna to

81

buy nets with which to carry my corn back from the coast. When I got back, I went to a meeting with other *Joseños* who had corn ready to harvest on the coast. We arranged to go harvest our corn on August 12.

❧ Obligatory Street Repair in San José
AUGUST 7, 1972

At 4:00 A.M. I woke up startled at the uproar of drums and flageolets. When I went to the street to ask the policeman what the ruckus was about, he declared that it was obligatory for me to help repair the road from San José to San Martín.[13] I really needed the money I could make from a day's work, but I decided that I had better contribute my labor to the roadwork to avoid a $3 fine for not cooperating with the officials. Besides, I think it is the duty of each citizen to work harmoniously with the municipality.

Nevertheless, during the entire day that 65 of us *Joseños* toiled on the road repair, I kept thinking about how poor I was and how I was losing a whole day's work. Finally, the municipal officials dismissed us at 4:00 P.M. As soon as I got home, I went to bathe in the lake to wash off the day's grime.

When I got back from the ten-minute walk from the lake, I was weary. I picked up a copy of my book the *New Testament* and started reading. I read the letter of Saint James, chapter 1, verses 5 through 9. This reading stimulated many thoughts about my religious life, comparing it with the words of the Bible.

❧ Poverty, Insomnia, and Illnesses
AUGUST 8–9, 1972

At 3:00 A.M. I woke up worrying about my poverty, my family, and what I could do to provide for them. My worry caused sleeplessness. I finally got out of bed without having slept much, gave thanks to God, and ate a meager breakfast.

During the morning I cleaned weeds from my *cuerda* of beans, stopping at noon to eat my lunch of tortillas and beans with salt. All I had to drink was a bottle of piped water. While I ate, I thought how sad and hard the life of a poor man is!

I finished my chores in the field at 3:00 P.M., and I went home to rest. I was ravenous, and my wife prepared dinner. After eating, to relax I opened the book *The Towns of Lake Atitlán* that my good friend Jaime had given me as a remembrance. I didn't stop reading this interesting book about the native towns where I live until 9:00 P.M. By this time it was getting too dark to read by candlelight, and besides my eyes were tired.

When I got up the next morning at 6:00 A.M., I asked my wife to fix breakfast for me, but she was unable to get out of bed. Because she had a fever, she could not cook. Thus, I fixed breakfast for my children and myself.

I debated over whether I should go to work in the fields, but I finally was too concerned about my wife's being sick. Instead of going to hoe, I went to the public health center in San José to ask for medicine.[14] Because I had no money, I could not go to a pharmacy.

After fixing lunch for the children at noon, I went with the Peruvian to interview two Protestant families about their reasons for changing religion. I got home around 6:30, and I prepared dinner because my wife was still too sick to work.

↷ Problems Over Tito's Study
AUGUST 10, 1972

At 3:30 P.M. I went out with the student from California to try to get an interview with a Protestant named Bernardo Coj Hernández. Tito and I tried to speak to him in Spanish, but he was not in the mind to answer any of our questions. I tried asking him in the Tzutuhil language because I thought that this was the only way he would talk about his beliefs. Then the man began to scold me in Tzutuhil.

"Why did you come to my house working with the gringos? What do you have to do with the subject of religion? It would be better for you to go to find work on the coast or somewhere else than to work with these people. I have no use for these gringos! You are working with them just because you are poor."

I didn't even try to answer him—he had totally offended me.

"You are a thief and you can't earn any money any other way than by working with the anthropologists. I don't have anything to do with anthropologists because I am a Protestant. I understand my

Bible. It says that on the outside there are sheepskins but on the inside there are voracious wolves."

"Very well," I said. "We did not come here to offend you but for an interview for which the man will pay you for the hour of your time that we use."

The more Señor Bernardo talked the more he chided me for helping the Peruvian student. He even threatened to throw me off his property with a stick. He never did allow us to interview him. He's very rude!

Later we went to the house of Señor Pascual Ixtamer Sumoza. It was the same thing as with Señor Bernardo all over again. Señor Pascual called me a thief and refused to be interviewed. Tito struggled for an interview, but he would not consent.

So we went to yet another member of the Central American church to ask for an interview. His name is José García Ramos. This man did not scold me for working with the anthropologists, but at first he refused to give us an interview. He was not going to talk to us because the Ladino pastor from Chimaltenango, who visits the chapel once or twice a month, told the entire congregation not to talk to the students. The pastor, who is not a missionary, proclaimed that anthropologists are good for nothing and their work is of no value. The membership of the chapel was instructed not to associate with them.

But gradually I convinced the Protestant to be interviewed. I explained the meanings of the questions and the reason for the work. I was patient, and I gained his confidence. We didn't leave his house until 6:30 P.M.

At 7:00 P.M. when I got back home my wife already had dinner prepared. We ate a simple meal, but we were thankful for what we had. Afterwards I went to a neighboring *tienda* [small shop] to buy some candles and cigarettes.

When I returned I began to write down what had happened. I thought that Tito might be having more difficulty with the Protestants than Don Jaime because Don Jaime's luck is better. I thought about a trip to Panajachel the next day, if God permits it.

At 4:00 A.M. I woke as I was having a nightmare. I was dreaming that some huge, mean bulls were chasing me because they wanted to kill me. To get out of their path, I climbed on top of the grill of a truck, and that is when I woke up. I started thinking about the significance of my dream. Maybe the bulls represented my enemies who are thinking bad things about me for working with the anthropologists.

❧ My Friend Tito Leaves San José
AUGUST 15, 1972

After lunch a tooth that has been bothering me for several days began to ache again so I took three sips of a pain killer in a glass of water. This brought some relief.

At 4:00 P.M. my Peruvian friend, Ruben Paredes, came to say good-bye because he was leaving San José for Peru. He had completed his study, and he was going to Peru to see his family before returning to the University of California at Los Angeles to resume his studies.

As we walked along the edge of the lake, I was overcome with a feeling of sorrow because we had become fast friends and shared many memories of his experience in San José. In addition to the Holy Bible he had given me for my birthday, he gave me a lantern and a T-shirt with the initials of his university (UCLA).

After seeing Tito and his wife off on the 4:30 P.M. launch, I returned to my house somewhat depressed at the departure of my friend. My tooth began to ache again, so I went to the health center and asked the medic for something to stop it. He gave me an injection and some pain pills.

At 7:00 P.M. we ate dinner, but I was too downcast to enjoy the meal. I went to bed about 9:00 P.M.

About 3:00 A.M. I dreamed I was flirting with some women. Among them was my sweetheart with whom I had been living before marrying my wife, Josefa. When I recognized my old lover in the crowd of women, I was embarrassed so I started walking away from them. At this moment I awoke. I was puzzled about the meaning of this dream.

❧ Fighting Over a Soccer Game
AUGUST 20, 1972

At 4:00 A.M. my wife and I slipped out of bed and walked down to bathe at the edge of the lake. At first the water was a bit chilly, but it was pleasant to swim in the hush of early morning.

We did not get around to eating breakfast until about 9:00 A.M. As we were finishing our meal, a fellow teammate from the Blue and White Sports Club came to ask me to referee a soccer game. I agreed.

Some of the players were from San José and others were from San Martín. I arrived at the soccer field in good spirits. I refereed the entire game, but in the last two minutes a couple of the guys from San Martín did not like the way I was controlling the play. They began to harass me with insults. I tried to contain myself, but they kept bothering me.

Finally, they challenged me to fight them. By this time I had had enough of their remarks and countered, "You name the place." One thing led to another, and they began to scuffle with me. Quickly, it erupted into a full-scale fistfight. Because I knew a little boxing, I beat one of them up pretty badly. Although I won the battle, I felt bad about it. My conscience bothered me for having slugged the guy the way I did. I resolved never to go to the soccer field again.

That afternoon 30 *quintales* [3,000 pounds] of my corn arrived from the coast with the two fellows I had sent to harvest it. Carrying the corn to my house fatigued the guys so I gave them some *tragos*. I kept half of the corn and sold the rest for $60.

In the evening I asked God for forgiveness from having fought on the soccer field, and I thanked him for the corn.

In the morning we had rabbit meat from my father-in-law's hunting in the mountains with his shotgun. Afterwards I spread the corn on the ground to dry in the sun because it was somewhat damp.

In the afternoon I arranged to talk with officials of the Catholic church and brotherhoods about information that Dr. [Clyde] Woods needed.[15] I asked them such things as the names of all the *principales,* how long they had been *principales,* how many brotherhoods exist in San José, and what the functions of the brotherhoods are.

For dinner, we ate fish and tortillas.

ᐁ Dreaming of Erupting Volcanoes and a Trip to Panajachel
AUGUST 22, 1972

About 4:00 A.M., I had another frightful dream. I dreamed that the San Diego and San Martín volcanoes were erupting—spewing rocks and sulfur. Hot boulders started smashing into San José, and at that point I woke up. I did not understand what this dream meant. It upset me so much I was unable to go back to sleep.[16]

After getting up and watering my onions, I walked over to the school to get some statistics for Dr. Woods from the school's director. I found out how many students are attending this year, how many are in each grade, how many are boys and how many are girls, the number of Indians and the number of Ladinos, and the number of teachers.

When I was eating lunch, I thought about going to see my friend Jaime in Panajachel. I decided to catch the afternoon launch, but when I arrived at Don Jaime's house, he was not there. Instead, he was in the United States.

I went to an inn named *Casa del Viajero* [House of the Traveler], but they charged me a lot—$1.50 for one night. In contrast, I can stay 24 hours in Guatemala City for just 50 cents. I concluded that life in Panajachel is very expensive by Guatemala's standards. I don't know why, but I think this is because a lot of gringos come to Panajachel, and they want to charge me the same price as they charge the gringos.

After sleeping peacefully in the hotel, I ate breakfast in the marketplace for 50 cents. Then I went to Dr. Wood's house where I chatted with him for a little while.

Dr. Woods, after talking a while, offered to take me back to San José in his boat. I was grateful, and he brought me back to San José without charging me a single penny.

ᓇ Catholics Battle a Protestant Mayor Over Property Boundaries
AUGUST 27, SUNDAY

I read my books *The New Testament* and *The Towns of Lake Atitlán* until lunch time at 2:00 P.M. After lunch I went to the Meeting Hall in the Catholic Church for a council meeting ordered by the President of Catholic Action. He wanted to confer with church members about a dispute that had emerged with the municipality.

The Protestant mayor, Antonio Sánchez López, would not give permission to cut down a dying tree that was about to fall on a house. Those who wanted to cut down the tree claimed that the mayor had no right to tell them they could not because it was really standing on land owned by the Catholic church. They got out the land title of the church, which indicated that the tree and the house were actually on church property. In turn the mayor got out the title of the municipality, which indicated that the tree is on municipal property. In fact the two titles indicated that the boundaries of the church and the municipality overlap. Members of the church wanted to measure the land to prove their title, which is older than the municipal title. They argued this would prove their position. The mayor and his policemen, however, threatened to throw anyone in jail who tried to measure the land. The Catholics then were afraid to check the boundaries. This seemed strange to me because we Catholics make up nearly the whole town—some 1,000 compared to the 25 municipal officials.

Everyone else was afraid to measure the property so I finally declared, "Let's look at the land and see how it is." I grabbed the tape measure and said, "If they throw me in jail, so be it!" But I measured the area, and the mayor and the policemen did nothing. When the other Catholics saw my courage, they congratulated me for doing the job.

In the end the mayor did nothing because it turned out that he was really afraid. The *principales,* the *cofradías,* and *Acción Católica* [Catholic Action] were all ready to hire lawyers to fight over this land in court. The mayor realized that although this town is not very big, there is power here [among the Catholics]—power is everything here!

What happened was that the mayor cut the tree down himself, with the permission of the members of the Catholic church who had wanted it done in the first place. After all the fuss, this is all that happened! It blew up into a big mess because the municipality wanted this, that, and the other thing. The mayor threatened to throw the Catholics in jail, and the Catholics, in turn, threatened to throw him in jail. In the end, it was really a crazy problem.

I didn't get home until about 8:00 P.M. After dinner my companions of the Blue and White Sports Club and I rehearsed a Biblical play *San Juan el Bautista* that we are going to present to the town tomorrow to commemorate the Blue and White Sports Club anniversary. I got home around midnight, but I was so restless I didn't go to sleep until about 2:00 A.M.

❧ The Story of San Juan el Bautista
AUGUST 28, 1972

About 4:00 P.M., after collecting some data for Dr. Woods about expenditures in the *cargos* [offices] of the religious brother-

hoods, I went with other members of my sports club to begin commemorating our anniversary. Six of us went to mass for the team.
After mass we made a pilgrimage to the cemetery to visit the grave
of a deceased member of the team. In the evening we presented the
play. Among the acts that we performed was one entitled, "The
Beheading of San Juan el Bautista." The play was made pleasant
by the playing of the marimba band *Alma Martinera* [Soul of San
Martín] from San Martín la Laguna.

*What were the other acts? Can you explain more about what
happened at the play?*

We borrowed a diesel motor from Father Jorge H. Rodríquez
to generate electricity for the light in the church where we would
produce our religious play. It was a German made machine with a
high capacity of 125 to 150 watts. We charged 5 cents for each adult
and 3 cents for each child in order to pay for the diesel fuel used
and to give Father Jorge $2 for rent.

Before the play began, we went over our lines that were
taken from the *New Testament* from the Evangelist San Mateo
[and San Lucas].

At last, 8:30 P.M., the moment of curtain call, arrived, and the
play commenced. Act I opened as the angel Gabriel (played by
Roberto Mendoza) appeared to Juan's father Zacarías (played by
Zacarías Pérez Pantzay), who was a priest during the days of
Herodes, King of Judea. As Zacarías was burning incense in the
Temple of God, Gabriel appeared to the right of the altar and astonished Zacarías. Gabriel told him to fear not and that his wife
Isabel (played by Mateo Sicay Vásquez, actually a boy dressed like
a woman) would bear him a son who should be named Juan and
who would be a prophet of God. Because Isabel was barren and
both she and Zacarías were getting old, Zacarías doubted Gabriel's
words. For this reason, Zacarías was deprived of his speech until
the birth would come to pass.

When Isabel [the cousin of María who would also be visited
by Gabriel to announce the immaculate conception of Jesús] bore a
son, her relatives and friends gathered and asked what they should
call the infant (played by my six-month old son Ramón). She told
them Juan, but they didn't believe her since no one in the family
had been named that. They then went to Zacarías to implore
whether the infant should be called Zacarías after his father. But
because Zacarías was still dumb, he gestured for a tablet. On it he
wrote, "His name shall be Juan!" [Immediately thereafter Zacarías

regained his speech and filled the people with fear and marvel.]

Act II dealt with Juan's role as prophet (played by Samuel Bizarro) who predicted the coming of Jesucristo. His companions at the River Jordan were played by Zacarías Pérez Pantzay [who also played Juan's father in Act I] and Alberto Coj Mendosa.

Act III of the program was the baptism of Señor Jesucristo in the River Jordan when he was 30 years old. This splendid act took all 20 members of our club to perform.

Act IV dealt with the last part of the life of Juan el Bautista—his beheading. King Herodes lusted for Herodias, who was his brother Felipe's wife—that is, his sister-in-law. Juan, who was a beloved prophet of the people, declared that Herodes had no right to Herodias. This infuriated Herodes. He would have preferred to put Juan to death, but he hesitated because he feared the people would rebel if he persecuted their prophet. Thus, Herodes just ordered his soldiers to throw Juan into prison.

Then King Herodes's birthday arrived. During the big fiesta with many guests, the daughter of Herodias danced and so pleased Herodes that he proclaimed in front of everyone that he would give her anything she desired. Her mother Herodias prompted her to say, "Give me here on a platter the head of Juan el Bautista!" Although King Herodes was dismayed at this request, he sent his soldiers to Juan's cell to carry out the execution.

The curtain fell as Herodes's soldiers were poised ready to cut off Juan's head. When the curtain opened again, Juan's head was on a table (but this was a false head of rubber with a lot of red painted on it to represent blood drawn from the sword).

And this is how the play ended. It had lasted about two hours, and the townspeople enjoyed it very much. Before the play, many of the people of San José had not known the story of Juan el Bautista, who is a patron saint of their town.

After we were congratulated by the people for the performance, members of the Blue and White Sports Club celebrated the play's success with wine and *aguardiente*. We recounted the ordeal of presenting the story of San Juan el Bautista's life, and we ended up drinking until dawn.

I didn't come to my senses until about 2:00 P.M. My wife told me that my companions from the club had come over to get me to eat lunch with them, but that she had been unable to wake me. I nursed my hangover with fish soup, and I didn't do anything else the entire day.

❧ A Dream about Fighting
SEPTEMBER 2, 1972

Yesterday, I stayed home on the eye doctor's advice. He gave me medicine for my eyes and advised me to rest. Because of the ache in my eyes, I did not sleep very well. Even though my eyes bothered me still, I had to work today because I did not have any money to buy corn.

I was too troubled to eat. I just read my Bible a little, said my prayers, and went to sleep.

About 2:00 A.M. I had a bad dream. I dreamed that a man wanted to fight me with a machete. Then in the dream I told him, "Not with a machete. If you are a man, fight with your fists." But then in the dream another man suddenly appeared. Nevertheless, I managed to punch both of them. In the dream, I beat up both of them. Then I woke up.

I went back to sleep again, but about 4:00 A.M. I started dreaming once more. This time I was walking in the countryside with a cousin of mine. Suddenly, a stranger appeared and wanted to capture me to throw me in jail. In the dream I told my cousin to run, and we began running away from my enemy. We ran so far that we could no longer see where he was. And that is when I awoke. I began to think about what the dream meant, but I was unable to understand it.

❧ Worrying over Poverty and a Dream of Persecution
SEPTEMBER 7, 1972

While working in the fields this afternoon, I pondered over my condition of poverty. I am longing for a change for the better in life so that I can live happier with my family. But I must wait and see if God will give me his blessings.

Returning from a hard day's work in the field, I rested awhile and then went to try my luck fishing in the lake. Fortunately, I caught two pounds of fish that my wife fixed for dinner.

At 3:00 A.M. I was dreaming again. I was walking down the road with a machete in my hand when suddenly two men appeared and began to chase me with stones. To dodge their barrage and escape their pursuit, I leaped 20 meters into the air and left my enemies far behind. At that point I awoke and looked at my watch.

I went back to sleep again. But the same dream continued. About ten men were chasing me with stones when suddenly my little son, José, appeared. I picked up a club to defend myself and José, and the pursuers ran away from us. I had won the confrontation in my dream. Then I woke up and looked at my watch. It was 4:00 A.M.

The significance of the dream worried me, and I could not get back to sleep. Maybe the ones who were after me were my enemies in San José. These were probably the ones who spoke badly of me because I had worked with the anthropologists from California.

❧ My Mother Is Gravely Ill
SEPTEMBER 21, 1972

After fishing this evening, I received news that my blood mother is gravely ill. She sent for me to come to her, and I had to respect her wishes. As I walked to her house, I thought a lot about her because she had not even reared me—she abandoned me when I was an infant!

Upon seeing my mother in such serious condition, I sent for a medic to come examine her. He could not help her. By 1:00 A.M. we arranged to carry her to the Sololá hospital for treatment.

None of us slept the whole night—we spent the entire time worrying!

At 4:00 A.M., I carried my mother on my back down the path to the pier to catch the morning launch for Panajachel. We arrived at the hospital in Sololá by bus at 9:00 A.M. and admitted her for treatment. The doctor told me that she would have to stay awhile. I felt sad leaving my mother in the hospital.

I went to the Sololá marketplace, but I didn't buy anything because I only had enough money for my boat passage from Panajachel to San José [40 cents]. Skipping lunch, I began the 8 kilometers down the mountain to Panajachel. It took me two hours.

I rested the half hour before the launch arrived at 3:30 P.M. By the time I reached San José at 5:00 P.M., I was ravenous.

❧ Recruiting Young Men for the Army
SEPTEMBER 25, 1972

I got out of bed feeling good this morning because I did not dream anything. I slept quite peacefully. I spent the whole day working for a man for 50 cents.

When I got off work, I received a summons to report to the Town Tribunal. I began to wonder what they would be calling me for, and I got ready to present myself before them.

When I arrived the commissioner for the army, Alejandro Ramos Cholotio, showed me and another fellow, who had also been a sergeant in the army, an order he had received from the commandant of the military reserves in Sololá. The telegram said that 15 militiamen had to be recruited for military service. Señor Alejandro pleaded, "Listen, please help me catch these young men."

The other ex-sergeant and I were given clubs to make the potential recruits respect us when we found them. We went all over the streets looking for eligible young men. All of them found out we were looking for them, and so they scrambled to hide. By 8:00 P.M. we had captured five fellows, all of whom we marched to the municipal police station.

An hour later a big uproar was brewing by the parents, brothers, sisters, and other relatives of the young men we had captured. They tried to talk us into letting them go, and when they saw we would not they began to cry and fuss over them.

Then about 9:30 P.M., two young boys from San Martín walked unsuspectingly through the streets of San José. We spotted them, pounced on them, and captured them for the army.

Fifteen minutes later we marched all of the recruits to San Martín. Then there was another disturbance by the families of the boys. With that the commissioner of San Martín gave us the keys to the jail, and we locked them all up. Needless to say, all of these newly recruited militiamen were extremely upset to be going off to the army. Some offered us money to set them free, but I refused to accept a bribe because it is prohibited by the law.

We guarded the men in the San Martín jail in shifts until 1:00 A.M. The walk back to San José was very cold. Finally, the turmoil was over about 2:00 A.M. I laid down and tried to sleep, but I could not. I live right on the corner of two main streets. There were many drunks making lots of noise!

❧Hoodlums on the Coast
SEPTEMBER 26–OCTOBER 5, 1972

Since I didn't get any sleep last night I was grumpy. I also woke up feeling somewhat sick, as if I am catching the flu. I couldn't muster enough initiative to go to work—I slept all morning.

At 3:00 P.M. I went to check on a *cuadrilla* in San Jorge to make sure they were still going to leave for the coast as scheduled. When I got home about 8:00 P.M., my cousin, Andrés Bizarro, came over, and we planned the trip until around 11:00 P.M. After writing this in my diary, I went to sleep.

We left with the crew early in the morning in a truck from San Martín. By noontime the rain caught up with us, and it rained heavily for two hours. Then we ran into a detachment of military police. They stopped us and demanded our license for recruiting crews. We did not have one yet because it was still being processed. To prevent them from writing us a fine, we gave them a $10 bribe.

We arrived at the Pangola Farm about 5:00 P.M., and the administrators accepted us for work. They gave us corn, beans, and salt for our sustenance, and they guided us to the encampment for the crew named *El Río* [The River] because it is next to a river. Around 7:00 P.M., Andrés and I ate dinner with the workers.

It began raining about 2:00 A.M., and at daybreak it was still raining. Nevertheless, the guys went to work, although it was somewhat cold for the coast.

The military police had told us that the only reason they were accepting our $10 was that we had to go to the office of the farm to ask for a clearance to recruit workers. Thus, Andrés and I went to the office to ask for one. The administrator understood what had happened to us, and immediately he granted us a bill of power, or clearance, and we were happy.

We didn't eat breakfast until noon. Afterwards, we passed a pleasant afternoon observing people from far away and pretty places. The coast is a very agreeable place—I like it very much. I chatted with many Ladinos.

At 3:00 A.M., I escorted Andrés to a village to put him on the right track back to San José. I stayed at the coast awhile to insure the work was satisfactory. Thanks to God, all of my townsmen were happy with their jobs. At noon, when the fellows returned from work, six of us chipped in and bought a chicken to eat.

Some things happen here at the coast that are difficult for me to understand. At 2:00 A.M. a thief entered our quarters and stole one of the worker's clothing. The robber woke us up, and a few of the guys chased him. But he did not let himself get caught. Yes, it is true that some very strange happenings take place in our country. This caused me to spend the whole day upset.

I wish I had brought one of my books to read to get my mind off last night's robbery, but unfortunately I did not bring any books. What happened last night makes it difficult to get to sleep. I am writing these things down while I am staying here in the camp.

Yet another disturbing and frightful thing happened here at camp. At 1:00 A.M. I was lying in bed, but not yet asleep. Suddenly three men surprised me with a machete—they were trying to kill me! I jumped out of bed and ran about 100 meters to where the other workers were sleeping. I shouted for help and three of the workers hurried out of bed to come to my defense. They were Zacarías Pérez Pantzay, Antonio Bizarro Yojcom, and Diego Vásquez Ujpán. When the hoodlums attacking me saw them coming, they turned and ran away.

Later I discovered that these guys had wanted to join the *Joseño* work crew. When they found out that I was here with the crew, they thought I had money on me and if they killed me they could take it. Actually, I did not have any money with me. Without doubt, it was my workers who saved me from death. I was so frightened by this event that I could not sleep at all the rest of the night. I thought about the meaning of my past dreams.

Daybreak found me quite depressed. I was thinking about how difficult and dangerous my job as a labor contractor is because to be on the coast is to be in a delicate [situation]—there are many bad people here!

About 8:00 A.M. a Ladino invited me to have breakfast with him. After eating, another Ladino and I went to an adjacent farm where we had been told that a soccer team from the capital was coming out to play against a team made up of guys on the farm.

The game began at 11:00 A.M., and it was very pleasant to watch. The players from Guatemala City demonstrated quite a few good techniques.

It rained heavily in the afternoon, and I began to think about going to Panajachel to confer with my good North American friend James Sexton. If God gives me life, tomorrow I will be in Panajachel, and I will give my friend the pages of my diary I have been working on.

On the morning of October 2, I woke up at 1:00 A.M. I had planned to take off for San José at this time, but because it was so early I was unable to get out of bed. I dozed off again, and this is when I had a bad dream. I was walking along the beach of San José. I took off my clothes and was ready to bathe when suddenly I saw a corpse lying on the beach. The dead body shocked me, and I didn't know what to do. Then I put my clothes back on and started running. That is when I awoke. When I looked at my watch, I saw that it was 3:00 A.M.

I got up, arranged my clothes, and started saying good-bye to the workers who were staying on the farm. I agreed to return in ten days to check to see how they were doing, to see whether they

needed anything such as medicine and whether the work and lodging were still satisfactory.

As I started walking the 8 kilometers to Texcuaco to catch a
bus, I was somewhat troubled. It was early (3:20 A.M.), and I did not
have a machete to protect myself in case someone else attacked me.

The bus that I caught in Cocales did not roll into Panajachel
until 3:45 P.M. As soon as I got off, I went to find my friend Jaime,
but he was not at home. Then I went to the marketplace to buy a
cup of coffee. It was almost time [October 4] for Panajachel's titular
fiesta, and there were already dancers performing for the public. I
watched the Dance of the Mexicans at the home of a *Panajacheleño*
[resident of Panajachel].

I left the private fiesta and bought a daily newspaper *El
Gráfico* and began to read it on the street. That's when my friend
Jaime spotted me and greeted me. He could only chat for a little
while because he was on his way to an interview with a
Panajacheleño. I agreed to go to his house a couple of hours later.

While I was passing time, some Ladino friends of mine in
Panajachel invited me for some drinks. I had a few with them, and
then I went to the North American's house. While we were chatting
about my autobiography and diary, I asked him for a beer. While I
was drinking the beer, this good friend of mine invited me to eat
dinner at a hotel. By the time we reached the restaurant, however, it
had already closed for the evening. We did not eat.

When I took leave of Señor Jaime, I was happy because he
gave me money for the work I had been doing on my diary. I went
back to the *pensión* [inn] where I had asked for a room, but at 9:00
P.M. friends of mine told me that my mother was still in the hospital.
I decided to go to see her. Without paying for the room, I caught a
bus to Sololá.

In Sololá I rented a room, but I did not sleep well because it
was too cold. I got up at 6:00 A.M. and went to the hospital. The aide
told me that I could not visit until 10:00 A.M., the proper hour.

When I finally got to enter my mother's room, I was relieved
because she looked much better. I was chatting with her when the
doctor arrived. He spoke to me, and in turn I respectfully greeted
him, thanking him for all he had done for my mother. Before I
realized it, half the day had passed.

After eating breakfast about 1:00 P.M., I went to say good-bye
to my mother. The bus carried me to Panajachel about 3:00 P.M.
While I was stepping off the bus, I ran into some friends. We went
into a bar to have some cokes. As soon as we finished, I walked over

to the house of my North American friend. I said good-bye to Don Jaime and headed for the pier to catch the launch to San José.

ᖆIllness, A Dream, and Listening to a Bicycle Race
OCTOBER 7–9, 1972

With $10 of the money Don Jaime gave me, I paid for a freight-order of corn. Today, I began preparing ground for planting coffee trees although I am sick with a headache. I was going to bathe in the lake, but my wife cautioned me not to because of my feeling ill. I had to respect her advice. While I was reading a book in the middle of the afternoon, I fell asleep.

When I woke up at 4:00 A.M., I realized I had been dreaming. In the dream, my family and I left for the coast with all of our belongings. But we were not riding in a bus or a truck. Instead, I was carrying all of our possessions on my back and in my arms. This was very difficult for me to do. I began looking for someone to help me, and then I awoke. I could not understand the meaning of this dream. I think dreaming is something strange.

I got up at 5:00 A.M., and I went to bathe in the lake. Afterwards, I asked my father-in-law to lend me his radio so that I could listen to the bicycle race because today is the final day of the circuit.

The champion turned out to be Manuel de Jesús Herrera. He won almost every stage of the competition. But the King of the Mountain was Saturnino Rustrian Caceres. On the slopes of the mountains, he won 51 points, and he lost the race to Señor Jesús only by three minutes and fifteen seconds. The race was really something because the foreigners in it came in only fourth and fifth place. The results pleased me, and I was very happy with the way the day had passed. In the afternoon I returned the radio to its owner.

In the evening a friend came over to celebrate the Guatemalan victory. We did not quit drinking until about 11:00 P.M. As I write these things down I am a bit drunk, but not very drunk. That is all until tomorrow.

I woke up with a severe stomachache because the drinks I had last night settled wrongly with me. Instead of going to work in the fields, I stayed in bed. I wanted to buy medicine for the pain in my belly, but I didn't have any money. A cup of coffee with a fair amount of lemon juice calmed the pain somewhat, but by this time it was already the middle of the afternoon. Thus the day passed.

❧ My Cousin, María Bizarro, Dies
OCTOBER 14, 1972

My wife and I have planted a lot of coffee seedlings. We wished we had the money to hire a helper for this arduous job, but we had to do it alone. Our children stayed with a neighbor as we worked. It has not rained in several days so we have to carry water to irrigate the plants from quite a distance.

I have been thinking about preparing land for planting tomatoes. I keep thinking, "I need to plant something. I know very well that cultivation is worthwhile—I am without money because I have nothing sowed." Finally, I grabbed my hoe and went to work on a patch near the shoreline.

Unfortunately, at 8:30 A.M. a telegram arrived for my Uncle Daniel Bizarro, which notified him that his daughter María had died in the hospital at Sololá. They told me this when I went to his house to investigate all the commotion. Since no one else seemed interested in traveling to Sololá to bring my cousin's body back for burial, I began trying to make the necessary arrangements to go by canoe. Finally, some other fellows decided to brave the midnight waters of the lake with me in order to fetch my cousin's remains. While I controlled the rudder, they paddled the long journey [10 kilometers] to Panajachel. Not until 2:00 A.M. did we arrive.

By foot we went the eight kilometers [up the mountain] to Sololá and arrived at the hospital at 5:30 A.M. The staff gave us a medical report and took us to identify the body in the morgue. Seeing my cousin in the plain casket really was stressful for me. Afterwards, I walked to the civil registry to obtain a death certificate to present to the governor of Sololá, who would permit us to transport the body back to San José. By 9:00 A.M. the permit was ready, but I took it to the police station to make sure it was in proper order. At 10:00 A.M. we were ready to begin carrying the corpse back to the cemetery in San José.

By the grace of God a North American priest did us the favor of driving the body back to the pier in Panajachel. Then we put the body in the canoe, and I briefly ran to say hello to my friend Jaime Sexton. When I returned, we shoved off paddling for San José.

It was a long, hard trip. By the time we reached the other side of the lake at 2:00 P.M., the whole town was on the lakeshore waiting for us. Many of the townspeople had water, beer, wine, and liquor to serve us, but I was more hungry than thirsty because I had not eaten in a long time. Later, I had some drinks, and eventually I became inebriated. However, it was not the drinks that caused my intoxication as much as it had been my being awake all night and extremely fatigued at having paddled the body back. I fell asleep exhausted, and I was unaware when they lowered my cousin's body into her grave.

❧Planting Tomato Seedlings
OCTOBER 23–25, 1972

I have been worried about not having any money for necessities. I have plenty of corn, but no money. Thus, for two days I cleaned a man's onion fields, and I earned $1.50.

My wife accompanied me to the tomato patch to plant seedlings that I bought from my friend David Ramos. We worked very hard all day. My wife prepared dinner, but I went walking with some friends instead of eating.

At 4:00 A.M. I dreamed that I was back in the barracks at Retalhuleu. I was walking around proudly through the streets of the town, dressed in my uniform.

At 5:00 A.M. I left to water the small tomato sprigs that we planted yesterday because here in San José one has to water such crops daily. If one does not, they simply dry up in the sun and die.

The rest of the day I spent gathering firewood in the hills, except for making a trip to San Martín to buy medicine for my children who are sick.

I did not sleep a wink last night—too much boisterousness in the street outside my house. My neighbors got drunk and made a fuss all night. I got up, watered my tomatoes, and took natural fertilizer to the field for them.

❧Working as an Ordinary Cotton Picker
NOVEMBER 8–DECEMBER 9, 1972

Early this morning, my wife and I settled the matter—I am going to work 30 days on the Primavera Farm as a cotton picker, and she will be left in charge of caring for the crops—watering and applying fertilizer.

The administrators accepted the crew for work, and they left me in charge as overseer. Tomorrow we start to work!

Because of the climate, I awoke this morning with a bit of a headache. After eating breakfast at 5:00 A.M., the workers started to pick cotton. We worked all day without eating lunch because there wasn't any food.

At 4:00 A.M. the tractors that pulled the carts arrived. It took us two hours to get back to camp riding in the carts from the cotton field. Upon arrival, I began to notice that there are a lot of different people here from different places—Quiché, Sololá, Cobán, Sacapulas, and San Marcos Oriente.

The food they give us here is really monotonous. We had tortillas and beans for breakfast, dinner and lunch. After work I read my Bible.

This morning [November 11] I woke up with a headache again. I tried to bathe but I could not do this peacefully because there are many people and little water.

Again, they are feeding us tortillas and beans—for breakfast and at noon in the fields. After riding back to camp for two hours in the carts, they feed us tortillas and beans for dinner.

The rest of the men are cheerful—they joked with one another after dinner.

It is still impossible for me to sleep peacefully here. I was awakened early in the morning by other workers because it is so crowded and there is a lot of noise. Also, we are still just eating beans and tortillas—three times a day! Many workers still accept the beans, but tomorrow I have resolved not to eat any of them!

At breakfast when they offered me tortillas and beans, I only took the tortillas—not the beans! Instead of beans I ate tortillas with chili sauce. For lunch I managed to get my hands on a little cheese and ate it instead of the beans. For dinner I ate tortillas and avocado.

After reading one of my books, *The Towns of Lake Atitlán,* I wrote this down in my diary at 9:00 P.M. I will say my prayers now and go to bed.

When dawn came this morning, I got up feeling a bit sad, thinking about my family and my tomato field. I am pleased with the work here, but not the food.

Unfortunately at 1:00 P.M. one of my workers was poisoned by some kind of insect bite. They took him to Escuintla for treatment. We shall see how well he is when they bring him back to camp.

In the afternoon we were offered the same old thing to eat, but I was too upset over my worker's being in the hospital to eat. I have read a while in my Bible, and now I am going to bed.

Despite the poor and monotonous food they give us here, the workers are generally content because they are earning on the average $1.50 to $2.00 per day. Since I am the overseer, I am only making $1.25 daily. I am not paid by the pound. But that is the way it goes.

It is still [November 17] difficult to sleep here because there are about 5,000 workers and space is limited. And after working hard all day in the fields, they are still only giving us tortillas and beans to eat.

Our friend came back from the hospital this evening. We were glad that his illness is arrested.

In the evening we went to stroll around a small town called Texcuaco. We saw several drunks fighting in the streets. We craved some beer ourselves, but we did not have any money—we could only look!

One really gets tired of eating the same old food all of the time—tortillas and beans. This is what we had today as usual for breakfast and lunch. But after the crew bathed in the river, some of us bought a chicken and ate it. What a delightful change!

This morning [November 20] I did not go out to the fields with the workers. I have a throbbing headache, but I have neither medicine nor money. Thus, the day passed rather unpleasantly.

The steady diet of beans and tortillas makes me feel like not eating! I had to get my hands on a piece of cheese today. This afternoon I read a newspaper.

Last night I had a pleasant dream, and I awoke happily. I dreamed that I was at my house in San José, and I went to the lakeside to water my growing tomatoes. I chuckled at the dream's content.

During the day I chatted with the administrator Jesús Lerin about life in my hometown San José, and he told me about the customs in Spain. The working hours passed very cheerfully.

In the afternoon, a surprise arrived from my wife in San José. It was fish from the lake.[17] We relished it! Later the whole crew gathered to tell stories and jokes.

I am a little disturbed because when I got up this morning two of my workers had indigestion and were vomiting because of the poor food we have been eating. I had to take both of them to a medic. They were given medicine, but they will have to pay for it when we are paid at the end of the month.

After this I went to the office to ask for $50 to give to the crew. Everyone got a dollar, and each was glad because tonight we will have something different to eat.

[November 27] We are so tired of the little black beans that some friends and I drank Coca Colas and set out for Texcuaco to buy a pound of meat to roast. Unfortunately, by the time we got there, all the meat had been sold. We could only buy shrimp, but this was a pleasant change from the steady diet of beans. We were so pleased that we spent the rest of the evening playing cards and chatting.

At 4:00 A.M. the entire crew went to bathe in the Coyolate River. We didn't eat breakfast until 7:00 A.M., and we arrived in the cotton field very late. We hardly earned a dollar each the whole day.

In the late afternoon we played a soccer game against a team from Cobán, who are our companions. We won.

At last it is December 1. This means there are only a few more days left to work on the farm here. The thought of going home made me happy until I realized that three of my men had come down with malaria. When I told the administrator, he took them to the infirmary.

I could only eat bread and coffee this afternoon for dinner.

This makes the second day that I have been sick. My whole body aches, especially my head. To make things worse, I was only able to get about three hours sleep last night because of the crowdedness and noise.

Although I have no money, I went to a village named Santa Odillia where a medic gave me a shot of antibiotics that cost me $1.50. I promised to pay him as soon as the farm pays me.

When I got up this morning I was still so sick that I didn't feel like eating. All I had eaten all day was some bananas when I spoke to the administrator. He offered to help me with a dollar to buy something besides beans to eat. I thanked him.

I am still [December 6] in too much pain to go to work. All I could do today was bathe.

Because of the excitement of going home today [December 8], we did not sleep at all last night. My cousin Andrés has arrived from San José. He reports that my family is well.

The entire work crew filed into the farm office to receive their pay. By the afternoon we were in Cocales headed home. We arrived in San José at 10:00 P.M. Was I glad to be back! We ate a delicious meal of chicken. I felt it had been a long 30 days at the coast! It is midnight.

After getting out of bed and having a breakfast of something other than tortillas and beans—meat—we went to San Martín to buy a few things. When we returned in the afternoon, friends of mine who are *mayordomos* of the *cofradía* Concepción came to my house to visit. They were drunk. I drank with them the two beers they gave me, and I stretched out in a twine hammock to smoke some cigarettes.

For dinner, we ate crabs [taken from the lake] in a broth.

❧ Paxte Almost Drowns Me
DECEMBER 10, 1972

In 1975 I asked Ignacio whether people believe that there are spirits in the lake. He answered yes, and he wrote the following account of his own experience that he had omitted from his diary.

Little did I know that when I woke up on December 10 my life would almost end. After visiting with a friend in the afternoon, I went to bathe in the lake about 3:00 P.M. I walked to the beach to a place called Jaibal where I have bathed before. I am a strong swimmer, and I wasn't very far out (about 40–50 meters) from the bank when I swam into a plant that we call *paxte del lago* [which looks like seaweed].

When I realized that I was swimming into this plant, I turned around and tried to head back to shore. But I couldn't. The plant encircled my feet. I tried to shake loose, but the more I wiggled my feet the more engulfed I became. As I got entangled I began yelling, "Help me! Help me! Help me!" I remember yelling only three or four times before the weed pulled me down and I lost consciousness.

Fortunately, Señor Simón Coj and his son were on the shore irrigating tomatoes and onions. They heard me yell and saw me sink. Immediately, they ran to a canoe to paddle out to save me. I was unaware when they pulled me out of the water. I didn't regain consciousness until about 20 minutes after the strength of the *paxte* overwhelmed me. When I came to, I was lying near a coffee grove, and they were getting water out of my mouth. I had swallowed a lot of water. Señor Simón declared that by the time he and his son reached me, I was like dead. They grabbed hold of my hair and pulled me into the canoe and took me to shore. Their coming was certainly a blessing, but I could not express my thanks because I was unable to speak.

I went home quite frightened. For three days I was unable to sleep, and I stayed close to my house. Nothing like this had ever happened before. It really troubled me.

Later, some folks of my town came to advise me that when I was near death it was not because of the *paxte* but the spirits of people who have drowned in the lake. They said that whenever a person dies in the lake, their spirits are permanently bound to the lake. This is because the water goddess is always looking for more servants and the spirits are not happy to be alone in the water so they want to pull in more persons to join them. Others say that when the water goddess wants food she commands the other spirits to capture another person, and this person has to die in the lake for the beautiful señorita.

I am inclined to believe what they tell me about all of this. It is certain that I almost remained dead in the lake. Before losing consciousness, I was aware of the *paxte* pulling me down. But the plant does not have much strength with which to pull a person under; after all *paxte* is just a plant! I believe maybe the spirits of the lake were pulling me down by my feet. The whole ordeal made me sick for a few days.

There is another part to this belief that is also supported by my own experience. That is, they say that if a person dies on the bank of the lake, the spirit of the person stays in that spot and will frighten anyone who passes by the spot at night. The spirit wants to chase them away.

On October 4, 1970, a young boy drowned. He was 11 years old and named Andrés Cholotio Ujpán, the son of Señor Domingo Cholotio Gonzáles and Señora Francisca Ujpán. When he dived off the pier, he did not come up again. Others went to find out why he didn't emerge, and they found him dead.

The corpse was taken to Sololá to obtain a death certificate, and the following day it was returned to San José for burial. A few days later the parents of the deceased went to a shaman to find out why their son had drowned. The shaman said that the younster had died because he happened to dive into the water at a dangerous time when the lake spirits were looking for someone to capture. The water spirits are able to watch people, and they saw him dive into the water.

It seems certain that where a person dies, his spirit remains because once I went fishing at night in a canoe that a friend of mine lent me. I was only about 25 meters away from the spot where Andrés had drowned when I heard a loud noise from the same place, and it sent a chill through me. When I mustered up the courage to go over to the place where he had died, I found nothing there, but I felt very, very cold! I have thought about what happened, and I think perhaps Andrés's spirit wanted to scare me.

❧ A Bountiful Tomato Harvest
FEBRUARY 8–22, 1973

After planting a pound of onion seeds that cost me $6, I watered my tomatoes, which are ready for harvesting. Then a man arrived asking to buy some tomatoes. We agreed on 150 pounds at 5 cents a pound. So my wife and I began to harvest my beautiful crop of red tomatoes. I finished weighing the luscious tomatoes at 3:00 P.M. I was extremely pleased because this was my first sale of the year.

After eating lunch with my wife, I went back to my tomato field to add more fertilizer. Tomorrow I will fumigate the plants with Antracol.

My wife and I got up early this morning [February 12] to harvest the ripe tomatoes in my field. The field is bursting with tomatoes, and all my neighbors in San José admire this field of mine because it is so full of tomatoes.

We picked eight *arrobas* [200 pounds], and I sold them at 5 cents a pound. In total we made $10 today, thanks to God.

After bathing early in the lake, I ate fish broth with lots of chili for breakfast. At 9:00 A.M. my wife and I went to pick tomatoes to sell in the Sololá market tomorrow. We picked 150 pounds, and, God willing, I will carry them to Sololá.

For dinner, we had *chicharrones* [fried pork skins] with tortillas and lots of coffee.

I got up at 4:00 A.M. to carry the boxes of tomatoes to the shore where I was catching the launch to Panajachel in route to Sololá. Immediately, my wife brought me hot coffee at the beach where I was arranging the tomatoes for the trip. It was very cold, and the coffee, which tasted good, warmed me.

In Sololá I sold the tomatoes at 7 cents a pound. I grossed $10.50. But by the time I paid my passage to Sololá and back ($2) and a few things to eat in the marketplace, I had only $5 left. Nevertheless, I was still happy because I had a lot of tomatoes to sell!

Today [February 12] after bringing firewood from the countryside and bathing in the lake, I decided to pick 100 pounds of
tomatoes to take to Santa Elena to sell. I will have to carry them on
my back and there is no highway from here to there so we will see if
God gives me the strength to do this.

I got up at 1:00 A.M. to ready the cargo. By 5:00 A.M. I passed
through Santa Ana [which is nearly straight up a mountain by a
narrow footpath from San José]. I passed through a place named
Kamibal, which is an *aldea* of Santa Elena, and at 9:00 A.M. I made it
to Santa Elena [a seven-hour walk over mountains]. After eating
breakfast, I sold the tomatoes at 8 cents a pound. That is, I made $8
by 12:30 P.M.

After the last tomato was sold, I bought a few things for the
house to take back with me to San José. I was not very happy when
I ate lunch because I was exhausted. What's more—for lunch the
meat broth that I bought had too much chili in it! A bit upset, I
walked out of Santa Elena at 2:00 P.M.

When I reached a place called Pamesebal, I drank two-
eighths of a quart of liquor because I felt so tired. With the liquor
relieving my aches, I began to walk more rapidly toward San José. I
made it home, finally, sometime around 7:00 P.M.—extremely tired.

ᖇ The Secretary Has My Brother-in-Law Jailed
FEBRUARY 23, 1973

I was still tired from yesterday, so I did not get up until
7:00 A.M. I went to the beach to walk around. When I returned
home, relatives came to tell me that my brother-in-law Roberto
Monroy, the medic, was being held in jail because of being drunk
and fighting with the municipal secretary. I went to see about it at
the courthouse, but the matter could not be settled because the
mayor is really a bad person. He would not even tell me what
the charges are; he just said that by the twenty-sixth Roberto will
be in prison in Sololá.

My sister Julia was very upset. Roberto and I are not really
brothers, but I will have to see what I can do for him anyway.
We will see how this thing turns out because the crime is not
even stated.

In the afternoon, I had a few drinks with friends. At 9:00 P.M.
I arrived at the jailhouse [which is a tiny house in back of the
Municipal Hall] to give Roberto a drink of liquor and some
cigars. We were visiting with one another when a municipal

policeman appeared and told me it is prohibited to talk with prisoners. At the same time he ordered me to present myself in front of the justice of the peace.

My having to appear before the tribunal bothered me very much. The mayor, who is also the judge, told me that it is a serious offense to visit prisoners at night. He sentenced me to a fine of $5.

When I got home my wife scolded me for allowing this to happen. Five dollars is a lot of money for poor people to lose on a fine. This just made me feel more angry so I went out and got drunk. I was really aggravated!

I awakened with a hangover. My wife fixed breakfast, but I did not eat contentedly. I kept thinking about Roberto because tomorrow he is going to prison in Sololá. For certain, I will have to go with my brother-in-law to Sololá to see how all of this turns out.

In the afternoon we went to San Martín to get money to be able to bail Roberto out of jail. I went to speak with the doctor for whom Roberto works so that he would not lose his job as a medic. My brother-in-law is a Ladino, and he can't work as we natives [Indians] can. If we don't have one kind of job we can go ask for another—at hard labor, if necessary. Or we can go to the mountains to collect firewood and go around selling it all over the place. But because he is a Ladino, he can't do that kind of work. He can better provide for his family with the kind of work he has as a doctor's aide. If he lost his job because of this problem, there would be a lot of suffering and hardships in the family.

In the evening some neighbors and family friends came over to console Roberto's wife. We were so upset we hardly slept.

At 2:00 A.M. they took Roberto to Sololá. There was no launch that afternoon, so we had to travel to Panajachel by canoe. We were able to eat breakfast at 8:00 A.M. when we arrived in Sololá by bus, but Roberto went to jail without any breakfast. As we were eating lunch in a dining hall, a great friend Bartolomé Dionisio saw us. I spoke to him about my brother-in-law. Shortly thereafter we went to a lawyer, and together we entered the tribunal. The first thing they told us was that Señor Roberto Monroy Peneleu is accused of four crimes—assault, threat, dissension, and insult.

Why did Roberto argue with the secretary?

According to my brother-in-law, the reason that he argued with the secretary was that the secretary wanted to have his wife hired to work in the health clinic in San José. The secretary did not want anyone else to work there except his wife, and this led to the disagreement between him and Roberto. Roberto had gone to ask about this in San Diego, and there they told him that they didn't want anyone else but him working in the clinic. When he got back to San José, the town secretary had appointed another medic to work there. Roberto got drunk and argued with the secretary over the issue. This in turn led the secretary to making accusations against Roberto.

How did it all turn out?

Well, it turned out to be just slander against my brother-in-law. I have political contacts in Sololá from the time I acted as the general director of the Partido Institucional Democrático (PID) in San José. This is the party that was started when General Arana became president. It is his party—the Partido Institucional. My political friends in Sololá helped me defend Roberto in court. It turned out that Roberto spent only 24 hours in jail in Sololá. If it hadn't been for me, I don't know how many months he would have spent in jail! He won his case, and the judge had to give him back the $40 that he put up for bail. He won mainly because I was thoughtful and chose to defend him against his enemies.

After Roberto won his case, he went to work in San Diego la Laguna. My half-sister, Julia, still lives here in San José, and Roberto paid me $1 a day to oversee the construction of a new house for her.

In the afternoon I was free to leave to look for people to work on the coast. When I had enough for a *cuadrilla,* I put my first cousin Andrés Bizarro in charge of transporting them to the coast.

❧My Uncle Is Attacked by His Neighbors
JANUARY 25, 1974

At this point in Ignacio's diary, almost a year lapses before a nonroutine and nonrepetitive event. I was uncertain whether Ignacio lost interest in keeping his diary or whether not much happened to him that he considered important enough to write about; so I queried Ignacio about the relatively few entries for this period. It seems rather that not much happened that was noteworthy than that he failed to record a significant event.

My wife and children and I took a very pleasant canoe ride to San Jorge. While I gave money to a *cuadrilla,* my family had a good

time at the fiesta. My wife persuaded me to leave before I got
drunk. We both recalled last year when I injured my shin rather
severely because I got too drunk and passed out.

We got home about 5:00 p.m., and I was rather pleased with
myself for not getting intoxicated. I walked to André's house, but
he was not home. Then I went to chat with my father-in-law. When
I returned home, my brother-in-law, Benjamín Coché, was waiting
for me at my house. We began talking, and I sent for beers. We
drank with gusto.

Then I heard a ruckus in the streets. When I looked out of
my window, I saw that some drunken neighbors were trying to kill
my uncle—my mother's brother. I didn't know if the drunks had
been drinking in the bar near my house or if they just were out
to be mean.

When I went outside to defend my uncle, my wife accompanied me. She was holding one of our little children in her arms
when one of the neighbors struck her in anger. That was really a sad
thing for me to witness.

Then the drunks grabbed me and tried to strike me. But they
were unable to hold on to me or hit me because they were too
drunk! I kicked them to defend myself because they were surely
out for blood.

I don't know why for sure they were doing all of this. I think
they are just jealous. My insulting neighbors' names are Benito
Ixtamer Toc, Calixto Pérez Sánchez, and Carmen Sánchez Cholotio.
These people made up a *calumnia* [slander] against me, and they
reported me to the justice of peace. They said that I had torn Señora
Carmen's slip, which was worth $10. They also claimed that I
caused her to lose a necklace valued at $20. Señor Calixto showed
up before the tribunal with an injury on his head, claiming that I
had put it there.

Then the justice of the peace ordered me to pay for the slip
and necklace. He also commanded me to pay $10 for Calixto's med-
ical treatment, including $1 a day for six days of medicine, or $6. By
the time he was through sentencing me, I had to pay $50 total. But
by the grace of God, I had saved $100, and I went home to get the
money the judge ordered me to pay.

The money they got out of me was clearly robbery. They knew
that I had money so they took advantage of me. It all gave me a
terribly bitter feeling against them, so I went to a bar and got drunk.
It cost me another $12 on liquor.

At 8:00 a.m. this morning [January 27], I left San José with a
work crew. I am writing this at the Pangola cotton farm. I am a little

sad about the money I lost—that is, that I had to give to my jealous neighbors. Only God can recoup for me the money I lost, little by little. If He is willing, I will return to San José tomorrow.

↬ San José Gets Electricity
JULY, 1974

When I was in San José in 1972, there was no electricity. Now [1975] there is. When did San José get electricity, and how did the people react to having it?

I was unaware of the exact date that the workers from the National Electric Company (NEC) arrived in San José to begin installing the electric outlets, but I know it was the beginning of July. Many workers came to both San José and San Martín, about 40 in each town.

I don't know how the rumor started, but the word spread quickly throughout the town of San José that the NEC workers kill people for light. They said that the electric plant in Santa María Quezaltenango needs people for the machine to work. Furthermore, when a person is killed he or she serves as food for the light, and when the machine is not fed food, it won't work. I really don't know how the neighbors of both towns heard about this, but they were so afraid that they wouldn't walk around at night after 7:00 P.M. because they thought to do so would be surrendering themselves to the NEC workers who would carry them off as food for the light. Thus, there was a period when at 9:00 P.M. there wasn't a soul on the streets.

The youngsters didn't go out in the afternoon to fish anymore because they thought they would be killed. Many people would run away when they saw one of the NEC workers. During the installation period, townspeople would secure their houses at 8:00 P.M. so that no one could take them away. There was a lot of fear in San José and even in San Martín. The women went to San Martín in groups of five or ten (for protection) to shop; and women from San Martín also walked in groups.

I don't know why but some *Joseños* thought bad things about me. They claimed that a friend of mine Diego José Ramos Rodríquez and I had some kind of obligation to the head of the electric institute to turn over to him a certain number of people from San José as food for light. I was unaware that people were thinking these bad things about me until Diego showed up at my house to tell me that some lady had said to him that he and I were committed to the NEC to kill people. The rumor got out and spread. Everyone was afraid of me, and they started saying bad things about me.

Finally, it was necessary for Diego and me to go to court to stop it. We filed a complaint against Señor Clemente Canajay, Señora Isabel Cholotio Cumes, and other members of their families because they went around spreading these lies about us. In court, Diego and I declared our innocence to their allegations, and the mayor, Don Daniel Bizarro T., charged each of them a $5 fine. Only then did the people calm down and lose their fear of us. It is true that the NEC men came to my house a lot, but I only sold them tomatoes and onions. The people, however, suspected something else.

I don't know if light needs people for food, but I believe it is a lie because during their stay in San José, the NEC men never did anything wrong. In the afternoon, after work, they would try to kill a dove or some other bird in our coffee fields, but they didn't kill any people.

The whole affair was fading away when they tried the lights for the first time in San José on September 10, 1974. With the coming of light, the people once again went out to walk with a real change—the streets were lighted!

The inauguration of the electric light took place on September 14. Then the people of San José quickly forgot about how afraid they had been. In San Martín, it was somewhat different from San José because the inauguration of the light wasn't until December before Christmas.[18]

Now, in these two towns, there are many changes, and the people don't remember if the machine needs people to eat. Furthermore, whenever there is a power failure, these same people make a big fuss about how they need the light, but before it came they wouldn't even talk about it.

I Fall Into the Hands of my Enemy, the Mayor
FEBRUARY 4, 1975

Today a friend of mine named David Sicay Pablo arrived at my home so drunk on *aguardiente* he could not walk. It was rather late at night so I went to help him home, making sure that he would not fall and hit his head or hurt his body.

Within a half-hour I returned home, but when I knocked on my door my wife refused to open it. Apparently, she thought I had gone to drink. It is a pity that she thought this because I had not drunk one cup—not a cup! I had not escorted the man home with the intention of drinking with him—only to keep him from hurting himself.

When I began to beat loudly on the door, my children opened it for me. But my wife began to quarrel a lot with me and would not stop. She finally made me so mad at her that I slapped her in the face. Mind you, it was not a hard slap. Nevertheless, she did not just take it. Instead, she went running to the justice of the peace the next morning to report me.

On the same day, the tribunal ordered me to appear before them. When I arrived before the mayor [who is also the judge], he interrogated me incessantly. "Has your house always existed in disgrace?" he repeated.

"No, this is the first time such a thing has happened in my house."

The *señor alcalde* Daniel Bizarro T. handed down sentences to me with relish. He claimed that walking at night is against the law (but it isn't) and fined me $10. Then he even fined my wife $6 for not opening the door. All of these penalties added up to $16 which is a lot of money to us poor folks.

The mayor was taking great pleasure in fining me because he is envious, or he has a certain amount of political animosity toward me. That is, he is the general secretary of the Partido Revolucionario whereas I am the general secretary of the Partido Institucional Democrático. While the Partido Revolucionario campaigned for Colonel Ernesto Paiz Novales for president during the 1973 election, we in the Partido Institucional Democrático supported General de Brigada Shel [Kjell] Eugenio Laugerud García. Colonel Paiz lost and General Laugerud is now the president of Guatemala. This is the reason for the rancor the mayor had for me. It was a pleasure for him when I committed my error. He must have said, "Good, Ignacio has fallen into my hands."

But I don't know why my wife and I fought. I think that in this world men always have their faults.

❧ Señor Emilio Lavarenzo Drowns in the Lake
FEBRUARY 1975

In 1975 I asked Ignacio whether he thought a strong wind whips up over the lake when someone dies. This is a popular belief among many natives. Ignacio gave the following accounts that he had not included in his diary.

I am not sure of the day, but in February Señor Emilio Lavarenzo, who is from San Martín, drowned in the lake at a place called Chuachoj. This happened when he went to take a bath. They found him dead the next day, and they took his body to Sololá for a death certificate. Since the accident took place in the jurisdiction of San José, I met his son 15 days after the death. He had been to a spiritualist in Mazatenango to talk with his father's spirit. He says that during the séance his father spoke to him (through the mouth of the spiritualist), telling him that he died because the spirits in the water pulled him under. His father went on to say, through the medium of the spiritualist, that he tried to fight off the spirits in the water, but there were too many of them.

The boy is a friend of mine, and he talked openly with me about his experience with the spiritualist. He said that for this session he spent about $35 dollars for candles, incense, flowers, *aguardiente,* and beer and money in effect (that is, apart from the cost of traveling to Mazatenango and paying for lodging).

When a person dies in the lake, a strong wind passes over the lake from north to south, the opposite of the wind *El Xocomil.* The wind after a death lasts from four to eight days, blowing day and night. It is certain that this happens each time someone drowns. I can affirm that when Andrés Cholotio Ujpán died, the same night we felt a strong wind for five days. And moreover, the same thing happened after Emilio Lavarenzo drowned—there was a very strong wind from the north. Thus, the townspeople know that when a strong wind comes, it signifies that someone has drowned in the lake, not just for the people of San José but other towns also. My town believes that when a person dies by drowning, the goddess of the lake discharges a strong wind to cast out the body of the fallen just as if one would cast out a stone. According to this belief, the goddess of the lake needs only the spirit of the deceased—not the body itself.

In June 1975 another case happened that supports this belief. This was when five persons from Tzancuil drowned in the lake. I do not know the exact date when they died because the case was told to me by a good friend Gabriel of Tzancuil.

The case involved a family from Tzancuil and a servant who were going to Sololá to the market. Since it is very difficult to negotiate the trip by foot, they decided to go in a canoe. I was told the señor had $80 with which he planned to buy two little bulls at the Friday market. His plan was to take his wife and two children and his servant all in the canoe to get to Sololá. Then the servant would return with the bulls on foot while he and his family returned via canoe.

In Sololá the señor did not spend all of his money for the bulls. He had enough left over to buy some drinks for himself, his wife and the servant. As they began to get drunk, they forgot that they had to return to Tzancuil by canoe. By the time they were ready to leave they were very intoxicated.

They all walked down to the lake and climbed in the canoe, including the servant who did not walk home after all. When they were well out on the lake, the canoe capsized, and everyone of them drowned—the man, his wife, their two children, and the servant!

The next day there was a strong wind from the north over the lake. The reason I know this is that I noticed the wind, and I asked my friend Gabriel why there was so much wind. He told me, "My dear friend, three days ago five of my countrymen [from Tzancuil] died. Each time someone dies by drowning for sure there has to be a strong wind." Because the goddess of the water does not want to see the dead bodies that sink below the water, she commands the wind to blow their bodies out among the stones and rocks of the shoreline. All the goddess wants is the spirits, not the bodies!

They say that if one does not want to be drawn into the lake, one must make a ceremony for the goddess. One must ask for permission to cross the water or to fish in the lake.

Do fishermen perform ceremonies before fishing in the lake?

I have not seen myself nor had one of these ceremonies performed. I am told that the fishermen perform a *costumbre* each year. They go with a shaman to a place on the bank of the lake, taking candles, incense, cups of liquor, and especially sweet smelling flowers and perfume because the owner is a woman (*dueña,* or goddess). The shaman asks for permission to use the lake and for the goddess to turn loose the fish so they might catch them. The men who fish do this ceremony once or twice a year.

I fish occasionally in the lake, but since I do not fish as an occupation and I usually only fish for what I intend to eat, it is not necessary for me to perform such a ceremony. I believe the 14 fishermen in San José perform the *costumbre* as a group. They are all Catholic; none is Protestant. The candles that they burn for the goddess are white for good luck, and they burn them clandestinely so that their townspeople won't gossip about them for performing such *costumbres.*

❧ The Good Mayor Unintentionally Resigns
JUNE 28, 1975

The good *alcalde* of San José, Señor Daniel Bizarro T., is the brother of my dear friend Andrés. He is also the one who fined me

$16 for fighting with my wife. As mayor he treated people of San José and San Martín very badly. He thought he was king—never pardoning anyone for anything. But then the hour arrived when no one asked him for a pardon.

His majesty the mayor began drinking on June 16, five days before the main fiesta of the town (San José). His wife joined him in the bars, and by the time June 24 arrived, he and his wife were on such a binge that they forgot there was a fiesta. The good *alcalde* was so tanked up on liquor from drinking all week that he failed to go to his office. On the day of the fiesta he is supposed to be in the tribunal with the *cofradías* and respected elders of the town and other important people. Instead, the office for him was a bar.

This prompted his companions to hold a conference. They commanded the syndic and the town secretary to write a letter of resignation. They wrote it in the words of the mayor—that is, as if he had written the document himself. In essence, the document said that he the mayor was unable to continue in his office and that he was resigning. But it was not the mayor in fact who wrote the letter—it was the syndic and the secretary.

As soon as the letter was finished, they sent an *alguacil* to the bar to ask the mayor to sign an official letter from Sololá. Little did he know that he signed his own resignation! He was, of course, too drunk to know what he was doing.

When the ex-mayor realized what he had done, he just began to drink even more. The words of God are certain because they say, "Do not judge and you will not be judged; do not condemn and you will not be condemned; forgive and you will be forgiven." If this man had been thinking of these words, he would still be mayor.

The present mayor is what we call an *accidental*, that is, an alderman temporarily made mayor. It is not likely that there will be another election until next year because people are not really interested in such things. They would argue it is a waste of time to fool around with another election when they should be busy working in the fields.

My Brother's Murderers Are Shot
JUNE, 1975

I wrote in my autobiography that my half-brother Santos Diego was murdered on November 30, 1972. He lost his life on the El Salvador Farm, which is a municipality of Chicacao in the department of Suchitépequez. My brother had been working for three days as a *comerciante ayudante* [assistant to a traveling merchant]

of Señor Domingo Quinillo from Santa Cruz del Quiché. They had
been selling clothing from farm to farm when two thugs cut them
down with machetes.

The two criminals were identified as Héctor Abel Mazariegos
and Rocael Ortiz Sánchez. Ortiz was the son of the administrator of
the El Salvador Farm, and Abel was the son of the *alcalde auxiliar*
[auxiliary, or deputy mayor found only on farms and *aldeas* who
enforces laws] of the same farm.

By order of the Supreme Court of Justice the criminals were
shot in this month of June 1975, on a Saturday. I read about the
execution in the newspaper and heard it on the radio.

☙ A Diviner in San Luis Predicts My Future
AUGUST 27, 1975

Today in San Luis, while waiting to catch the launch for
Panajachel, I met a man who is a diviner. He tells the future with
little green birds. When he asks the birds, they tell him what a
person's luck will be.

Well, I was curious about this, and I paid him 10 cents to read
my luck. He did it with three little birds, but I am not sure what to
think about his prophecy.

"I am projecting a business," he told me. "On your route you
will earn some things, but be careful." This is what one little bird
told him.

The other bird, according to the man, said, "In your work do
not go with bad friends and do not believe everything you are told.
You have enemies; take care."

The last bird said, "You have six children. Protect them well
and never arrive home rude in your house."

These small birds are supposed to be able to understand their
master, who is from Totonicapán. He was in San Luis only for the
fiesta. He tells the birds that such and such a person needs to know
what his luck will be, puts them down on a table, and interprets
their actions.

☙ Heavy Rains Bring Misfortune with Cuadrillas
SEPTEMBER 5 – 13, 1975

Gabriel Celado came to my house from Santa Rosa la Laguna
to offer me a 25-man *cuadrilla* that he would have ready to leave by

Saturday, but I refused his offer because of the small number of men. On the other hand, Jorge González of Santa Ana came and offered 60 men to take to the coast. I agreed with the latter to make a trip Monday, September 8.

Sunday afternoon I went to San Martín with my assistants Julián Chorol and Lorenzo Pérez Hernández to talk to the owner of a truck to see if he would lend me $300 to give to the crew. The truck owner, named Lucas Mendoza, told me that he would give me money but not until later in the afternoon. When we went again to his house, however, Señor Lucas refused. "I can't give you money," he stated, "you owe a lot of people."

It turned out that Manuel Alejandro Ujpán and Marcos Vásquez Castro told him these falsehoods because I hired a new assistant Señor Pérez García. Señor Mendoza believed them, and this gave me a bad feeling in my heart that is difficult to explain. It was nothing more than a fraud against me.

Later I went to my friend Miguel T. Ixtamer who also owns a truck. He received me in a friendly manner. I told him about the deceit that was being perpetrated against me, and then I asked him for a loan. Happily he lent me the money.

Because Señor Miguel's truck was on the way to Cocales carrying corn, we arranged for one of my helpers to take the bus to Cocales via Guatemala City to tell the truck driver to meet me and part of the crew at a junction in Samayac.

At 1:00 A.M. Monday, my assistant Julián Chorol left to get the truck, and I departed for Santa Ana to get ten members of the crew. I arrived at 4:00 A.M., and woke them up, giving them their advance money. Then we boarded the bus headed for Quezaltenango.

Unfortunately, the bus had only traveled about one kilometer when a landslide tumbled down blocking the road. My ten workers and I began walking toward the junction in Samayac while the rest of the passengers went back to Santa Ana.

The road was uphill and slippery from rain. We had just a little distance to go to make it to the top when hunger and exhaustion overwhelmed me, and I could walk no farther. I fainted. When I recovered, I walked little by little to the junction, arriving about 10:00 A.M. We waited there for Señor Miguel's truck.

To pass the time we told little old-time stories. But eventually, I got so hungry that I went to a nearby house to ask for breakfast. Lamentably, I did not get any.

At last the truck arrived at 1:00 P.M. Julián stayed with the ten men at the junction while I went with the truck looking for the rest of the crew in Santa Clara Tecpán. The road was fine until it ran out of asphalt. Rain had made the dirt slippery, and one kilometer after the end of the pavement, the truck skidded, and we nearly fell into a 600-meter gorge. This gave us a terrific fright! We were only seven kilometers away from Santa Clara, but after spending a laborious hour getting the truck out to a safe place on the road, we decided to go back because the road was too dangerous to continue on to Santa Clara.

We didn't get back to the Samayac junction where we had left the few workers from Santa Ana until 4:00 P.M. By this time the driver and his assistant were too scared to try to drive to the coast so we did not make the trip. I had to pay the men from Santa Ana for one-day's work, and they went back to their home town.

I finally got to eat breakfast at 6:00 P.M. at a place called Los Encuentros [a bus stop on the Pan American Highway]. Afterwards, I had some drinks with my friend Julián Chorol and the truck driver.

We arrived in Panajachel at 9:00 P.M. and looked for a place to spend the night. We ended up in an inn for 20 cents a person. When I was counting my money, I discovered that I was missing $40 (either lost or stolen). The truck left, and my helper and I stayed in Panajachel.

Tuesday morning we got up at 3:00 A.M. to catch the 4:00 A.M. launch to San José. We arrived home in an hour and a half, but it was a sad homecoming because the money I had borrowed had been wasted.

In the afternoon I went to San Martín to tell Señor Miguel T. Ixtamer what had happened to me on the road. Well, he obliged me to pay him for the truck trip—it was $100. But since I don't have this much money, I will have to pay him in four installments.

Because of the rainy weather, I suffered hunger, thirst, fatigue, pain, and a loss of money on the trip.

On Wednesday I left on another trip for the coast with 20 people for the Pangolita Farm. This time, however, the workers were from San José. It rained hard along the way, and we were scared because we remembered what had happened to us last Monday. But we arrived without incident.

When it dawned Thursday, it was raining. The people could not go out to work because of the wetness.

On the same day, they paid one of my crews that had just finished working a month. I left with them at 3:00 P.M. headed back to San José in the same truck.

We stopped in Cocales for dinner where we had quite a few drinks. I was quite enraged that my trips keep turning out badly for me.

Only ten kilometers from San Martín la Laguna and at 2:00 A.M., the truck got stuck in a mud slide. Julián Chorol and I struggled to get the mud off the road, but it was impossible because so much had slid down the mountain. To make matters worse, nobody would help us because the entire crew was drunk. It didn't matter to them at all! Thus we passed the rest of the night.

It was Friday morning and we still couldn't get the truck out of the mud. Many cars passed us going downhill, but because we were going uphill, they were unable to help. Finally, about 8:00 A.M. Señor Miguel T. Ixtamer arrived in a van with some workers with hoes. Working in the rain, we began to move all the mud from the road.

By the time we finally rolled into San Martín, I was drenched, ravenous, thirsty, exhausted, and worried. After chatting with Señor Miguel for a little while, I got to my house to eat breakfast about 11:30 A.M. Gabriel Celado arrived from Samayac. He, Julián, and I started drinking. I told Gabriel what had happened to us. He stated that he thought that other contractors had practiced witchcraft against me. This would explain our six days of suffering. But I don't know if Gabriel's belief is correct. My thinking is that our misfortune is due to the weather. In any case, I lost $190—a lot of money. I don't know what I'll do to pay the debt because it is so much. But I will ask God to bless me—to help me find a way to pay back the money.

In the afternoon, *profesor* Arturo came to my house to ask for help in buying fuel for the vehicle that is going to Quezaltenango to bring back the torch that represents the glorious liberty of Guatemala. This will be part of the activities of Independence Day on September 15. I gave him $5 and my assistant Julián gave him $1.

I woke up Saturday aching from having drunk too much *aguardiente*. The hangover was so painful that I didn't go to work.

Celebrating Independence Day
SEPTEMBER 14–15, 1975

Profesores Arturo and Guido arranged with several sports clubs to have athletes run the torch from Quezaltenango to San José. These clubs included the Municipal Sports Club, the Cholotio Sports Club, the Quetzal Sports Club, and the Blue and White Sports Club. They all agreed to take turns running with the torch. But at the last minute all of the teams except the Blue and White Sports Club backed out of going. Eight members of this club and an enthusiastic volunteer from San Martín kept their commitment. The fellow from San Martín does not belong to the soccer team, but he carries in his heart the importance of a free Guatemala. These young men asked me to accompany them to Quezaltenango, but I was unable despite being a member of the club.

They set out for Quezaltenango in the pickup of the North American Reverend Father from San Diego la Laguna. He didn't charge any rent for the use of his truck. Thus, the only expense was for gasoline.

The rain caused the young athletes much strife while they were running. But they are good fellows. It was a marathon run, and they took turns every 2 kilometers. While one ran, the others rode in the pickup. The distance between Quezaltenango and San José is 150 kilometers, and even with nine young men running, it is very tiring.

At 12:00 midnight when they arrived in San José and placed the torch beneath the National Pavilion on the municipal atrium, almost all the townspeople—men, women, and children—watched. All of the old people were asking from what the torch was made, and they seemed pleased when they were told. This was the first time that such a thing was done in San José. Although this is the first time that the liberty torch was seen in this little corner of Guatemala, I don't know if young men next year will get as excited about participating in such events. Only God knows!

Dawn came early on this holiday. The school children, townspeople, town officials and workers, the members of the cofradías, and the members of Catholic Action all paraded to the municipal soccer field to attend the reading of the Declaration of Independence of Guatemala.

Afterwards the Municipal Sports Team was planning on an exciting game of soccer against the team for the Portuario Company from Guatemala City, but these guys from Guatemala failed to come. And there was no game.

I suppose that things turn out to be a disappointment sometimes. But I believe the reason is that people are at times misleading. For example, the Municipal Sports Club had also promised to go to Quezaltenango to help carry the torch back, but in the end they didn't go. They misled the guys from the Blue and White Sports Club. In turn, they were deceived by the fellows from Guatemala. My feeling is that it is better not to mislead so as not to be misled. This should be clearly understood.

℞An Encounter with Maximón
SEPTEMBER 20, 1975

Late Saturday night, I was returning from San Martín after waiting for a truck that never showed. I was just entering my house when the shaman Eduardo Flores spoke to me. He was accompanied by a noted shaman from San Martín named Santiago Cojox, and he invited me to go to his house where the [new] *Maximón* brotherhood had gathered.[19]

About 15 minutes later I headed for his house. When I arrived the shaman from San Martín was sitting with the image of Maximón, and Señor Eduardo was making a fire with live coals in the corridor in order to burn myrrh incense. I don't know what *costumbre* they were performing, but when I entered, they asked me if I had any money with which to visit Maximón. I answered, "No." With my answer they got angry, and they ordered me to leave. So then I told them, "I didn't come here to argue with you." As I was talking, Eduardo's father, Jorge Flores, entered the room and told me that if I didn't leave from there, they would have to throw me out with sticks. As I was making my exit, they told me that they were going to bewitch me because I did not leave them any money.

By now it was 2:00 A.M. I decided to walk back to San Martín to see if the truck had arrived. It was not there. And my assistant Julián was already in Santa Clara Tecpán waiting for the truck. Suddenly, I felt hopeless. Although reluctant, Señor Miguel T. Ixtamer had lent me another $100 to give to the waiting crew. So another trip has turned out bad because of the poor timing of the truck. But such is my luck!

℞ Celebration of the Cofradía Santo Domingo Guzmán
OCTOBER 4, 1975

It is customary for the brotherhood Santo Domingo Guzmán to celebrate this day of Saint Francis of Assisi. The head of this brotherhood traditionally invites the brotherhoods San Juan Bautista and Virgen Concepción for food and drink.

On this day Señor José Sicay Méndez Ramos, the head of the Virgin of Conception fraternity, and Bartolo Sicay Cholotio, his first officer, gave a good *borrachera* [drunken party with lots of food and drink]. When these two men were pretty well inebriated, they cut open the head of Señor Ricardo García Pantzay with a wine bottle, inflicting a severe wound.

Subsequently, the two culprits were called before the tribunal, and the injured man proclaimed that he intended to sue them in Sololá. But Señor José and Señor Bartolo convinced the victim not to sue, and eventually he pardoned them. Nevertheless, the officers of the *cofradía* had to pay a $20 fine as well as half of the $16 medical bill. Señor José Sicay was able to produce the money for the damages because he has a little shop that does well. But Señor Bartolo Sicay Cholotio didn't have any money. He had to borrow it from another person to pay the penalty.

Two days after the incident, I left for the coast to work so that I can pay off my debt to Señor Miguel Ixtamer in San Martín.

ᕦ My Half-Sister Gets Married on my Son's Birthday
OCTOBER 30, THURSDAY, 1975

Today is my son José's birthday. Thanks to God Almighty, he is nine years old. We did not throw a party for him because we are short of money. Still my wife and I bought some bread and a few pounds of meat to eat with relatives and friends of the family. José was born at 10:00 P.M. so we should have celebrated at night. But instead we did it in the morning because one of my half-sisters Catarina Micaela García Bizarro invited us to her marriage to a young man named Geraldo Vásquez Canajay to take place in the afternoon.

When we arrived with my family at the courthouse, I was embarrassed because there were three couples all getting married on the same day. The other two couples had been living together for several years, and for that reason they had a lot of family and friends there to watch. Because the mayor's office is too small to accommodate everyone, there were some 50 people crowded outside.

One couple who had been living together, but not legally, is Cristóbal Ovalle Hernández and Alejandra Coché Ujpán. Their children are already big—the eldest being about 15 years old. The other couple, Carlos Cholotio Ajpop and Angelica Sumosa Cholotio, had been living together for four years, but also not by law.

I felt ashamed because the acting mayor was not paying much attention to what he was doing. He left all of the guests, parents, and godparents standing outside in front of the courthouse. It would have been better to have performed the ceremonies in the public assembly room where there is ample space. What do we have councilmen for if they can't even think? And besides we have a secretary who is Ladino (who should know better). Why didn't he tell the mayor how to perform the marriages properly?

I think we have a secretary who is shameless. He is from Santa Ana la Laguna, and he has three brothers; all of them are bad. They are envious and slanderous, and they enjoy mistreating people. This is the same secretary who slandered my brother-in-law Roberto, who forced the elected mayor to resign during the fiesta, and who has accused the teachers of not working and teaching the children anything.

A fourth wedding would have taken place on the same day, but the officials in the municipality would not allow it because they said the couple, Señor Jaime Velásquez and Señora Elena Pérez González, are relatives. Actually, Señora Elena's grandfather was Pedro Pérez who is a brother to Señora María Pérez who in turn is also the grandmother of Señor Jaime Velásquez. [That is, the couple are second cousins, children of grandparents who are siblings.] Since they were denied marriage in the courthouse of San José, they went all the way to Sololá where the judge of the Primary Court of Claims married them.

After the wedding proceedings in San José, the newlyweds and guests went to the parochial assembly room at the special invitation of the president of Catholic Action. But there wasn't anything to eat or drink so I went with my friend Diego Velásquez Méndez to have some beers at his house. Finally, I got home and rested after all the festivities.

❧A Drowning at San Diego la Laguna
NOVEMBER 24, 1975

Last Monday, November 17, Señor Antonio Castro drowned while taking a bath at Panan—a beach at San Diego la Laguna. I heard this news on the radio around noon.

At 3:00 P.M. a strong wind started to whip up to the north. This wind from the north lasted eight days. They call this wind the fury of the devils. It did not calm down until 10:00 A.M. today [Monday]. It is true that when a person dies in Lake Atitlán a strong wind always comes down [from the north at the command of the water goddess].

❧ A Boat Sinks and Crew Has Problems
SUNDAY, DECEMBER 14–TUESDAY, DECEMBER 16, 1975

At 4:00 P.M., after arranging a *cuadrilla* with my friend Gabriel Celado Sánchez in Tzancuil I headed back for San José. I was high in the mountains when I spotted about three kilometers below a launch on Lake Atitlán that was headed south. I watched the boat until I came to a dip in the road and my view was blocked. When I emerged, I could still see the launch, but it was no longer moving—it was completely out of order. The *Xocomil* (wind) was very strong, and the launch was about to capsize. A curve in the road blocked my vision of the distressed launch again, and when I reached the point where I could see the general area where the launch had been, it was no longer in sight. It apparently had sunk completely.

Because I was still very far away from both the launch and home, I did not think much more about it. By the time I got home it was 7:00 P.M., and I was exhausted. I just went to sleep.

Today [Monday] a strong wind was blowing at dawn, but I was unable to determine the nature of the wind [its significance]. I went to San Martín to contract a truck to take the *cuadrilla*.

At dawn I distributed a little money to some of the men who were going to work on the coast. At 8:00 A.M. Señor Miguel Ixtamer's truck arrived to pick up the portion of the crew who were from San José. From there we all went to San Martín to wait for people from Tzancuil who were supposed to arrive in a passenger canoe [a large one].

We waited for a long time. When the boat finally appeared the wind over the lake was quite strong. Just as the canoe was about three meters from the bank, it capsized. This was a pitiful sight because the canoe carried seven women and three children among the 35 workers aboard. The other men from San Martín and I plunged into the water to pull them to safety and prevent them from drowning. The water was rough, and our clothes got soaked, but thanks to God no one was hurt.

The whole ordeal scared the people from Tzancuil so much that they lost their desire to go to the coast to work. Eventually, I helped them overcome their fear, and I gave them money to buy a few things to eat.

My friend Gabriel told me later that when they passed in the direction of San Benito, they saw a sunken launch about ten meters down. This was the first thing that had frightened them. I replied that I thought the launch must have sunk Sunday afternoon, but neither of us knew whether anyone had drowned.

At 1:00 P.M. we left San Martín for the coast, but unfortunately we had traveled only eight kilometers to a place called Tzancacay when the truck broke down. We had to wait there while the driver and his assistant returned on foot to bring another truck from San Martín. While we waited, the people built a fire to warm themselves because the altitude was high, and it was cold.

The spare truck that arrived was in good running condition, and we left in it at 5:00 P.M. We arrived in Cocales by 9:00 P.M. and bought dinner there. But we did not tarry more than 20 minutes. It was 10:30 at night by the time we reached Río Pantaleón. We had almost made it across the river when the tires got stuck in the mud. We struggled to free them, but in vain. We could not budge them. We labored to free them until midnight—until everyone was exhausted. We were delayed again!

Because we could not free the tires, we had no choice but to spend the night in the truck. Unfortunately, there wasn't room for everyone inside. Neither my friend Geofredo nor I had brought bedding. What Geofredo did was to cut four leaves of manaque, or green palm—two for himself and two for me. We used one for a mat and the other for a poncho. But who can sleep on the bank of a river that is very wet and cold and swarming with mosquitos. Needless to say, we just suffered until Wednesday dawned.

At 5:00 A.M. a bus, *Flor de mi Tierra*, [Flower of My Land] passed. I flagged it down and talked with the driver Victor, asking him to advise Don Federico to send a bus to transport the *cuadrilla* because the truck was stuck fast and it was only getting worse under the weight of the people loaded in it.

At 6:30 A.M. the bus that I had sent for arrived, and I talked with Federico's brother who was on it. I asked him to transport the *cuadrilla* the rest of the way, and he said that he would be happy to do so.

The people were delighted to climb aboard the bus after so much trouble in the trucks. After saying good-bye to Heberto, who was waiting behind with the driver and his assistant for a tractor to pull the truck out, I headed out anew with my *cuadrilla* toward the Pangolita Farm.

We arrived at the sheds at 8:00 A.M. Because it was late in the morning and the people had not yet eaten breakfast, they did not want to work. Instead, while some went to bathe in the Coyolate River, others went to look for firewood for cooking. I went to the company storeroom to draw their provisions of cooking material, corn, beans, salt and lime.

When I had finished getting all of these things, a car passed that was driven by a man selling newspapers. I bought the *Prensa Libre* and began to read. I noticed an article about the launch that I saw stranded on the lake last Sunday. The *Prensa* said that the launch was found in the vicinity of San Martín la Laguna and that an engineer and his wife and three children lost their lives. Also navigating with them was a señor from Germany, but he did not drown. They found him on Tuesday on the Pacayal Farm in the jurisdiction of San Martín, but he was in a state of shock. He could neither eat nor speak. They transferred him immediately by helicopter to Guatemala City. The bodies of the engineer's wife and three children were found but not the body of the engineer himself. That is what I read in the paper. I remembered the launch that I had seen Sunday when I went to talk with Gabriel in Tzancuil. The launch was in distress and the *Xocomil* was very strong, and when I walked past a turn in the road, I could no longer see it. That was when it sank.

On December 15, a strong wind fell in the morning, blowing hard from the north. The same thing happened Tuesday when the canoe that was bringing the workers to San Martín capsized; it was because of the strong winds. I don't know why, but when a person dies in the lake it is certain that a day later a very strong wind blows for eight days. We are witnessing this phenomenon this very hour— it is not a lie; it is true, but I do not know why it is so.

The old people of San José say that it is because only the spirit of the person who drowns is needed by the water goddess, not the body. Thus, she makes a strong wind to cast out the corpse because she does not want it to remain permanently in the interior of the lake. She wishes to keep the lake very clean and clear. I am not sure this is the reason for the strong winds when a person dies, but I am certain that a wind will whip up when there is a drowning.

❧ The Season of Christmas and New Year
DECEMBER 23, 1975–JANUARY 15, 1976

Last Saturday [December 20] my wife and I went to buy clothing for our children and ourselves in San Martín. We spent $45, but we did not purchase many pieces because clothing is very expensive.

At 3:30 A.M. [Tuesday, December 23] we left San Martín for the farm Pangolita to pick up a crew that had been working. At 1:00 P.M. the truck stopped at a *comedor* so that we could eat a simple lunch. They charged us $2 each. These times are very expensive for poor people. For those who have money the high prices are all right, but for a poor person like me, they are excessive.

The crew whom we were transporting was paid at 4:00 P.M., but we delayed leaving for quite some time to allow the workers to buy their little items such as sugar, meat, bread, and cheese.

By the grace of God we made the trip without much happening. The only thing that took place was in an *aldea* called Cerro Colorado. A detachment of military mobile police would not let us pass. The only reason they gave us was that the truck did not have a license to carry passengers. They ordered me to unload all the people from the truck; then they escorted the truck to a storage place for transit vehicles. All of this hassle bothered me very much because it was at night and it prevented me from taking the crew home.

The driver offered to give the policemen money, but the policemen claimed that they did not want any. The truth, however, was that they wanted a great deal more than the driver offered. Finally, after all the hassling, they asked for $10 each. Because there were three of them, this meant that we had to produce $30. Not until I gave $15 and the driver gave $15 did they let us proceed. These are the señor policemen! I wondered how much money they rob from the poor working people because I know very well that all trucks carrying *cuadrillas* must pass this checkpoint. I think the reason they are doing this is that it is near Christmas. They need a lot of money to buy gifts for their children because they only asked for $2 to let us pass on previous trips. Luckily, this time I had $198 from the work of the crew as well as the $45 remaining from the cost of the passage of the truck. That is, in total, I had $243.

On Christmas Eve, December 24, my wife and I went to San Martín to buy things to eat. In the afternoon she cooked tamales and bread to eat late at night and Christmas day.

In the evening I went for a stroll with some friends, and we ended up drinking some *tragos*. Around 11:00 P.M. I returned home and ate tamales with my wife and little ones and my friends, Julián Chorol and Fernando Jorge. We had a fiesta. Then my wife went to church while I stayed home to watch the children who had gone to sleep. But I continued drinking with my friends, and, well, we drank a lot. When my wife returned, my friends and I were

pretty intoxicated. I told them good-bye around 2:00 A.M., and I
went to bed.

I did not get up until 8:00 A.M. The entire day passed very
pleasantly. But I am not sure how it was for others because there
were many drunks in the streets. Most of the people of San José
celebrated Christmas, the day Jesus Christ was born, by drinking
their *tragos.*

To me there is a delightful custom in our town during Christmas. On this day there is no preference with whom one may eat.
One can dine with whomever one chooses. *Joseños* give one another tamales, bread, chocolates, Coca Cola, beer and liquor. But
this is done only after mass, that is, after the people are free from
their religious services. People begin to visit one another only
after mass.

In total my expenses for the twenty-fourth and twenty-fifth
of December were $50, all of it spent on food and drink. This
Christmas passed very pleasantly with my family and friends, but
next year who knows what it will be like.

Do Joseños *exchange gifts during Christmas?*

Christmas is a very important day for the people of San José—
the most important day of the year. In fact it is the day that is most
important in almost all of Guatemala. If one wants to go to mass,
there is an early morning mass. Since above all it is a religious
holiday, there is no *marimba* or carnival atmosphere as there is
during a fiesta of a patron saint. On Christmas one just tries to be
happy and to have a good time for a little while. It is the custom to
give Christmas gifts by some, but we usually don't give gifts because we are too poor. If one has money, one may give some toys to
the kids, or one may give a hat or shirt to members of the family. We
poor people would like to exchange gifts, but we don't always have
the means. Thus we usually give something to eat—a tamale, some
bread, a cup of chocolate, or lunch.

This New Year's Eve falls on Wednesday. All I did was to
pass time in my house, waiting to say good-bye to 1975, until about
6:00 P.M. when my friend, David Coché Ramos, came to my house
and asked me to take a walk with him to San Martín.

"Very well," I said. "Let's go!"

We walked a while and eventually arrived at a bar where we
began to drink beer—we drank a lot!

At 10:00 P.M. we returned to San José with my friend Miguel Tuc Ixtamer in his truck. When we reached my house, I discussed with my friend, Miguel, the debt I owed him since the month of September when I took two trips that turned out to be failures and lost $190, the cost of the service of the truck. (As I wrote in my diary last year, 1975, the failures were because of bad weather.)

Well, Señor Miguel Tuc Ixtamer agreed to reduce the debt with one condition—that I pay the balance right now. I consented and paid him only $140, a reduction of $50. This man finally considered the unfortunate circumstances of the indebtedness because $190 is a lot of money to pay for trips that did not even carry people to work and turned out bad because of the rain. But I was glad that we reached a compromise because I cancelled the entire debt that I had incurred with him.

Afterwards, we continued drinking until it dawned the first of January, 1976. I was quite content because my debt was paid in full by the end of December.

How is New Year's Day celebrated? Do people make resolutions?

On this day people tend to have private fiestas. It's almost like Christmas with the exception that sometimes there is a *marimba* sponsored by the municipality to mark the day that the offices *alguaciles* change for another year.

It is the custom to make resolutions—to use better deportment, not to get drunk and start fights, but to be a good person the whole year. We have a belief in this town that if one does something bad on the first day of the year, it is an omen that nothing will go well for the person during the entire year. Consequently, one usually does nothing on the first of the year. He just stays home and rests.

Today, January 6, is *Santos Reyes* [the Day of the Holy Kings, when the Magi, or wise men from the East, three in number, came to give presents to the infant Jesus]. On this day, which is a religious holiday, they take the image of baby Jesus from house to house where the Catholics kiss it. All of the Catholic Actionists go to Church to visit the image.

Generally, *Joseños* do not exchange gifts on this day [as do people in other Latin American communities]. The Day of the Three Kings is a day for gift-giving but mostly only Ladinos do this. We Indians do not have the means to give gifts. Because not everyone stays home and observes this religious holiday, the Day of the Three Kings is not as important in San José as is Christmas.

On January 15, practically no one in San José worked because it is a very holy day called *El Día de Nuestro Señor de Esquipulas* [The Day of Our Lord of Esquipulas, also known as the Black Christ of Esquipulas]. There were several drunks all over town. All I did was to bathe in the lake and read my books.

❧ The Day of the Fiesta of San Jorge
JANUARY 25, 1976

Today is the fiesta of San Jorge la Laguna. Although I did not go to it, I was able to see many trucks and buses and people on foot headed in that direction. This is because my house sits along the side of the main road to San Jorge [a new road replacing the former footpath].

About 10:00 AM. Señor Felix García Sánchez arrived at my house with his wife. He is from San Luis, but his wife is a *Joseña* who is kin to my wife. I really don't know what happened to him, but when he came to my house at dawn, he was drunk. He said that yesterday the justice of the peace [the mayor] fined him and he began drinking. The bartender gave him so much liquor that he squandered all of his money. His wife got angry and did not want to return to San Luis. In any case, he did not have enough money to get back to San Luis so he asked me to lend him $4. I gave it to him explaining that when I need something he can return the favor. Perhaps I might be trying to sell vegetables someday, and he can go with me to find the municipal market in a town like Santa Lucía Cotzumalguapa.

After giving him the money, I bought two liters of beer to drink with my friend, and we ate a breakfast of beef and lots of vegetables. When he left I did not continue drinking. The afternoon was very tranquil.

❧ Completing a New House
JANUARY 28, 1976

On this day I began to plaster the adobe walls of my new house. I hired Señor Domingo Mendoza S. of San Martín to help me. The job will cost $125 for his labor, and I have to arrange to get all the needed material such as lime, sand, cement, and small gravel.

For a house of 12 *varas* long [about 33 feet] and 5½ *varas* wide [about 15 feet] with a porch, I have to buy 35 *quintales* [about 3,500 pounds] of lime, 8 *quintales* [about 800 pounds] of cement, 100 *cargas* [loads] of fine sand, 100 *cargas* of small rocks, and 15 loads of second-grade sand. I need all of these materials, but right now I only have 12 *quintales* of lime, 8 of cement, and 24 *cargas* of fine sand. This is enough for Señor Domingo to begin. I did not have to buy the sand because I exchange dirt for it with my friend, Samuel Pérez Có. He will make adobe from the dirt. My friends helped me a lot in transporting the material. Señor Lorenzo Pérez García and my brother, Geraldo Ujpán, helped me carry the sand and dirt, and Señor Nicolás of San Martín brought the lime from Guatemala [City].

Today [January 29, Thursday] I worked at home on my new house taking out dirt to prepare the sides of the floor for laying cement. After eating a pleasant lunch, my wife and I began to plan a trip we will make on Saturday to Esquipulas in the eastern part of the country to visit *El Santo Cristo de Esquipulas*. We plan to return Wednesday, February 4.

❧ Pilgrimage to the Black Christ of Esquipulas
JANUARY 30–FEBRUARY 2, 1976

Dawn came very tranquilly as I was giving thanks to God that my family is happy, poor but content. Tomorrow will be our trip to Esquipulas. We are going to take our son, José Juan, along with us. But to take all of the children—María, Ramón Antonio, Erasmo Ignacio, as well as José—would be too expensive. We will leave the other three with my mother-in-law. Of course, we are going to give her beans and corn and everything else that she will need for them during the five days that we will be gone. In addition we will leave her some spending money to make them all happy.

This afternoon we are packing everything that we will take with us. We will depart at daybreak tomorrow to catch the bus in San Martín la Laguna to Guatemala City. When the trip is over, I will write down everything that happens—both the good and the bad—in my diary.

I got up at 1:00 A.M. Saturday to arrange the notions we will carry with us, and my wife prepared food to take. At 2:00 A.M.

we left San José for San Martín on foot to catch the 3:00 A.M. bus *Transportes Rebuli*. We made it to San Martín on time, and we caught the bus.

Although it was very cold riding in the bus, my wife was fascinated when we passed through all the towns—Godínez, Patzún, Patzicía, Chimaltenago, Santo Sacatepéquez, San Lucas Sacatepéquez, and many other places. This was the first time she had ever seen these places, and she soon forgot the cold! Because I was familiar with all of these towns from previous trips, I was not quite as infatuated.

We arrived in Guatemala City at 8:00 A.M. Here we were supposed to change buses to the line *Galilea*. During the trip from Lake Atitlán, I asked the bus driver what time the line left Guatemala for Esquipulas, and he told me at 9:00 A.M. For this reason, I was confident that we had plenty of time to make the connection, but the driver did not tell me that on Saturdays the other line left at 7:45. When we arrived in Guatemala, we could not find the bus so I asked at the office in the station. They told me that the bus had already left for Esquipulas, but that there is service on the hour to Esquipulas on the line *Rutas Orientales*. To catch this bus, we would have to go to the central part of the city.

Then I flagged down a taxi and paid the driver $1 to take us to the office of *Rutas Orientales*. When we reached the depot, I paid the ticket agent $5 ($2.50 per person) for the 9:00 A.M. departure. The organization on this line is really superb—when a passenger pays his tickets, he knows exactly what seat he has. Ours were 44 and 45, the last seats in the big, streamlined bus. José would ride in our laps.

We still had not eaten breakfast, and we were by now very hungry. By the grace of God, my wife had thought to bring food. As soon as the bus pulled out of Guatemala City we ate breakfast with orange juice instead of coffee. We ate quite quickly.

As we headed east in the direction of Esquipulas, we passed many places that we were both seeing for the first time—people and towns with different kinds of clothing and customs that we had never seen before. It was all very interesting. I did not know the names of these towns, and when I would ask other passengers they said they didn't know them either. Because I began to read a newspaper, I soon paid less attention to the towns we were passing through.

We rolled into a town called Zacapa which is very warm. The heat in this town is much more unbearable than the heat in the

Pacific Coast towns. We had to buy some oranges to quench our thirst. As we passed through the town, the heat put my son, José, to sleep.

At 1:00 P.M. we arrived at Chiquimula. I was thinking that we had arrived in Esquipulas because I was unfamiliar with the eastern part of Guatemala. But the bus only stopped for five minutes for servicing, and during this time I was unable to inquire about the name of the said city.

An hour later, at 2:00 P.M., we arrived in the blessed town of Esquipulas. A man next to me told us that we had arrived, and he asked us if we wanted to rent a room. I told him, "Thank you very much, sir, we will go to your place." This señor turned out to be the owner of a pension named *Hospedaje Esquipulas*. He gave us a very clean room with a bath and electricity, and only charged us $2 for each 24 hours.

After taking a bath to rid ourselves of road grime, we locked our clothes in the room and went to visit the Holy Temple. It was beautiful, and many other people were visiting there too. Afterwards, we went to eat lunch.

Immediately after lunch, we returned again to the temple to attend the *Santa Misa* [Holy Mass] that is officiated in the afternoon. After this sacred mass, we returned to the inn where we ate at 8:00 P.M. We did not go out again. Instead we went to bed and slept soundly.

At 5:00 A.M. Sunday we went again to *Santa Misa* and received the sacred communion. Then we went back to the pension for breakfast. At 10:00 A.M. we went to *Santa Misa* again for an hour. Then we walked around the town to buy a few things.

Instead of eating lunch in a *comedor,* we bought three dozen radishes, two lemons, salt, a knife, and a new plate. We bought tortillas and prepared our own vegetable lunch.

For some reason we began thinking that it would be better to return to San José on Monday instead of Wednesday as we had earlier planned [for our pilgrimage to visit the Black Christ in Esquipulas]. By now we were already acquainted with the town and its [famous] temple, and we didn't really care to stay another two days. Thus we agreed to leave in the morning.

We went back to the temple to say good-bye to the *Santo Cristo* [a colonial sculpture of the Savior made of balsam to give it a dark complexion like the Indians that has turned shiny black from burning candles and incense since 1595 when it was installed]. For the last time we received the Holy Communion and the mass ended at 6:00 P.M. As remembrances, I bought a picture with an image of the Black Christ and little items such as sweets, ornaments, and a religious book. Afterwards, we ate dinner at a Chinese restaurant. We had never eaten Chinese food before—it was excellent!

At 3:00 A.M. we boarded the Galilea bus to Guatemala City and sat in our assigned seats. When we reached Chiquimula, we noticed that the vehicle was taking a different route back to Guatemala City. Although this route had plenty of sharp curves, we didn't mind because we got to see another part of the country.

At 7:00 A.M. we arrived in a town called Agua Blanca where the conductors of the bus ate breakfast. Unfortunately, the *comedor* was tiny, and there wasn't enough room for all the passengers to fit. For that reason, a lot of us were unable to eat, and this made us uncomfortable. As soon as these señores were full of breakfast, we continued our journey, and we reached Santa Catarina Mita by 8:30 A.M. In this town I was able to buy my wife and José orange juice. I didn't want any juice—tortillas was what I needed to satisfy my hunger!

By 9:00 A.M. we left the department of Progreso behind; at 10:00 A.M. we reached the capital city of the department of Jutiapa. From Jutiapa the bus made no more stops during the 150 kilometers to Guatemala City, which we rolled into at noon.

We were able to grab a bite to eat at last, but I had to go to the highway to be able to flag down the 12:30 P.M. bus, *Reina Martinera*, which goes to San Martín. Lamentably, there wasn't time for my wife to get acquainted with the central part of the capital, but I think later she will have another opportunity to visit Guatemala City.

We finally reached San José at 8:00 P.M., but when we entered the house there was nothing in it to eat. I was starved, and I ran to a neighboring shop to buy bread and soda water. I was not able to get any tortillas!

Traveling many hours exhausted us. Although the trip to Esquipulas took 11 hours, the return trip took 17. We were glad to be home, and we quickly fell fast asleep.

This morning, February 3, Tuesday, I got up very late, eating breakfast about 9:00 A.M. I went to San Martín to buy meat, and we had a good lunch. Afterwards, my wife and I drank a few cups of liquor. It was a very beautiful afternoon that we spent with all of our children. I figured that the entire trip had cost us $65. We went to bed early.

❧The February 4 Earthquake
FEBRUARY 4–6, 1976

At 1:30 A.M. I woke up because I was no longer sleepy. I turned on the radio softly to listen to the program, the "Club of the Vigilants," on the channel Radio Ciros of Guatemala. It was 2:00 A.M., and I was by now wide awake.

At 2:40 A.M. two men passed by my house on the road to San Martín. When I opened my window, I only recognized Señor Cornelio López. I asked where he had been at this hour. He replied that he was going to San Martín to catch the 3:00 A.M. bus to Guatemala City, but that he must not tarry lest he miss the bus.

As soon as he left, I laid down again on my bed, but I could not get to sleep. I was just turning on a light when suddenly a monstrous earthquake hit! I managed to get out of bed. My wife got out of bed, but we could not reach the children. It was terrible! We were not able to walk, and then the lights went out! We remained in complete darkness in the dead of night. At last I was able to reach my horrified children and get them out of the house onto the patio. It was 3:02 A.M. Wednesday.

Immediately we heard a great bustle of people from the other houses. Like us, my neighbors were very frightened. Some were crying, others were on their knees praying for God's mercy. We spent the rest of this dreadful night outside our house in the patio. Otherwise, if another quake hit, we might be crushed if the house collapsed and the heavy roof fell on us.

I turned on my radio again to learn the extent of damage and injury, but not one station in Guatemala was functioning. Each one had collapsed and gone off the air. Of course, this made the situation worse because we agonized over what might have happened.

At 4:00 A.M. we were able finally to tune in a station, Radio KUU, on a new wave of Honduras. It reported that Port Cortez of San Pedro Sula had sunk. Two guards were known dead—one from the said port and another from a hacienda. However, they said nothing about what had happened to Guatemala.

Finally, it was dawn, and we gave thanks to God for having given us anew the light of day! As the sun came out and provided light, we calmed down somewhat. By day, one is able to control himself better.

Not until 6:00 A.M. did a Guatemalan radio station return to the air to provide the first information of the result of the earthquake. It said that the Rushbel Hospital was on fire. At once we were filled with dread because in this hospital was institutionalized a señora who is a relative of my wife. We worried that if she were still alive she might perish in the flames.

Slowly we heard the news of the towns Chimaltenango, Patzún, Tecpán, Patzicía, San Juan Comalapa, San José Poaquil, Joyabaj of El Quiché. These were the ones most damaged by the earthquakes and with many casualties. It was truly disheartening to hear that some of the towns we had just passed through on our trip were completely destroyed along with vast numbers of their people!

For example, in Salcaja there was hardly anything left. The town tumbled down, and only 50 were left living. In Joyabaj 400 persons died; in Antigua Guatemala 38 were killed; in Patzún 198 fell when the town was leveled. These were the first results we learned of very early in the morning. But the aftershocks continued! Little by little the number of reported dead increased.

The radio station that did a superb job in reporting these events was Radio Victoria of the capital of the department of Mazatenango. Also the station Del Venado was good in informing us what had taken place.

I was able to learn about San José, San Jorge and San Martín at first hand. By God's grace there was little damage in these towns. Not one house had fallen nor was there one death in San José because of the titanic quake [7.5 on the Richter seismological scale and described in *Time* magazine on February 23, 1976, page 26, as one of the most destructive earthquakes ever to hit the Western Hemisphere.]

At 12:00 noon we heard on the news that an express bus plunged into Lake Atitlán, entrapping all the passengers on board. The name of the line was not reported, and this alarmed us *Joseños* because we feared the bus could have been one of the Rebuli line that leaves from San Martín at 3:00 A.M. each day for Guatemala City. Or it could have been the line *Reina Martinera* that travels Wednesdays to Chicacao on the coast. On either of these lines, many *Joseños* and *Martineros* travel each day. We kept listening in agony to find out which bus had sunk to the bottom of the lake with all its passengers, but we were unable to find out.

At 3:00 P.M. Señor Cornelio López, whom I had briefly talked to this morning as he was hurrying to catch the bus for Guatemala City, arrived at my house. I was astonished to see him because I had thought something horrible must have happened while he was riding the bus. But he reported that the bus got as far as Tamalaj [an *aldea* of San Luis near the lakeside], and they were almost to San Diego la Laguna when the quake hit at 3:00 A.M. Señor López said that everyone on the bus did not feel the seismic movement. Nevertheless, the bus came to a fissure in the earth where many rocks had tumbled down, and to prevent a collision, it had to stop. Neither cars leaving from San Martín and San Luis, nor those coming from the coast or from Guatemala City, were able to pass.

Señor López was especially upset with the bus driver and his collector of tariffs. The collector had already taken $1.50 from each passenger for the fare to Guatemala City. Señor López said that all of the passengers asked him to return the dollar because the fare from San Martín to San Diego is only 50 cents. But the collector kept the money and got violent when the passengers argued with him. When these poor passengers went to present their complaint to the justice of the peace in San Martín the judge sided in favor of the collector. He did this, apparently, because the bus driver is kin to him. According to Señor López, it had been a swindle!

The earthquakes caused a lot of grief, and what a pity it was for all those people to die! Lamentably, we heard that thieves were looting damaged buildings and houses.

In the afternoon I talked with Señor Jerónimo Mendoza Tzal, the owner of a neighboring shop. He was grieved and worried because he was here in San José but his family was in San Martín. We discussed the bus that had plunged into the lake. The radio announced that it had been located with bodies inside, but that no one was able to pull it out of the water.[20]

Night came with panic and pain. We ate dinner nervously because every minute there was a tremor. We bedded down in the patio of the house in the open air, but we were still full of fear.

The Tremors Continue
FEBRUARY 5–14, 1976

When dawn came our clothing was soaked from the night dew. The night had been windy and cold and every minute we felt a tremor. As the sun was coming out, almost the whole town was giving thanks to God for having preserved their lives and the lives of their children.

We turned on the radio to hear the newscasters report an ever increasing number of dead and demolished houses in different parts of the country. The mayor of San José sent the town crier through the streets accompanied with a drummer to proclaim that no one was to leave for work. He ordered that everyone stay home to take care of his family and vacate his dwelling, taking what he could outside his house to save his possessions from destruction in the event of another strong quake.

By 5:00 A.M. all of the radio stations in Guatemala were on the air with updates on the effect of the earthquake. We listened all day, mainly to Radio Victoria of Mazatenango since it was providing the best coverage.

With the darkness of night came agony and discomfort from having to remain out-of-doors. The night dew, strong wind, and severe cold made it unbearable. It was impossible to sleep, and the night passed with a lot of suffering.

It is Friday, February 6, and the tremors continue to torment the whole town. People argue with one another about the cause of the telluric movement. Some say that the sin of us Gentiles is increasing and for that reason God sends us his punishment. Others claim it is the end of the world. Yet others believe the gods of the volcanoes are moving the ground to kill people in order to capture their spirits as servants. The oldest people say that the god of the ocean shook the earth and tore up the hills because he wants to join Lake Atitlán with the Pacific Ocean. But the lake and the ocean are resisting because they don't want to mix their water—the lake is sweet [fresh] and the ocean is saline. At times these intense debates are interrupted suddenly with another tremor—they quickly forget what they were talking about.

Again we braved the soaking, night dew and immense cold because we are too afraid to sleep inside our houses. My youngsters have all taken sick because of the exposure to the elements. They are ill with influenza and head colds. I had to go to the health clinic to ask the medic for medicine, but when I arrived the nurse, Señor Hernández, was crying unabashedly for his parents. He said that they lived in Tecpán but the town was completely destroyed by the earthquake. He did not know the whereabouts of his parents, whether they were alive or dead. He wanted to go to Tecpán to look for them, but he did not have money for passage, and even if he had he could not travel there because the highway is blocked due to landslides. I sympathized with him, and finally this poor friend gave me pills for my sick youngsters.

Sunday [February 8] we experienced eight more tremors, fortunately not strong ones. We moved from the patio to the porch

because the porch offers at least minimal protection from the dew
and cold. But still we had the fearful tremors.

At 10:00 A.M. I went to the beach to pick a few tomatoes from
my plants. Until now all the people had forgotten about their culti-
vations. As they remembered their fields, they thanked God that
they were still there and began to irrigate onions, tomatoes, and
other vegetables.

At 11:00 A.M. a large launch arrived at the pier. It was full of
Guatemalan soldiers who were surveying the destruction and
searching for wounded. But by God's grace in this town there is
little personal or material damage.

About 12:00 noon another launch arrived carrying the governor of Sololá. His mission was to set up two emergency com-
mittees—one in the municipality and another in the Catholic
Church. By the afternoon the officials began to announce by
loudspeaker the collection of foodstuffs and money for relief. Many
Joseños gave in the municipality, but most gave in the Catholic
Church. I contributed my small help of $5 in the municipality. I
would have liked to have given more, but I just didn't have the
money.

The Evangelist (Central American) Church did not collect a
thing. They were saying that it was not their sins that brought on
the disaster, and for that reason these Protestants did not care to
help with donations.

Today, Monday, despite many friends telling me that it would
be better not to finish plastering my house [the earthquakes might
shake it down, and I would lose my investment], Señor Domingo
Mendoza Sánchez continued working on my house. Because I now
had all the materials needed, I decided it would be better to go
ahead and finish building it. If the house falls, so be my luck. My
family will just have to do without one. Nevertheless, we continued
to sleep on the porch. That is, the way things are now. I have a
new house [after all these years of hard work], but we are not sleeping in it.

If people ridiculed us for building a new house and not sleeping in it, they must have been those having houses of cane walls
and straw roofs. The earthquake is not an enemy to these people
because if the house collapses, the light weight of the cane and
straw will do little damage. On the other hand, adobe, tile, and
sheet metal are heavy and dangerous. If they fall someone inside
will surely get hurt or killed!

Today, Tuesday, I continued working on my house. The children play without much fear, but the tremors continue. We are almost accustomed to them now.

When I turned on the radio, I heard that 23,000 have died and 80,000 are wounded and 1,000,000 are homeless. How pitiful was this news! We were in deep agony because we still felt the many tremors, and any time another strong one could hit again.[21]

Today, Wednesday, we got up the courage to sleep inside the house again. We worried the whole night because if another quake should hit, we would have a difficult time getting the children out to safety. We gave in to sleeping in the house because my children are very ill and my wife has also come down sick. Nearly the entire family is ill. To make things worse, we did not have any firewood because the vendors are not coming. They are from Patzilín, and they have to walk two hours to reach San José. Before arriving, they must walk down a rather steep hill called Paquixtán. This hill is full of rocks, and the vendors do not want to chance carrying a load of wood on their backs because they are fearful that a quake will hit as they are descending and they will lose their lives.

For this reason, almost the whole town is short of firewood. This is a pity because for us Indians firewood is of great importance. We must have it for cooking and warmth. Not one soul in this town has a stove. We are all too poor to afford one!

Although I was somewhat sick, I got my tumpline and rope and took off to the mountains to cut a load of wood. It is a dire necessity, and I have to leave to cut it myself.

Today [Thursday] we braved sleeping inside my new house again, but we left the doors open in order to be able to run out quickly in case another quake hit. By God's grace, we slept peacefully the whole night. We were so weary that we didn't know whether any tremors had come in the night.

We carried the small stones needed to prepare the floor of the house. My friend, José Coché Criado, helped me fix the floor, but we didn't know if my family and I were going to be able to sleep on it or not. The radio predicted a continuation of the tremors!

Also, on this day, many groups of catechists, both men and women, went around visiting with families on the order of the president of Catholic Action, Roberto Chavajay Toc. Their mission was to orient families toward God—that is, one must love one's neighbor; one must not say bad things, steal, or get drunk because sooner or later or perhaps in a short while [because of the quakes] we may die. The catechists also recited prayers to God with the families.

I appreciated what the catechists were doing, but I am not sure everyone did. That is, the Evangelists were saying bad things about the Catholics. They claimed that the strong earthquake of February 4 struck because the Catholics did not believe in God. I do not know why they say this. I do know that Catholics worship the same living God that Protestants worship.

The Protestants are saying, furthermore, that if the Catholics do not come and repent in the Protestant Church, the earthquakes will continue for another year. For this reason, they say that a number of Catholics have converted to Protestantism in San Martín la Laguna, but I don't know their names. (Maybe I will go later to San Martín to find out who they are and write their names on the back of this page of my diary.)

Today [Friday, February 13] officers of Catholic Action sent a contribution of $175 for relief of earthquake victims throughout Sololá, not just San José. The officials entrusted this money to Father Jorge H. Rodríquez of the parish of San Martín la Laguna [who also serves the church in San José because there still is no resident priest]. He will send the money to the bishop of the diocese of Sololá who will take charge of the distributions to the people in need. I think this is a very good thing!

This afternoon the municipal mayor gave notice to get corn and beans for cooking and sending to the needy. He said that the municipality sent the provisions two days earlier, but the poor people could not accept them because they had no place to cook them. For that reason, the *Joseños* would have to cook the food, but the municipality would pay for grinding the corn into dough at the miller's house.

My wife and I did not go to the municipality to get corn and beans. We would contribute our share of corn. My wife cooked 40 pounds in lime. About 7:00 P.M. we took the kernels to the mill for grinding into dough. Immediately thereafter, my wife began cooking tortillas until Saturday dawned. During the night I only slept two hours.

I arose this morning at 6:00 A.M. and packed the tortillas in a cardboard box. Then I delivered it to the alderman of the municipality. He asked the name of my wife because when the women had come to pick up the corn in the municipality they left their names. Upon returning with the tortillas, he checked their names off the list.

At 8:00 A.M. the pickup owned by Señor Alfonso García Sumosa left toward Tecpán carrying the food that the women of San José had spent the whole night preparing.

The same thing happened in San Martín la Laguna because *Joseños* heard Mayor Francisco Coj ordering over a loudspeaker that women come to the municipality to get corn to make into tortillas to send to Tecpán.

It was peaceful during lunch, but we kept thinking about the necessity of sleeping on the ground rather than in the beds in our houses. We were all very tired by now, but this is the way it had to be because of the limited strength of the human constitution.

ᕽ My Friend, José, Is Refused a License to Marry His Fiancée
FEBRUARY 15, 1976

In the afternoon my friend, José, came to discuss a problem he has with his fiancée. He was ready to contract marriage with Señorita Catarina Vásquez, but the municipal secretary who is in charge of the civil registry does not want to extend the certificate of residence to the señorita. The problem is that the señorita possesses the second surname of her father and not her mother. Her father is Señor Alejandro Ixtamer Vásquez, and her mother is Señora Rebeca Pérez. Her full name is verified on her birth certificate that is signed by her father. He had not thought she would have any problems with the name Catarina Vásquez.

José told me that last Friday they all went to Sololá. The secretary got them a license, but for fixing the name of the girl, he asked José for $100 to pay the lawyer's fee. However, José said that he did not agree to pay that much money because it is a lot for a poor person such as himself.

I told José that if he wanted I gladly would help him with his problem. I was confident that a very good friend of mine in Sololá would be able to solve it because my friend is a leader of my political party (PID). But because the launch does not come until Tuesday, we would have to wait until then to take care of the matter. As if to punctuate our agreement, a quake moved the ground below us.

There would be no remedy for sleeping on the porch of the house. We spent a very cold and windy night sleeping on the porch. I don't know why but when the quake passed yesterday a strong north wind fell over the lake.

The only thing I did today was to carry fine sand for plastering my house.

We spent the whole night on the porch of my house. At 4:30 A.M. José arrived with his fiancée and her father to get me for the trip to Sololá. I prepared my papers and went to the wharf to catch the boat. Such a cold had settled over the lake that I shivered while I waited.

When we arrived in Panajachel, all of the buses were full. But I told my friends not to despair and if they were patient another bus would pass soon. And within 15 minutes one did.

When we arrived in Sololá, the girl's father thought it would be best to arrange an urgent appointment with the judge at 1:00 P.M. I answered, "Wait a little while for me!"

I went to my friend, who is named Andrés Sáenz López. I told him about the problem, and he answered that he could solve it if I would wait a half-hour for him to have breakfast.

At 9:00 A.M. my friend Andrés, who is nothing more than an inspector of statistics, arrived at his office. Then I showed him the testimony of the age of Catarina Vásquez. He read it, and he took us to a lawyer and notary. The lawyer told me that he could correct the registry of birth, but he could not do it right then. He said he would do it on Friday, February 20.

We did not prolong our visit in his office. We went to breakfast. I looked for the market to buy things, but it turned out that the market had been closed. Not a soul could be found in the marketplace because of the damage by the earthquakes. The marketplace had been moved to the municipal soccer field near the Santa Teresita Hospital.

I was surprised because this had been my first trip to Sololá since the earthquake. Many buildings had fallen down, but these were often very old structures with dangerously aged wood.

I went to talk to my friend, Juan Mendoza Ovalle, who works in the National Police force. All of the persons in this institution were lodged in a field of canvas tents that had been erected in the city park. The chief's camp was a smaller tent and separate from the rest. The building that they had formerly occupied was dangerously cracked.

I walked to the central part of the city to the front of the Calvary Church. People were not allowed to pass through the street because they were beginning to repair the church. As I stood there inspecting the damage a lot of Indians began to work in front of me. They claimed that they would have a new church constructed in record time.

I could not find the former office of the justice of the peace because it was housed in an old tile and wood dwelling that collapsed.

Several newspaper boys were selling papers on the streets. Some of the papers said that many of those who died on February 4 were cremated because there had not been room for them in the cemeteries. Others said that the dead were buried in mass graves. The vendors carried three different newspapers, but I could not determine which one was best.

I had brought my son Ramón Antonio with us, and at noon we went to eat lunch in a *comedor*. We caught the 1:30 bus to Panajachel, and once we got there I had a beer at a bar.

At 3:00 P.M. we went to the same pier where the launch let us debark, but we discovered that we would not be able to embark from the same place. We had to walk about three kilometers on the eastern side of Panajachel [to Jucanya]. I did not mind as much for myself as for those who were carrying *cargas* on their backs. For them it was a sacrifice to get to where the boat was leaving. We had to cross the Panajachel River, and the men carrying loads suffered. They say the reason we had to walk the extra three kilometers is that the owner of the line [who is an Indian with a private wharf on the Jucanya beach] wants to raise the price of passage [which is now 40 cents one way]. He has been unable to do this, and he is punishing the passengers by making them walk farther. I don't know, however, whether these allegations are rumor or truth.[22]

When I arrived home, my wife had a good dinner waiting for me. I was delighted with her thoughtfulness.

At 7:00 P.M. this evening [February 19] Señor Juan Mendoza Ovalle came to my house to invite me to a political meeting at the home of Señor Mario Ramos Pop who is a member of the Partido Institucional Democrático (PID).

At the meeting we conferred with members of the Movimiento de Liberación Nacional (MLN) to draw up a list of integrated candidates for municipal office. It turned out to be a long debate with much discussion. Finally, the directors of the two parties agreed on the following pre-candidate slate:

(1) *Alcalde* [mayor], Juan Mendoza Ovalle, PID
(2) *Síndico* [syndic], Ignacio Bizarro Ujpán, PID
(3) *Regidor 1* [First alderman], Tobías Savala Soto, MLN
(4) *Regidor 2* [Second alderman], Bernardino Ujpán Flores, PID
(5) *Regidor 3* [Third alderman], Jorge Ixtamer Lavarenzo, PID

(6) *Regidor 4* [Fourth alderman], Jorge Hernández Nicolás, MLN

(7) *Regidor 5* [Fifth alderman], Agustín Toc López, MLN

(8) *Suplentes* [Substitutes]

    (a) *Concejal 1* [First Councilman], Julián Canajay Ramos, PID

    (b) *Concejal 2* [Second Councilman], Cornelio Cholotio Sumosa, PID

I don't know if the list we made up will be final because the person who is running for mayor has to meet with the national police. He must run openly for office [cannot retain a government job while running].

When we realized the hour was getting late (10:00 P.M.), Juan Mendoza Ovalle sent for two bottles of liquor. We finished these and sent for more. We drank until we became inebriated.

I didn't get home until around 2:00 A.M. I only got two hours sleep because at 4:00 A.M. José came to wake me for the trip to Sololá [February 20]. I got up, but I was still drunk. Too much liquor and lack of sleep combined to make me feel awful, but I arranged my papers and stumbled to the beach with my little daughter María. I was taking her since she pleaded to go.

By the time we reached the town I was very much in need of a drink to quench my thirst. I went into a bar and had a beer to get rid of my hangover. My friends went to eat breakfast in the marketplace, but I did not go with them because all I wanted was another beer. I could not resist my craving.

At 9:00 A.M. I went to the office of my friend Andrés Sáenz López. He immediately took us to the lawyer Francisco Damian to arrange the marriage papers of José and Catarina. Catarina's parents were there to participate as was José's mother (his father died 18 years ago). Andrés Sáenz and I acted as witnesses.

For all of this the lawyer only charged $15. This made José happy. Also, Catarina's father Señor Alejandro Ixtamer Vásquez was pleased because it would have been a major problem to accomplish this in San José. We all went merrily to a small restaurant where José ordered beers for everyone. When these were drunk, Señor Ixtamer ordered another round. We ended up drinking a lot!

These two men invited me to eat lunch with them, but before leaving the canteen the town mayor entered with two of his officers, Dons Bartolo Lavarenzo and Ricardo Gonzáles, who are my friends. They introduced me to the mayor as their friend, and we all began to drink. I bought them a round, and they offered to help me whenever I have any problems. By now I was feeling drunk so I said good-bye to them and went to eat lunch with my daughter María and my *Joseño* friends.

After a lunch that was difficult for me to eat, I went to rest in a bus and to ponder over all that had happened. The bus left for Panajachel about 2:00 P.M., and when we got there I did not drink anymore. I just went to catch the launch.

While we were cruising over the lake toward San José, I chatted with Señor Pedro Ixtamer Ujpán, a *Joseño* friend. He offered me a *cuerda* [.178 acre] of onions for the price of $135.

Despite the horror of the earthquakes and tremors, many people were celebrating in San José. Today is the day of our national hero Tecún Umán, who fought against the Spanish conquerors. Señor Pedro Ixtamer came with me to my house and sent for a beer to drink as we visited on the porch. I did not go out again. Rather, I just reflected on how this day had turned out to be so beautiful!

On Thursday [February 26] at 4:00 A.M. I went to the justice of the peace with José Coché and Catarina Vásquez for the lecture on the act of matrimony to conform with the law. It was a peaceful union, and the judge instructed them each of their obligations as man and wife.

After the civil ceremony they invited me to the home of Alejandro Ixtamer for dinner. But before it was ready, we indulged in a few cups of wine.

They asked me to accompany them during their ecclesiastical ceremony which is going to be performed on the first Sunday in March.

✎ Lent Begins
MARCH 3, WEDNESDAY, 1976

On this day begins Lent, when there are only 45 days until Good Friday. This is the day most respected in the Catholic Church. Every good Catholic is prohibited from any kind of work. The day is called Ash Wednesday. This is because of the ceremony performed by the priest. Before giving mass, he makes the sign of the cross on the face of each Christian with black ashes. This black cross signifies the mark of a good Christian who walks faithfully with the church and preserves the service of the saint until death.

❧ My Wife Is Expecting a Baby
MARCH 4, 1976

Today I hired two boys to help me harvest a parcel of onions. By evening we had cleaned and bundled all of the onions in order to haul them to the central marketplace in Guatemala City.

I hated to leave my house because my wife is bedfast expecting to give birth to a new baby any day. Nevertheless, selling onions is necessary so I left at 7:00 A.M. The truck went very slow because it carried a lot of cargo. For the truck owners, it is better to travel by night so that they can carry the cargo and its owner at the same time. The trucks are designed especially for cargo, not passengers. To avoid the daytime police, the drivers travel at night so they won't be fined. We reached Guatemala at 3:00 A.M.

I sold the onions at a good price, but I could not keep from worrying about my wife. When I got back home, she was still bedridden and expecting.

On Saturday at 8:00 P.M. Enrique Pantzay arrived at my house to discuss business concerning onions. Shortly, he invited me to a bar to talk things over, but before we could swallow a drop, an earthquake of great intensity hit, making us flee into the street. It was 9:30 P.M. My first thought was to race home and see if my wife and children were all right, but I finally decided to stay and continue our business chat.

We cautiously walked back into the bar and drank the cups of liquor. But only ten minutes later, at 9:40, a second powerful quake hit. This made us vanish back to our homes. When I arrived, my wife was petrified and my children were crying.

I carried the bedding outside to sleep on the bare ground again before the order arrived from the municipality by the town crier that no one was to sleep inside his house tonight. Needless to say, nobody did.

At daybreak Sunday [March 7] the whole town was panicked because of the two strong quakes and tremors. Today, several couples decided to get married because they have been living together, and they say that if they die unmarried their souls will be lost forever [because they were living together].

The first wedding in San José was that of my friend José Coché Criado and Catarina Vásquez. The second marriage was that of Domingo Tuc García and Clara Pérez Có. The latter two

couples had been living together for several years and only now
decided to contract marriage according to the Church.

Not only were there several marriages in San José, there were
many in other towns. In San Jorge 40 couples had the ceremony
performed. I know this is true because the municipal secretary Joel
Mendoza Cotúc, an Indian native of San Martín, told me. He reported that before the quakes that many couples of San Jorge
refused marriage. Most of them lived *juntos* [as common law man
and wife]. They married to save their souls in case they are
killed in future quakes. Now they believe whatever happens to
them may happen.

Another Tremendous Earthquake
MARCH 8, 1976

Tonight my little daughter María was too frightened to agree
to sleep in the house. We finally convinced her at 11:00 P.M. that
everything was going to be all right. Shortly thereafter we were all
fast asleep.

At 2:00 A.M. a very powerful earthquake hit. I managed to get
up out of bed, but I could not find the children to take them outside.
I was shaking with nervousness. Finally, I calmed myself and
looked at my watch. We took all of our bedding outside on the porch
despite my wife being bedfast and regardless of the strong wind,
night dew, and extreme cold.

My wife and I were so shocked we could not sleep. The children fell asleep soon, and to protect them from the night dew we
covered them with *nylon* [plastic sheet]. Nevertheless, we all
awoke soaked.

From 2:00 A.M. until 4:00 A.M. four different strong quakes hit
us. We were terrified!

When dawn finally came, the mayor of the town ordered a
commission to see how many houses had fallen down and how
many people were injured. We expected the worse, but by some
miracle not one house had fallen nor had one person been hurt.

My Wife Gives Birth and the Quakes Continue
MARCH 11, 1976

I arrived home from a trip to Guatemala City to sell onions to
learn that my wife had given birth at 11:00 P.M. the night before to a

baby girl. We named her Susana Julia. I was so happy I went and drank a beer!

This morning [March 12] I did not go anywhere. Instead, I stayed home with the youngsters and prepared meals because my wife is not able to work.

It is Saturday this morning [March 13], and I got up at dawn without anything new taking place during the night. I thanked God for having enough mercy to let me still be alive.

At 8:00 a.m. I went to talk with Señor Domingo Mendoza Sánchez about finishing the floor of the porch of my house. He told me that we needed 300 pounds of cement and if I got it that he would be able to do the job on Monday.

Señor Lucas Mendoza, a *Martinero* who has established a butcher shop here in San José, sells building supplies such as cement and lime. I went to his meat store, and he told me that he had the cement but that it was at his home in San Martín. I told him I would walk there to get the cement. Meanwhile, I bought two pounds of beef to take home for lunch.

I put the beef in a kettle to stew, and I placed the older children in charge of tending it. Immediately, I set out for San Martín to fetch the cement. I was only about three *cuadras* [825 feet] from Señor Lucas's house when I met a friend, Zacarías, who is a chauffeur, and my *compadre* Diego Gonzáles, who is godparent to Ramón Antonio. Just as we were greeting one another, an intense earthquake (equal to the one of February 4) struck.

My coparent exclaimed that his wife was seriously ill suffering from a nervous breakdown because of the persistent quakes and tremors, and he rushed off to go to her aid. Likewise, I felt desperate to hurry back to my wife, explaining to Zacarías that she was still bedfast with an infant who is scarcely four days old. The distance from San Martín to San José is two kilometers over a hilly [and unpaved] road so I started to run home. Then my friend Zacarías grabbed my arm and advised, "Ignacio, you should not run. Only God can save your wife now. To run in panic is too dangerous." His words calmed my nerves, and I took his advice.

I began walking as fast as I could down the rocky road to San José. It would have been difficult to run anyway. Everyone in San Martín had abandoned his house. Flocks of terrified people were in the streets. Some believed the world was ending. Women and children were crying; others were praying. Two teachers collapsed with heart attacks. Rocks and land were sliding down from the volcano, San Martín, horrifying people. In the distance across the lake, we could see land sliding down in San Miguel and in Santa

Apolonia. A strong wind whipped up dust clouds from the land-slides, and within a few minutes we could no longer see the other towns on the lakeshore.

It seemed like an eternity getting home from San Martín although the distance is really not that far. When I reached my house, I found my wife recovering from shock. During the quake she had wanted to get out of the house, but she was in bed and unable to move. When neighbors rushed in to see whether she was all right, she was so frightened that she could not speak. Thank God she had not been physically injured. She was sobbing, but she was able to speak to me in a normal fashion.

The quake hit at 10:30 A.M.

After comforting my wife and children, I cooked tortillas to eat with the meat broth that had been stewing. At 1:00 P.M. just as we were finishing lunch another strong quake hit. Our youngsters flew out of the house, but I stayed inside at the side of my wife and infant to protect them as much as I could.

As soon as the movement of the earth subsided and we collected our wits, I ran to get materials to construct a shed to protect my wife and infant. I obtained planks, field cane, forked poles, beams, and sheets of nylon. My uncle, Samuel, and my younger brother, Jorge, came to help me build the little shelter. We worked feverishly, and we had it done by 6:00 P.M. (before nightfall). Even though my house is new and well built, a strong earthquake could knock it down regardless.

[It is March 18, and] we have been sleeping in the little house for five days. But the wind and cold have become so severe we can no longer endure spending the nights in the tiny shelter. Today we are moving back into the house, and we will spend the night there.

~ The Day of San José
MARCH 19

This morning I went to the civil registry to record the birth of my little daughter, Susana Julia. Because it is the day of San José, the townspeople are jubilant and celebrating.

The image of San José is sponsored by its brotherhood. The head of the fraternity is a town elder. Unlike the other *cofradías*, the head of this one has to work only when there is a marriage. The couples, who are about to be married, gather in the house of the image of San José [usually in a separate room of the head of the *cofradía*] with the *principales* and catechists of Catholic Action. Together they all march to the church singing hymns and setting off a lot of *bombas* [bombs, mortarized fireworks shot into the air before exploding] that produce a lot of noise and smoke. After the ecclesiastical marriage, the newly joined couples invited their guests to a fiesta. To serve food and drink, the couples may borrow china entrusted to the *cofradía* of San José. These are not made of porcelain, but fine clay. They were purchased in Totonicapán in 1952. They are cheap but taken care of well.

The *alcalde* of San José, who was turning his office over to a new *alcalde* [for a year's service], was Señor Pascual Ixtamer. His sons, Señores Juan Catalina Ixtamer Sumosa and Roberto Ixtamer Morales, had a double wedding. Because Roberto's new wife is from San Martín, a lot of people from that town showed up for the wedding. They had quite a fiesta with a lot of *bombas*.

The day passed very pleasantly.

❧ A Shaman from Sololá Explains the Earthquakes
MARCH 21, 1976

This morning I hired a worker to help me clean and bundle onions to take to the Central Market in Guatemala City to sell. I left at 3:00 P.M. with the cargo and arrived at 9:00 P.M. Since it was somewhat late by the time I sold the onions, I decided to sleep in the truck terminal with two other guys who had come to sell their harvest in the market.

One fellow was from San Miguel la Laguna and the other from Sololá. Our conversation soon turned to earthquakes. The señor from Sololá said that he is a shaman. He claimed that the reason we are having earthquakes is that the people in this day and age have forgotten to perform the *costumbres* to the Sacred World. They no longer burn *pom* (myrrh) incense, and candles. For that reason, *El Dueño del Santo Mundo* [God of the Sacred World] is angry. In fury he moves the earth because his children do not remember to give him offerings. The shaman used Tecpán and Patzún [where damage was devastating and casualties were heavy] as examples, stating that all of the people who died in these towns were Protestant.

However, I don't know if what he says is certain. The news only said that most of the people who died were in Tecpán, Patzún, and Chimaltenango. I don't know if all of these people were Protestants.

❧A Political Trip to Guatemala City
MARCH 25, 1976

On this day Thursday I went to the Congress of the Republic in Guatemala City. But the señor president of the Congress, *licenciado* [lawyer] Donald Alvarez Ruiz, was very busy, and I was unable to talk to him. Thus what I did was talk to *licenciado* Marure Navarro, the coordinator for the department of Sololá of the Partido Institucional Democrático, instead. We discussed the registration of the list of candidates for municipal governments. The conversation with *licenciado* Navarro went very well. I was able to talk intelligently with him, and he told me he is going to pay a visit to San José.

Because the truck returning me to San Martín had a tire fall off, I did not get back to San José until 5:00 A.M. this morning. When I asked my wife to open the door, I noticed that her parents were there, and I thought immediately that something bad must have happened.

When everyone was awake, they told me that my cow had died, but they did not know what illness had caused the death. This was a sad surprise for me because when I had left for Guatemala City, the cow was all right.

My father-in-law said that they noticed that the cow had taken sick at 2:00 A.M. At that time they went to wake up a neighbor, Antonio Castro Bizarro, who knows how to make a remedy of cooked grass for sick cows. Señor Castro realized that the cow was suffering, but the medicine he concocted did not work. Seeing that something else had to be done, my wife's parents summoned Benjamín Coché who had cured a lot of animals with his pure intelligence. But finally, he was not able to cure the cow either, and lamentably it died at 9:00 A.M.

My wife's father said that he went to the municipality to ask for help to carry the animal out of the *sitio* where it had died. The tribunal ordered many neighbors to help carry the body to a place far from town. When this was done, they say that my father-in-law gathered with a few neighbors. They drank a lot of *aguardiente* and ended up drunk.

Although I did not see all of these things happen because I was not home, my wife serves as witness to these events.

At 10:00 A.M. on this same day, some of my relatives arrived to console me over the loss of my cow. We drank with them some beer until lunchtime. Because I had a stomachache from something I had eaten in Guatemala City, I stayed in bed after lunch.

At 8:00 P.M. my friend José arrived to bring me some drinks to solace me over the loss of my precious cow, and I was a bit sad for having lost it because it was worth $100—a lot of money for us poor folks. To pay for such an expensive animal and then lose it because of illness is depressing.

José told me that some witchcraft had been performed against me, and this was the reason for the death of the animal. But, I only believe in God [not sorcery]. I know very well that in the life of a man things are both good and bad. Furthermore, the loss of a cow can be remedied [another one can be bought]; it is not like losing a member of one's family.

❧ A Tzancuil Cuadrilla Abandons Their Work
MARCH 30, 1976

My brother Geraldo arrived in the morning at my house to offer me some drinks, but I was unable to drink with him because I was still sick to my stomach. He passed out at 11:00 A.M. and did not wake up until 3:00 P.M. When he awoke, he left to drink more liquor in the streets. But the police surprised him and carried him off to jail because his wife had complained that he struck her last night while drunk.

Later Geraldo's mother told me that Geraldo was still in jail but that his wife had gone to Panajachel to sell used clothing [to the tourist shops]. His mother said that his wife had robbed Geraldo of $120 that Señor Lucas Mendoza had paid him for a bull. But, I am not sure what Geraldo's mother tells me is true because his money also belongs to his wife.

On this same day I received disheartening news. The crew whom I had left at the Pangolita Finca had abandoned their work. It meant that I had lost $350—an awful lot of money for a poor *Joseño* like me. The money does not belong to me but to Señor Lucas Mendoza who lent it to me. Only God can help me recover it. I don't know what I can do because I don't have any money with which to arrange other crews to earn the money back. The crew was from Tzancuil. I had given the money to advance the people to my assistant who lives in this town because he knows the people better. Although I trusted this assistant, I am responsible for the money that I borrowed from the owner of the truck.

At 6:00 P.M. I had to go to the health clinic, because when I heard that my crew had run away, the pain in my stomach got even worse. I passed the jail and noticed that my brother Geraldo was

creating quite an uproar because he was still incarcerated. When I
got home, I swallowed two of the pills and two spoonfuls of
medicine that they gave me, but I don't know what it is.

When night fell, I did not sleep at all. I was too worried about
the great loss of money. Suddenly it occurred to me that my great
friend James Sexton might help me with a loan.

This afternoon [March 31] I arrived in Guatemala to send a
letter to my good friend. In Zone 1, I got a room in an inn named
San Judas Tadeo. But because of the fleas and drunks, I was not
able to sleep peacefully. I did not have money to rent a private room
in a better inn.

When I awoke this morning, I hardly had a stomachache, but
my mind was troubled still. I got up at 5:00 A.M. and wrote a letter to
my friend James. By 9:00 A.M. I put the letter in the mail and prayed
that it would reach his hands safely.

At 10:00 A.M. I caught a bus, *Flor de mi Tierra*, to the Pangolita
Farm. The señor supervisor of work, Don Gabriel García, who is a
Spaniard, told me that the workers left because they did not want to
work. But since the work was good, he was somewhat baffled at
their departure.

For dinner, I borrowed a meal from a señora whom I know
well, promising to pay her later. During the night I did not sleep
well because I had to sleep beneath an almond tree. I would doze a
little, but then I would wake up startled because I was afraid of the
many drunks who passed by carrying machetes. They were coming
and going to a nearby fiesta. I had asked some ladies to let me sleep
in a bus with them, but they refused. Perhaps they thought I was a
robber, but that certainly is not the case because I know very well
that my honor is worth more than anything else. True, I am broke,
but I cannot become a thief because it is certain that, "stealing is
worse than dying—it is better to die than to steal!"

> *If the workers did not want to continue working on the Pan-
> golita Farm, what do you think might have been the reason?*

It could have been many things: the workers were not
trustworthy, but they had worked for me before; the temperature
in March was too hot for them; the field boss was rude to them;
the food was bad; or all of these things could have influenced
them to leave.

ᐁMy Wife Uses a Temascal
APRIL 3, 1976

I got up feeling good because my stomachache is gone finally. After breakfast I went to irrigate tomatoes. Since they were infested with insects and fungus, I made insecticide and fungicide and sprayed them.

After eating lunch, I went to clean land for sowing. I quit at 6:00 P.M., but I still had a lot to do. This land will serve me well for planting corn and beans when God gives me the blessing to do so, that is to say, when the first rains fall. Here in San José I have to plant a lot of fields to have enough corn to last the whole year. It seems certain that I am not going to be able to plant corn on the coast this season because I am short of money.

At 8:00 P.M. tonight my wife went to a *temascal* [sweat house] because she felt very cold in her muscles. For us natives the *temascal* is a great thing with which to give warmth to the body. The one that she used belongs to her father, and it is located about three *cuadras* [about 825 feet] from our house. There used to be a lot more *temascals*. Nowadays only a few Indians have them, and those of us who do not must take the owner of one a gift of bread or meat and tortillas if we wish to use the *temascal*.

For the first time we took our daughter Susana Julia for a stroll in the streets—24 days after her birth. Our neighbors admired the beautiful baby girl. And my wife's parents liked her name very much. We returned home very contented.

Today is the eve of the anniversary of the Society of the Daughters of Mary who organize a fiesta in the Catholic Action Church. Young girls belong to this society until about the age of 14 when they get married. The society was established in San José eleven years ago. When we chatted with a girl who belongs to this group, I asked her how many anniversaries she thought the organization will celebrate. I was surprised when she told me that she did not know. Imagine, it was sad for me to realize that some young people participate in fiestas without really knowing the meaning of what they are doing nor how long they plan to keep the spirit of the celebrations alive. It happens that this señorita is the secretary of the Daughters of Mary, but she does not care to speculate how many years this organization will witness.

In the evening, I was told that my brother Geraldo was sentenced to 40 days in jail for hitting his wife on March 29. This made me sad because 40 days in jail is a lot of time for us poor folks. Morever, it is close to Good Friday—while my brother is in jail, his family will be alone during the festivities. My own family will probably spend the fiesta in one another's company. Lamentably, Geraldo received the pain of jail—not a fine! The señor mayor and señor secretary did it to him because of envy; that is, my brother is the secretary of propaganda for the Partido Institucional Democrático, but these señores belong to the Partido Democrático Cristiano. It is for this reason they dislike my brother and me. They would love for me to fall into their hands, but I have not done so yet.

If our party wins the political battle, God willing, we will put into office our own mayor, Juan Mendoza Ovalle. Then we will get rid of the present secretary, and the town will be more tranquil.

It is the secretary who is making the town unpleasant. He is doing it because he is Ladino, and because we are Indians we are unimportant to him. But before God and before the law we are all one—there is no preference to color and size.

The present secretary is the person who [with the mayor] administers justice and fines. If a person [defendant] is Ladino, he finds no fault with them, but if he is Indian, he finds them guilty and penalizes them. The acting mayor allows the secretary to give most of the orders.

Also the *Martineros* are severely persecuted by their town secretary [who is also Ladino]. It happens that in the neighboring towns of San José and San Martín, the two secretaries are brothers. The brother in San Martín is elder, and he is named Nicolás Antonio Ramos Lorenzo. The one in San José is younger, and he is called Marcos Erasmo Ramos Lorenzo. The *Martineros* are also fighting for the official party, and if they win they are also going to put into office a good mayor and secretary.

Such injustices we are suffering now, and I am writing them down at 11:00 P.M. I ask God to protect my family until morning.

San José Gets Its First *Radiola*
APRIL 4, 1976

When I arrived home from a trip to San Martín, there were many drunks in the streets of San José because a *radiola* [large cabinet radio with record player] had arrived in town. The one who bought it for his home is Señor Francisco González Criado. It is the first such apparatus to appear in town, and it was creating quite a disturbance.

I met with my father-in-law who told me that some men had tried to kill him with sticks and machetes. They are shamans who were drinking and fighting in the streets over their clients. Señor Antonio Castro Cholotio received a patron, and Señor Remigo Castro Cholotio was envious. This caused a ruckus. But it is not worthwhile to fight over superstitious things—such things are unimportant. If they were important, these men would not fight over them and be more like professional doctors. Shamans fight over one having more intelligence than another, but if one is smarter than the other it is because he knows how to work, how to think well, and how to deal with people.

❧ A Strange Case of Polyandry in Guatemala
APRIL 7, 1976

At 2:00 P.M. a friend of mine selling firewood arrived at my house from Totonicapán. I was chatting with him when a worker from NEC [the electric company] arrived. We began to talk with him, and the friend from Totonicapán told a story about a family in San Juan Argueta.

He said that when he was selling firewood in San Juan he discovered that two males, both plank-makers for a sawmill, and one woman with three children comprise a family. That is, the woman has two husbands [which would make it a rare case of polyandry for Middle America]. The two men are very good friends with one another, and they leave their house to go to work at the same time. They also buy their clothing together. But sleeping arrangements require that the woman sleep one week with one man at a time. That is, she alternates husbands every other week. The woman has three children, but she does not know who the actual father of each child is. Although the children do not know which is their real father, they are quite fond of both men. This is the first case that I have heard of a woman having two husbands in Guatemala.

Once in a while, it is reported that men have two women, especially in the town of Samayac. And many men have concubines. An example is a señor who lives in Panaranjo, which is in the municipality of Santa Clara Tecpán. I learned of him when I had the opportunity to travel to Panaranjo, accompanying my brother-in-law, Roberto Peneleu, who was selling medicine there. This señor has four women and seven children with each woman. Altogether he has 28 children. But they say this man is the richest person in the area because he has a lot of coffee farms, two bars, two *tiendas*, and a *comedor*.

At 10:30 P.M. I was in my house listening to a soccer game on the radio with my friends Jorge and José. We were listening to the game between the champions of Guatemala and the champions of El Salvador. The team from Guatemala is called Aurora de Guatemala, and the one from El Salvador is named Aguila de San Miguel del Salvador. Although both of these teams played very hard, the game ended in a tie—zero to zero; neither team won.

Early this morning [April 8] I was sleeping peacefully when my wife woke me up asking what time it was. I answered 4:30 A.M., and when I noticed she was crying I asked her why. She replied that she was having a nightmare. She was dreaming that I had died. She said that I had been killed on the coast near Mazatenango. In her dreams the town first received a telegram advising everyone that the officials had my body. When my corpse arrived in San José, she saw it clearly in my coffin. My wife said that two children with flowers of many colors walked in front of my coffin as I was carried into my father-in-law's house. She said that a lot of people were crying for me, but others were glad to see me dead.

This was the content of my wife's dream. Among us Indians there is a belief that when we dream at dawn [from 3–5:00 A.M.] the dream will come to pass. But I do not really believe this because sometimes a person will dream bad things because of eating bad food and having indigestion and debility. Occasionally, however, the dream comes true. One simply prays to God Almighty that such a dream will not happen. [I believe] the God of the universe accompanies me on my trips. He watches over my leaving and coming, now and forever.

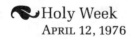 Holy Week
APRIL 12, 1976

Today, Monday, begins Holy Week. The whole town is preparing actively for the celebration, cleaning produce and weaving clothing for the fiesta. Some harvest tomatoes, while others pull up onions or pick chickpeas and beans for the markets of Sololá, San Luis, and Santa Ana. Most of the people of San José, San Martín,

San Benito, and Santa Bárbara go to sell and buy in the market of Santa Ana. Others do the same in the markets closest to their hometowns.

San Benito is the town that is the most remote, but even it is only 12 kilometers away. None of these towns has a good road. Everyone who wishes to sell items in the marketplace usually carries them on his back or head. Some who go to San Luis may travel in trucks, but the poorest must go by canoe because the fare is only 10 cents per *carga* compared with 30 cents per *carga* by truck. Nowadays, men with a little money may travel to Sololá to buy clothing for their wives and children.

On Tuesday of Holy Week I took my son José with me on foot to sell tomatoes in Santa Ana. Had we arrived earlier in the morning (about 4:00 A.M.), we might have sold them for 8 cents a pound instead of 5.

Wednesday of Holy Week is the day that people build a monument representing the mountain of Calvary where they crucified Jesus Christ. They construct it with fragrant leaves and many kinds of flowers. Also, they make a figure of Judas of Iscariot who is called Maximón, the one who sold Jesus into the hands of his enemies. They make the figure of Judas by stuffing banana leaves into old clothing, using an ancient mask for a face, and placing a sombrero on the head.

The image of Judas is placed in a church window, and a cigar is put into his mouth to indicate that Judas is an enemy of the church. But a lot of people respect and fear him rather than scorn him.

The old people say that during this time Maximón walks around at night in the form of a person looking to persecute people strolling in the streets. He is thus equated with the devil, and for this reason children are afraid to leave their houses at night.

Well, what they say about Maximón is true because it happened to me on Wednesday of Holy Week when I was 12 years old. I asked for permission to go outside for a walk at night, but I had to promise not to talk. I was acting foolishly, like the rest of the youngsters who accompanied me. We were creating a ruckus and being disrespectful on the grandest day of all. We played on a corner where there were no houses, and about 10:00 P.M. we became so exhausted that we began returning home. When we passed a part of town where there was a lot of grass, a man suddenly appeared wearing a sombrero. He scared us! We flew to the church which was the closest safe place. By the time we were inside the

man had disappeared. Horrified, we shouted for help. The townspeople came running, carrying candles and lanterns to see who
the stranger was, but when they arrived he was not to be seen.
When we led them to the place where we had seen the man
emerge, we could find no one there.

I went home very frightened. By the time I got there my
mother was sleeping. I was terrified, and I pleaded for her to open
the door for me.

The next day when I got out of bed, I told my mother what
had happened to me. She said that Maximón had visited us. The
other people in the town told me the same thing. My mother took
me to church to ask for forgiveness for my disrespect during this
[Holy] week.

Unlike nowadays, in the past, Holy Week was much more
pleasant. On Thursdays, we would make a procession at 8:00 P.M.
Because there were no street lights then, all of the people carried
candles. In front of the procession, a *mayordomo* of María Concepción carried a cross. He wore a heavy white dress made of cloth
manufactured completely in San José (these days only a couple of
people still make this kind of material). On either side of the cross-
bearer, two *texeles* [rank and file female members of *cofradías*]
carried great big candles weighing eight to ten pounds each.
The *mayordomo* who bore the cross was obliged not to sleep in
his house but in the *cofradía* to insure that he would not have
slept with his wife—a great sin on this holy day. During the procession the townspeople consumed a lot of liquor. (Those who had
to pay for the costs of the procession were the *cofrades* [members]
of the *cofradía* Santo Domingo Guzmán.)

The nature of this procession began to change twenty-two
years ago. It still began at 8:00 P.M. but without a drunken party and
quite solemn—only religious hymns were sung. However, last year
the *cofrades* began to drink again, and the officials of Catholic
Action forbade them to drink any more during the celebration.
They told the *cofrades* that they were not acting within the dictates of Catholic Actionism. They also forbade the *cofrades* from
making an image of Maximón on order of Padre Jorge H. Rodríquez
of San Martín. So in 1976, this year, no one made an image.

These days the ordinary Catholics of Catholic Action are
equating Maximón with the devil, and they do not have much respect for him. However, the shamans are so respectful of Maximón
that they only address him as Don Pedro de Alvarado. They say that
he is a saint because he conquered Guatemala and was valiant.

More or less he is another god to them, and they always refer to him as Don Pedro.

This Wednesday [April 14] of Holy Week I was in my house when I received notice that my adoptive father, Martín, who is also a baker, needed my assistance. He has had his own *horno* [large outdoor oven] since about 1965. He makes sweet bread and French bread which he sells on the farms on the coast through a *mozo* [helper].

Although I am not a baker, I have a little knowledge as a baker's assistant, and Señor Martín wanted me to help him. When we finished making all the bread around 7:00 P.M., he asked me how much I was going to charge him for my labor, and I answered, "Nothing." Then he gave me a lot of bread, which pleased me very much. I returned home with my arms full of bread.

On this Thursday of Holy Week I ate a very contented breakfast of chicken. For lunch we ate bread with honey and chocolate.

In the afternoon I went with my family to mass. Immediately afterwards I returned home and read the *New Testament* on the subject of the passion and death of Señor Jesus Christ. I did not leave the house for the rest of the night.

Because there was not much cold air at dawn, I got up very happy. After breakfast, my wife went to the butcher to buy meat for lunch, but when she arrived they told her there was no meat left. Thus for lunch we ate potatoes and string beans with a flower named *hisote* [a white, tasty flower from a small tree].

Some friends, Lucas Ujpán Cabrero, José Coché, and my brother Geraldo arrived to listen to a soccer game on the radio. The game was between Cuba and Guatemala, and it was played in Havana. When Cuba made a goal during the first half, my friends became very unhappy. Guatemala did not score, and my friends began to drink. The first one to buy a bottle for *tragos* was Lucas; then the others bought rounds. I didn't much want to drink, but they persuaded me, and we drank quite a lot.

In the second half Guatemala made a goal and Cuba did not. We became very happy and bought more drinks to celebrate. The game ended in a tie—one to one.

About 2:00 P.M. we began to eat, but by this time we were very drunk. As we ate, we talked about previous matches between the two countries. When the teams met in Guatemala, Guatemala won; when they played in Mexico, the game was a tie; the game just played in Cuba was a tie also. So Guatemala was ahead in the series.

Wasn't your brother Geraldo supposed to be in jail?

The reason that my brother Geraldo was able to listen to the game with us rather than stay in jail is that on Sundays the municipal officers let him go free because he works for them during the week. Had he not agreed to work for the tribunal, he would have to spend the entire time in jail.

Are all prisoners treated that way?

Most municipal prisoners are treated in a similar fashion. Some are too dangerous to let loose, and others may not be liked by the officers. If the prisoner is not married, it is a custom that the mayor order the *alguacil* to go around to the houses to collect food for the prisoner. If a family only has tortillas and salt to spare, which is often the case, that is all the prisoner eats. Sometimes it may be convenient to get food by becoming a prisoner, but not always.

At 3:00 P.M. Señor Delfino Cotúc of San Martín la Laguna arrived at my house with the message that Señor Juan Cortés, the supervisor of the Pangola Farm, wanted to talk with me. When we arrived at the place in San Martín where the señor had spent the night, he told me that he needed some good workers. I told him, "Don Juan Cortés, these days I am unable to work with *cuadrillas* because I don't have money to give to the people, the reason being that I lost the money in March when a crew did not want to continue to work and left." This was the gist of the conversation that I had with this señor, and when we finished, I returned to my house in San José, and he went back to the coast.

This morning [April 26] I got up with a hangover, but before I had a chance to wash my friend Gustavo Cholotio Dionisio arrived to tell me that his son had just died and that he needed money to bury him. It was a pity that I did not have any money—no more than $4. His son had died of parasites (that is to say, worms in his stomach killed him). I could only give my friend $2 and some planks to make a box for his dead son. Sadly, that's the way it was, and Gustavo left for his house.

After he left, I went to bathe, but before I reached the lake, a woman told me that Señora Josefa Ujpán, the wife of David Pérez Mogollón, had died. She died one month after giving birth to a baby girl. After her delivery, she was unable to get out of bed, and food did not settle well in her stomach. Because her family did not have any money, they did not take her to a doctor. But I think that half the people of San José are afraid of doctors and hospitals. They say, for example, that if one is going to die, it is better to die in one's own house. The poor señora was only 19 years old.

At 9:00 A.M. Lucas came to my house again, sick with a hangover like me. We both had a beer to ease the pain.

At 2:00 P.M. I went to visit my friend Gustavo. When I arrived at his house there were a lot of people drinking, and Gustavo was very drunk. His son had already been buried. They offered me a lot of drinks, but I only accepted two, no more. What I did was to stay near Gustavo to protect him from injury until he went to sleep. Then I carefully put him into his bed.

❧ A Visit With a Student From Flagstaff, Arizona
APRIL 27, 1976

On Tuesday I was still feeling very bad because of the great quantity of liquor I drank on Sunday and the few additional *tragos* that I had Monday. I was not hungry this morning; I just went to the beach to work my crops.

At 9:30 A.M. a student named John Peterkin from Flagstaff, Arizona, arrived to talk to me. He came with another North American student, a señorita called San Brin who was dressed in *tejidos* [Indian dress]. John began to speak in English, but I do not understand this language. Fortunately, the señorita knew Spanish well, and I asked her to do me the favor of explaining what John was saying. Until she translated for me, I did not understand that he was talking about my diary and more pages that I had for Dr. James Sexton. I replied that it would be better to talk in the afternoon because at the moment I was quite occupied. We agreed to meet in front of the church in San Martín at 5:00 P.M.

When I arrived, they were waiting for me in the door of the church. I talked a while with these two friends. John told me that he was going to be in Guatemala until August and that he was living in an apartment in Guatemala City near the theater Lido. If I wished, he would send any completed pages of my diary to Dr. Sexton, providing I bring them to him.

We finished our conversation, and I returned to my house in San José.

About 8:00 P.M. a friend, Agustín María, arrived at my house to chat. About 10:00 P.M., when I was very sleepy, a strong earthquake hit, and later another, which lasted about eight seconds and was also strong. This gave us a great fright! It was a pity that my son José was sick with a fever and the other children were sleeping. Instead of running outside, we just waited out the tremor inside our house.

Ignacito, my smallest son, was also sick, and he was not sleeping when the quakes hit. They gave him such a scare that his temperature increased.

My wife and I were so frightened that neither of us could get to sleep. An hour later at 11:00 P.M. yet another quake struck and scared us even more. But I felt I could not take the children outside because one of them was too sick. We entrusted our lives to God. And this is how we spent the entire night until it dawned. We did not sleep at all!

❧ A Trip to San Diego to Talk With the Father About a Loan
APRIL 28, 1976

Today I remembered that I had to go to San Diego to chat with Father Tomás Criado about a loan I discussed with him on the twenty-third of this month when I went to Guatemala. I had told him of the money I had lost when the *cuadrilla* left their uncompleted work, and he had offered to help me with a loan to establish my own business.

At 8:00 A.M. I was rowed in a canoe from San Martín to San Luis. From San Luis I caught a bus that reached San Diego la Laguna by 1:00 P.M. When I arrived at Father Tomás's house in San Diego, the señor priest was not at home. Thus, I went to the beach to take a stroll and pass time until he returned.

San Diego does not have much of a beach like the rest of the [lakeside] towns, but it is nevertheless pretty. There are a lot of launches docked at the pier, and there are more fishermen in San Diego than in San José. I spent an hour on the dock, and then I returned to the father's house. Still, I could not find him, and night was falling.

Since I was hungry, I went to eat at a *comedor*. They charged me 35 cents for the meal.

After dinner, I went to the house of my half-sister who is now living with her husband, Roberto Peneleu, a medic at the health center in San Diego. They were glad to see me, and they offered me dinner. But I had already eaten. After visiting awhile with them, I jotted down notes to write in my diary all that had happened from the twenty-fifth until today. As I write this, I am about ready to go to sleep at 11:00 P.M. Tomorrow I will see whether the father will give me the money he offered me earlier.

Thursday [April 29] dawned with me in San Diego la Laguna, and I got up at 4:00 A.M., having slept very peacefully.

My sister gave me breakfast, and afterwards I went to the house of Father Tomás again. When I arrived he was still sleeping. I waited until 8:30 when he got out of bed. He greeted me and asked me to wait a half-hour.

At 9:00 A.M. he took me to his office to talk about the loan. He told me that he would be pleased to lend me money. And I asked him for $500, explaining that I would spend $300 on fertilizer and $200 on corn in Guatemala City where I could buy them cheap and that I would sell them in San José at a profit.

When the father realized that I asked for a large loan, he took me to the cooperative of credit and savings in San Diego to talk with the señor president of the cooperative. This man, who is an Indian, said that he would give me fertilizer on credit but at the price of $10 per 100 pounds. And he would give me the corn also but at the cost of $7 per 100 pounds. However, I would have to deposit the title to my house [as security against the loan].

In short they agreed to give me fertilizer and corn, but at a very high price—it sells for the same price in San José. It was clear that I could not make any money on this kind of business venture, and I did not accept. Because they were asking the same price that was the selling price in San José, I would not make a cent!

If the father had given me the actual money, I could have gone to the capital to buy fertilizer because I know well that I can buy it at a place in Guatemala—12th Street and 12th Avenue, Zone 1 —where it cost only $6 per 100 pounds. It would only cost me 50 cents per 100 pounds to transport the commodities to San José. With this kind of business, I could make a little on the fertilizer and at least 50 cents per 100 pounds on the corn. But if I paid the price that the president of the cooperative wanted, I would still have to pay for transporting the products to San José from San Diego. I would lose money on the deal!

To me what the father did was a great deceit because he offered me one thing [money] and then changed his offer to something else [fertilizer and corn through the cooperative]. One should not mislead another like this because what he ended up offering me was neither what he originally promised nor what I had asked of him. But this is the way the world is. There are a lot of people in it, and each one has certain faults.

I am sitting beneath the branches of a large tree as I write all of this down. I am about two kilometers outside of San Diego, and there are hardly any people around. It is peaceful here. As I write I am waiting for a car that will give me a ride to San Luis. It's 11:00 A.M., and I will rest awhile here.

❧The Worker's Day
MAY 1, 1976

On this day, which is called *El Día del Trabajador* [the Worker's Day], no one works. There is a custom in our town that all of the workers bathe early in the morning, about 2:00 or 3:00 A.M. The most faithful bathe at 2:00 A.M., but the less enthused bathe about 4:00 A.M. Our old people tell us that if one does not want to bathe on this day that everyone will be sick the entire year. Therefore almost all of the men bathe on this date. Even some women bathe, but later in the morning. Everyone bathes in the lake.

The older people also say that those who bathe late in the day will absorb all of the laziness and sickness that the earlier ones washed off. So if a person bathes around 6:00 A.M., he will catch all of the illness that was washed off by others earlier. If the person does not bathe at all on this day, he will be sick the entire year. These are the reasons that nearly all of the men of San José bathed in the lake today, including myself. I took my bath about 4:00 A.M.

How many women participate in this custom?

Only about 25 percent of the women bathe, and they do it about 5:00 or 6:00 A.M. Women work mostly in their homes, and it is not believed that they will catch the laziness and sickness that the men wash off earlier. True, women sometimes work picking cotton on the coast in the *cuadrillas*, but they do not do this all the time as some men do [and thus they are generally exempt from the custom].

In addition to bathing themselves, men also bathe their horses, bulls, and dogs in the lake whenever possible to prevent their getting sick the next year. And thus the day passed.

❧The Celebration of Santa Cruz
MAY 3, 1976

This is the day that Santa Cruz is celebrated. In past years, one celebrated mass in the church. All of the Catholics celebrated for the great day that it is. Every Christian had to have a cross in his house adorned with distinct kinds of flowers as respect shown for Santa Cruz. One should do this because our Señor Jesucristo died on a cross. But I don't know what has happened in my town. These customs are disappearing, because I noticed that this third of May is the day of Santa Cruz, and lamentably nothing was done about it in the church. They performed neither mass nor *misterio* [a local, older word used to express going to the church to worship God, which is now equivalent to *rosario*, or rosary].

When this was celebrated by all the people in the past, it was very pleasant. Times, however, have changed. Santa Cruz is still celebrated, but it is celebrated by the Flores brothers who are shamans and who have the *cofradía* Maximón. Although I did not witness their celebration myself because I did not go to their house, my friend Diego José Ramos went. He told me that at their *sitio* there were bombas, a *chirimía* [flute and drum], and periodic drinking bouts. While I did not go myself, I could hear the sounds of the *chirimía* and exploding *bombas*.

The three shamans are Señores Eduardo Flores Tziac, Manuel Flores Tziac, and Ruben Flores Tziac [the last had performed for Felipe's spirit]. Also, they have a nephew, Remigo Jaime Flores, who is a shaman's apprentice. When these men saw that there was not going to be a celebration in the church, they improvised a fiesta in their *sitio* [where they have a room devoted to Maximón].

All of these men claim to be shamans, but they have only recently declared that they are. And most have had less than three years of experience. I believe that they are out to deceive the people into thinking that they are real shamans, but so far, few believe them. In these times, people are more knowledgeable and cognizant, and they will not allow themselves to be deceived easily.

Eduardo, one of the three brothers, lived in Guatemala City for about six years where he bought an image of Maximón that he says cost $300. He brought the image back to San José, but [despite the image] the brothers do not have many clients because people see them drunk in the bars and rude in the streets.

The Nine Days of Sympathy for San José
MAY 4–MAY 5, 1976

As I was walking to the beach to bathe at 5:00 A.M., I passed in front of the church. The bells were ringing out the low sound of grief, the sound of death. I asked the señor treasurer for whom the bells were tolling, and he told me that Señora Dominga Peréz Cholotio, the wife of Señor Pascual Ixtamer Sumosa who is president of Catholic Action, had died. This caused me a great sadness because she was the aunt of my wife. Her dying, however, was no great surprise because I knew that this señora had been ill. But lamentably I had not known before the sounding of the bells, which is the custom at the time of death in my town, that she lost her life. When I spoke to my wife about her, she said that she had visited her and that the señora had been gravely ill.

I went to the funeral with hundreds of Catholics. We accompanied her body to the cemetery. But first they took her to church because it is the custom to allow friends and relatives to say their last good-byes there. She was there for a half-hour, and they made many prayers and canticles for her. Next they took her to the cemetery where they performed many liturgies and canticles. Finally, they lowered her corpse into her grave. Such was the funeral for Señora Dominga Peréz.

There was much sadness in the town. After the burial, Señor Pascual Ixtamer, the widower, invited everyone who had accompanied the body of his deceased wife to the cemetery to his house to drink beer and liquor. I suppose this all cost the man a lot of money, but he did it because he wanted to.

All night there were hundreds of drunks in the town—men and women—crying for the deceased.

May 5 dawned with many drunks still in the streets. But Señor Pascual Ixtamer did not drink. It wasn't that he was not sad; he just didn't feel like drinking.

The last nine days, from April 26 to May 4, have been named the Nine Days of Sympathy for the town. During these days, five persons have died. On April 26, the Señora Josefa Ujpán, wife of Señor David Pérez Mogollón, and the son of my friend Gustavo Cholotio Dionisio both passed away. I wrote about my friend's misfortune already. They say that when I went to San Diego that Señora María Sacrin and the son of my friend, Francisco Vásquez, died. I did not record these last two deaths in my diary because I was not in town when they died. On Monday, May 4, the Señora Dominga Pérez Cholotio died.

It is the custom in my town that when a person dies, his friends and family in mourning should not have to preoccupy themselves with the burial—that is, they should not have to bother with such things as digging the grave. Instead, those in charge of this work are the *cofrades* of the three *cofradías*—San Juan Bautista,

Santo Domingo Guzmán, and María Concepción. As soon as the *cofrades* have the grave ready for burial, they go to inform the officers of the Catholic Church who in turn begin to toll the bells, signifying they are ready to carry the corpse to the grave.

In the municipal cemetery of my town, there are only four *nichos* [pantheons] because *Joseños* are usually too poor to afford anything but a simple burial in the ground. Only a few can afford above-the-ground tombs.

Among us Catholics it is the custom to erect a cross over the spot where the deceased is buried. The deceased's family must do this nine days after the burial to protect the spirit of the fallen and to prevent it from haunting surviving members of the family. The cross is made of wood, stone or cement.

People of other religions do not burn candles or incense nor place a cross over their dead in the same manner as we Catholics. But I have witnessed two cases in which Protestants behave as we Catholics. Once I was passing through San Martín when I noticed a funeral. When I asked who had died, they told me that it was Señora Petrona Soto, the mother of a Protestant pastor Luciano Puzul Soto whose house is situated on the side of the street that I was walking on. When I entered the house to console the grieving family, I saw that a lot of incense and candles were burning and some of the family were drinking beer, even though their religion prohibits it. The second case was on May 4 of this year when we were burying Dominga Pérez Cholotio. This day had completed the nine days since Josefa Ujpán had died, and her husband, parents, and kin, all of whom belong to the Central American church, were also at the cemetery. They had brought a lot of candles, and they were constructing a cross over her tomb. Protestants had never done this before, but now they were doing almost the same things as we Catholics do. I saw these two cases with my own eyes.

The Election Campaign Begins
MAY 6, 1976

At 10:00 P.M. I received a telegram from the señor president of the Congress of the Republic, *licenciado* Donaldo Alvarez Ruiz, who is the national director of the Partido Institucional Democrático. It asked me to bring the mayoral candidate to Panajachel to discuss campaign strategy.

But I really was not prepared for a trip to Panajachel because I received the telegram late at night. Furthermore, the mayoral candidate Juan Mendoza Ovalle was working at the national police headquarters in Sololá.

Isn't he the person who was mayor of San José when I lived there in 1970?

Yes. Señor Mendoza, our candidate for mayor, was mayor of San José in 1970, and he stayed in office for 20 months. Since 1972, he has been working as a policeman in Sololá. He is the sergeant in charge of the radio, making $117.22 monthly plus the cost of his uniforms. He accepted the candidacy for mayor again mainly because the people asked him to get rid of the secretary.

How will he do this if he is elected?

He will only have to consult with the other municipal officers and gain their backing in order to fire the current secretary. But he must write a letter asking for the secretary's resignation. The tribunal agrees on the length of time it will wait for the secretary to hand in his resignation. If this amount of time passes, and he has not resigned, the mayor must write another letter giving him a shorter length of time to resign. If this second letter fails, the mayor must write a third letter giving him even a shorter period of time to resign. Usually, the first letter allows eight days, the second three days, and the third 24 hours. If the secretary still does not want to leave, the mayor takes away his keys.

It takes, however, a strong mayor to get rid of an unwanted secretary. Since a secretary is appointed by the tribunal (the mayor, syndic and aldermen) and is not elected, he may remain in the job for several years, and the mayors may be afraid to initiate action to get rid of him because he becomes politically powerful.

Also, since in towns such as San José, the mayor does not earn a wage, the secretaries may pay them something on the side, and the mayors in return may feel indebted to them. In all of Guatemala the towns have to pay the secretary and the treasurer through taxes. In some towns there are two paid officers, but in towns like San José the same person fills both offices. In the months of January, February, and March everyone who is at least 18 years old has to pay a $1 tax which goes to pay the secretary and treasurer. In San José, the secretary gets paid $60 for being secretary and $30 for being treasurer.

With a new mandate the small town mayors may remain in office for four years instead of two, and that is a long time to go without pay. Since our candidate for mayor is earning a salary with the police department, he has mentioned to me that if the town does not come up with a salary, he will resign and go back to work for the police department after he fires the undesired secretary. For this reason we are trying to find money either locally or through the national government to pay him something, at least a small wage. When he officially runs for office, he will have to resign his position as police sergeant.

On this day [Friday, May 7] I went to Sololá to ask the chief of police to let Juan Mendoza Ovalle attend the meeting with the national director of our party at the Casa Contenta Hotel in Panajachel. It was granted.

In Panajachel Señor Donaldo Alvarez Ruiz received us very well. Unfortunately, however, not all of the candidates affiliated with the party showed. Of 18 municipalities where we have candidates running for office, only representatives from ten came to the meeting. The Señor Alvarez Ruiz became very upset because the rest did not show. I don't understand what happened to their telegrams because we got ours last night. We waited some time for the rest of our companions before beginning the meeting, but they never arrived, and we finally held it without them.

The señor president gave us good advice—do not mistreat the people of the other party; show respect for your neighbors within each town; and fight politically whenever you see it possible. But fight a political battle cleanly and democratically. This was the advice he gave to all of us. At the same time he gave us provisions and money ($40) with which to wage propaganda in the *aldeas* and to pay for the use of a loudspeaker. The more people in a town, the more money the party leaders received. Also, we received propaganda posters and handouts for each of the town's candidates.

Later in the day we returned to San José. In the night many neighbors gathered in my house to learn what had taken place at the session with the president of the congress. Juan addressed the town publicly over the loudspeaker, stating that if he were elected he would fire the secretary. (The secretary could hear him say these words.) In addition Juan promised that he would give all the people his attention and that he would serve all of his neighbors. Juan's words pleased the crowd.

The main reason Juan Mendoza O. accepted the candidacy for mayor is that he does not like the [Ladino] secretary. Even though Juan presently lives in Sololá, he has land and kin in San José and an interest in what happens to them. The secretary has offended him also, and he wishes to fire him.

One of the *principales* sent a runner to buy *aguardiente* in order to seal the agreement that we would get rid of the secretary if we win the election. We all began to drink happily, but we had some reservations about winning because the other parties are also fighting to win. And the town secretary has passed out some money to keep his position. But I don't think this will do him any good, and, God willing, we will win.

A lot of people stayed in my house until midnight drinking.

ᕦ The Anniversary of the Director of the Catholic Church
MAY 13, 1976

On this day they celebrated the third anniversary of Señor Juan Bizarro Gómez as director of the Catholic church. It has been three years since the Señor Bishop of Sololá Angelico Melotto and Father Jorgé H. Rodríquez appointed him director of the church. He is the oldest man in San José, and they say that he is the most intelligent. He is the uncle of my deceased adoptive mother María. The same kind of celebration took place for Señor Enrique Tzal in San Martín. Only in San José and San Martín of the Department of Sololá are there presidents (directors) of the [Catholic] churches. I believe the reason is that few people in the towns want to lose so much time with all the responsibilities [of the office]. The duties require that one be in church all the time and instruct people in the proper ways of the church. Only men who have many years of experience in Catholic Action become presidents.

Well, for the fiesta in San José there were many gifts and a *marimba* for Señor Juan Bizarro. Father Rodríquez honored him especially, decorating him with a gold medal for the last three years of valuable service to the Catholic Church. Since I was invited by the president of the Young Catholics, I went to watch these services.

And there were other activities. Father Rodríquez gave two masses; there was a basketball game between the Daughters of Mary of San José and a team from the secondary school, The Basic Institute of Santa Bárbara. San José enjoyed a 40-point margin over the visitors, winning the game with a score of 48–8.

ᗰ The Election Campaign Continues
MAY 14–JUNE 6, 1976

Today I went to Sololá to discuss campaign strategy with Juan Mendoza. We decided that tomorrow we will travel to the three *aldeas*—Tzarayá, Patzilín, and Pachichaj—to campaign for office. The chief of police told me that Juan could have three days off. Then I got a license from the governor's office to make political propaganda. The señor governor of Sololá extended a permit in my name as representative of PID, and in the name of Lucas Ujpán Cabrero as representative of MLN. The license allows us to pass out campaign material and to use a loudspeaker in the municipality of San José until the day before the election, providing we abide by the Electoral Law in operation under articles 72 and 73 and that we follow the regulations for voice and sound.

When we arrived in San José on the launch, we went to arrange our *papeletas* [slips of paper, 6″ × 8″, with a list of the candidates running for the combined parties of the PID and MLN and with the symbols of the parties and a picture of Juan Mendoza Ovalle] to pass out and post around town and in the *aldeas*. After all of this work, Señor Mendoza went to sleep, but I did not. A lot of political friends arrived at my house to chat about the content of our platform. I did not sleep at all.

At 2:00 A.M. I went to wake Señor Mendoza and our companions Lucas Ujpán C., Eduardo Cholotio Hernández, Geraldo Ujpán, and Alejandro Morales. At 3:00 we took off for the *aldea* Patzilín, and we arrived by 6:00. We talked to a group of citizens, asking for their help to win the election.

At 10:00 A.M., we arrived in the *aldea* Pachichaj where the people received us warmly. The brothers Tuc, members of a big family, gave us breakfast. When we told them the reason for our visit, they agreed to vote for and support us on election day but with the condition that we fire the secretary when we get into office. We agreed to do what these citizens asked us, and then we told them what they would have to do in order to vote. Señor Juan Mendoza offered his help for this *aldea* if he wins the election. In turn the people offered us some drinks.

At 1:00 P.M. we left Pachichaj. By this time our companions —Lucas, Eduardo, Geraldo and Alejandro—were completely drunk. But Juan and I were not. We did not want to drink in front of the people because we were running for office, and we did not want to compromise ourselves.

At 4:00 P.M. we arrived in Patzilín on our return trip to San José. In this *aldea*, our friends of the two parties PID and MLN were waiting for us with more bottles of liquor. Our companions continued drinking, but Señor Juan Mendoza and I did not drink at all—not one drink. Instead, what we did was to address ourselves to the citizens of this *aldea*, warning them not to allow themselves to be deceived by the other party.

We arrived at 7:00 P.M. with our colleagues still totally drunk. They went to their houses, but after all of this campaigning, Juan and I drank some beers [in privacy], and we went to sleep.

Today [Sunday, May 16] I was so tired I did not go to a single place. I just stayed home.

On Friday [May 21] I attended another meeting at the Hotel Casa Contenta in Panajachel. This time it was directed by Doctor José Trinidad Ucles Ramírez, the ex-minister of public health, who is now the counselor of state of the politics of PID. Dr. Ramírez told each leader what his obligations would be on June 6, election day. He also encouraged us to fight hard until this time. If our party wins, he offered to help each municipality get public works such as schools, potable water, electricity and roads. He also promised to visit each town personally to help win the election.

On Sunday morning [May 23], I went to bathe in the lake, and then I ate breakfast about 8:00 A.M. Because a car suddenly appeared with a loudspeaker and a person talking political propaganda, I ran to see it. The man turned out to be *señor licenciado* Emilio Samayoa Muñoz, who is the coordinator of the MLN. He was campaigning for Juan Mendoza. I greeted him, and he was very friendly. I explained to him that it would be better to say his speech in Tzutuhil rather than Spanish. Since he could not speak the language of our town, he gave me the microphone, and I began to speak.

We passed through the streets of the town three times, and finally I got tired of talking. But Señor Samayoa was very happy with what I had done. Although we do not belong to the same party, we are fighting for the same candidates, and this is why I did it.

In the morning of May 27, I went to the house of my uncle Señor Bizarro Mendoza who has a *marimba* band. He rented us his loudspeaker for $3 an hour, which is cheap because an owner of a loudspeaker in San Martín charges $5 an hour.

We began our propaganda at 7:00 P.M. First we talked at the house of Señor Mendoza Ovalle for an hour and a half. Then we went to my house and stayed the same length of time with the apparatus. In all we used it for three hours, which cost us $9. A crowd of people came to my house to hear what we had to say.

What did you say?

I spoke my words on the microphone trying to attract the attention of the town but without offending anyone. I spoke in both Spanish and Tzutuhil these words:

> Town and citizens of San José la Laguna. I am talking with you as director of the party. The names of the two parties that I represent are the Movimiento de Liberación Nacional and the Partido Institucional Democrático. You know very well that voting will be on June 6, a Sunday. We have for you a candidate for mayor who is Señor Juan Mendoza Ovalle, a man of capability and dynamism, to lead the municipal tribunal. Citizens of this town, moreover, you have seen this man Señor Mendoza when he was mayor in 1970 and 1971. He worked in this town and treated his citizens well.
>
> I urge all of you to vote on the sixth of June by making an "X" over the *mazorca* [the emblem of an ear of corn representing the PID] or an "X" over the *bandera* [the emblem of a flag representing the MLN]. If you prefer the PID, then all of you mark the *mazorca* with an "X", and then you will have more hope for progress in our town.
>
> You realize we are dominated by a secretary because he is Ladino. This is the reason. Señores, we offer, if we win the election, to fire the señor secretary for you. This is not slander or envy. You realize what has happened in our town. With the help of God and your vote we will be able to take to the tribunal the resident Juan Mendoza Ovalle.
>
> We ask for your votes to allow San José to have a better future. We do not offer you money, as the other parties are offering you. They are offering money to the people to vote for their candidate Jorge Sicay Tuc. We know well that the money is not of their party [the Partido Democrático Cristiano (PDC) and the Partido Revolucionario (PR) combined for the elections] but of the town secretary. This man gave $100 to people to save him from having to leave this town [if we win].
>
> I am not mistreating nor offending the candidate of the opposition. If the town votes for him, it is certain that we other candidates are not going to lose anything, but we will continue with the same señores in office and the same kind of treatment we are getting now we will continue to get.

After my speech the citizens shouted, "We are going to vote for you, but it is certain that you must fire the secretary!" I reiterated that we would fire him for sure. With this the citizens applauded and shouted approval. I repeated these same things many times in Spanish and Tzutuhil.

In the afternoon of June 1, my friends came to my house to tell me that the opposition parties were looking for a way to discredit our platform and list of candidates. My companions said our opponents were saying bad things about us and that they did not want Juan to become mayor nor me syndic. But I did not take any personal interest or affront in what they were saying, and neither did my family. If we win the election, fine. If we lose, we will just have more of the same mistreatment in the town. Furthermore, these offices are voluntary, and there isn't any pay for holding them. If there were a salary involved for them, there would be a good fight to win them. The main thing we are struggling to gain votes for is to be able to defend the town and get rid of the secretary who is tormenting the citizens.

Just as our two parties, the PID and the MLN, are joined together with their single list of candidates for office, the PR and the PDC chose their own candidates and are working to put into office the Señor Jorge Sicay Tuc for mayor.[23] They are misinforming the people about our candidate. These people are saying that if Juan Mendoza wins, he will place a tax on everything. This is slander; there are doing this to demoralize the citizens. But I think the people know best for whom to vote.

Both the Revolucionarios and the Democratacristianos speak badly about Juan Mendoza for not having contracted a civil nor a religious marriage in church. But this señor is arranging for marriage with his woman (he has grown children but he has never been officially married). However, Juan says that he is not going to marry her in San José because he must go to the secretary to do so. Thus his marriage will take place in San Jorge la Laguna. But I still do not know the date for it.

On this day [June 3] I am sick with a headache and sore throat. At 10:00 A.M. my friend Juan arrived to talk with me. He said that he is going to be married in San Jorge, and he asked me to accompany him. But I could not go because I was too sick. The enemy [the opposition party members] did not know this señor was going to be married [which means that their propaganda on this issue against him would be false].

At 5:00 A.M. [June 4] members of my party arrived at my house, obliging me to go to the *aldeas* with them because there are now only two days left before the election. I was still sick with a sore throat, and I did not want to go much, but finally they persuaded me.

We left at 6:00 A.M., and we arrived in Patzilín to talk with the committee for constructing a new school [because the old one had collapsed during the earthquake] and a group of citizens of this *aldea*. They would like a larger school with more grades. We had a pleasant talk with the people, and they gave us a good breakfast of beef, rice soup, and a lot of tortillas and coffee.

After breakfast we walked in the direction of the *aldea* Pachichaj. When we arrived, the acting mayor of San José, Francisco Mendoza Rodríquez, who actually is the first *regidor*, was also there campaigning for himself and his party. He was with the town secretary and other members of the opposition party, the Democráticos Cristianos. He was speaking on behalf of Jorge Sicay Tuc, and we were able to see and hear well what was happening.

What happened?

As we entered I noticed that six local citizens had gathered to tell the members of the opposition party what had been happening to them in this *aldea*. The campaigners offered all kinds of help—a new school, among other things. But then a citizen, Señor Federico Navichoc Paz, spoke:

> Señor Municipal Mayor, thanks for the visit, but now is not the time for you to come to offer us things that will be good for the *aldea*. You are offering things now that you cannot provide. Within a few days you will not be mayor. Besides, what you are offering us now, you have offered us before. Do you remember, Señor Mayor, that after the earthquake, we of this *aldea* went to your office to ask for your help in reconstructing our school. You answered us as the secretary answered, that there was not much money for rebuilding a school. Now, you come to us to offer help because now is the time for the next election.

Then the secretary replied:

> Señores of the *aldea*, get the votes for Jorge Sicay, and then I will try to help you. When our mayor takes his place in the tribunal, we are going to build a new school and other public works.

Then the *señor principal don* Victor Toc Gonzáles replied:

> Señor Secretary, please, we don't want to talk to you anymore. Remember, Señor Secretary, in your office you believed that you were a great king. Each time we needed something you did little for us. Now you would like to gain our confidence because you think we are going to fire you. We do not agree with Jorge Sicay. We are more favorable toward Don Juan Mendoza Ovalle who is going to see to our needs better

in this *aldea*. Thus, the time has passed that you can deceive the people; we are going to arrive on the sixth of June to deposit our votes in favor of the official party [PID].

Lucas Ujpán Cabrero, Jorge Ixtamer Lavarenzo, and I all heard these words well. Juanito [Juan Mendoza] did not hear them because he had gone with friends in the *aldea* to pass out more pamphlets.

Because no one wanted to listen to them, the members of the opposition left. But the citizens accepted our delegation eagerly, giving us lunch of chicken and plenty of beer. We talked with these citizens, and we offered to help improve their *aldea*. They promised in turn to vote for us.

We left Pachichaj at 2:00 P.M. under a heavy rain. When we arrived in Patzilín on our return trip, the citizens were also waiting for us with lunch, but I did not eat. I was too full from lunch in Pachichaj.

At 7:00 P.M. we arrived in the *aldea* Tzarayá, and the people there received us in a good frame of mind. We conversed with these people until 10:00 P.M.

Finally, at midnight we arrived in San José very tired and soaked, having suffered a lot on the campaign [trail] without earning a single cent from our efforts. When we arrived in San José, we headed for my house to drink a cup of liquor and relax. But when we reached my house we discovered that our colleagues were waiting to tell us what had happened while we were away.

They said that at 7:00 P.M. a car arrived with a loudspeaker making propaganda for Jorge Sicay. This group of Democráticos Cristianos began to say bad things about us in *lengua* [Tzutuhil] throughout the streets of San José. They said that it was better to vote for the Señor Sicay because when they won the election they would sponsor a *marimba* and give out all kinds of drinks to the townspeople. After airing this propaganda, they said that the señor secretary bought a lot of liquor for those who went to a party at the house of Antonio Ramos Cholotio.

Friday afternoon [June 4] at 4:00 P.M. we aired our propaganda again even though I was still sick—my body ached with a cold. We used the rented loudspeaker of my uncle, Huberto, in my house and in my father-in-law's house, the latter being in the center of town.

My words were discreet. They did not offend anyone nor abuse our opponents. When they heard my words, many townsmen offered their votes on Sunday, election day. By the time we left my father-in-law's house at 11:00 P.M., I was really sick and very sleepy. But I had to do these things for my party and for the great love of my town. I want to defend it from the hands of the municipal secretary Marcos Erasmo Ramos Lorenzo who has acted against the people on many occasions.

The members of the opposition parties, the Revolucionarios and the Democráticos Cristianos, also produced their own propaganda in the streets and in the house of Antonio Ramos Cholotío. Those who spoke into the microphone were Señores Cornelio Rufo López, Sivinica Méndez Pantzay, and Sebastián López García.

The words that Señor López uttered over a loudspeaker in a car were especially offensive. I remember well the favorable words that he had for his own mayoral candidate:

> It is better to vote for Jorge Sicay because this man is honorable and is married before the law and in the church. Moreover, he has an office in the church as third catechist. Also, he had already been president of Catholic Action.

His malicious words were against our own mayoral candidate. First, he claimed that Juan was not able to be our mayor again because his parents are not natives of San José but of Quiché [another department adjacent to Sololá]. If Juanito wanted to be mayor, it would be better that he go to the land of his parents. Furthermore, Juanito could not be mayor because he is not married by law nor by the church, and the townspeople should not vote for this candidate of the official party [the party of the current president of Guatemala]. He claimed that Juanito could not be mayor because when he was mayor before he had a concubine. In contrast, the town secretary was an honorable person who should continue working in the municipality. If the secretary had committed some fault with the town, he promised that Jorge Sicay Tuc would rectify it. He asked that the town mark an "X" over the map [the symbol] of the Partido Revolucionario or over the star, the symbol of the Partido Democrático Cristiano.

The other members of the opposition parties said the same kind of things about our candidate, Juan Mendoza. But for the grace of God, they did not say anything bad about me in private or over the loudspeaker.

It is true that Señor Juan renounced his position as mayor in 1972. He left his woman in San José with whom he had children but had not married, and he ran off to Panajachel with a mistress who also abandoned her man by whom she also had children. She went to work in Panajachel in the Comedor Ramírez, and Juanito got a job in the police department in Sololá. Eventually, he returned to San José and spent three days with his other woman. When he returned to Panajachel, he broke off his relationship with his concubine there. She remained in Panajachel about six months before she finally returned to her man and children in San José again. The reason that Juan had to resign his job as mayor in San José is that he believed he was making a scandal and embarrassing the townspeople. In any case, as far as most of the town was concerned, all of this was a private concern, and they did not want him to resign in 1972. He was doing a good job in the municipality, and he got along well with the people.

I do not think that Señor López thought carefully about what he was saying against Juanito. That is, he said that Juanito's parents were not natives of San José, but the mother of Señor Jorge Sicay Tuc was born in San Luis, not in San José. By this reasoning we also would be able to say that Jorge Sicay's parents were not natives. And Señor López criticized Señor Mendoza for not getting married, but Señor López has not married his wife either. [By this logic] how can he be elected first *regidor,* the office he is seeking if these are substantial grounds for denying Juanito the office of mayor. Furthermore, Rufo López spoke critically about Juan because of his resigning from the tribunal and taking up with another woman in Panajachel. But this was a private matter, and it had nothing to do with the town. The fact is that Señor Rufo López has also spent a period of time away from San José. He spent five years working for the national police in Guatemala City to earn money to construct a new house. During this period, he left his woman behind in San José, and after he was there a few months he gradually forgot about her and his children in San José. Eventually he took up with another woman and had a child by her. Later he was transferred to Coatepeque, and he began living with yet another woman by whom he had a daughter named Florencia.

Despite Señor Lopez' remarks against our candidate, we did not make public any of his same kind of behavior. The truth is that the whole town knows about his other two women and other children. I think it better not to criticize others so readily because we all have our faults.

In the morning of Saturday, June 5, *licenciado* Marure Navarro arrived in San José to give our delegates their credentials. He suggested that I rent a loudspeaker and continue campaigning for our platform. But I realized that I could not do this anymore because I was too sick and it would be better for me to stay home so that I could consult with anyone who might want to know how to vote. I felt I had to represent our party on the day before the election, and Señor Navarro agreed.

During the night, a friend came to my house to inform me of a scheme of the opposition. What they were planning to do was to present a document to the election officials which will prove that our candidate is still on the national police force. They say that the chief of police has not yet produced a certificate of resignation, and if Juanito wins the election after the votes are counted, they will demand the certificate of resignation. If he does not have it, all of the votes for our party will be nullified.

I was quite bothered with news of this plan because I don't know whether Juanito actually has a certificate of discharge. I went to ask him about it, and he confirmed that he had not received it yet. So we went together to my house to meet with other members of our party to plan what to do. I told Juan that if he would write a note for the police chief, I would seal it in a letter with rubber [sealing cement] and sign it as the general director of the party. The note should ask the chief to extend the certificate of discharge immediately. But by now my friend Juanito was so nervous about not having his discharge, he could not write. So I took out my pen and began to write an official letter to the señor chief, explaining very carefully that he needed to serve us this certificate tomorrow before the hour the votes are counted.

Luckily, tomorrow is Sunday and the launch from Panajachel will arrive. We chose Erasmo Coché Morales to take the letter to Sololá.

After working out our counter strategy, we decided to hold a raffle to predict who would win tomorrow. On a piece of paper I wrote the name of Jorge Sicay Tuc, and on another I wrote the name of Juan Mendoza Ovalle. I folded the two pieces of paper well and threw them three times into the air, letting them land on the floor. Then I asked my little daughter María to pick up one piece and hand it to me. When I unfolded the piece that she handed me, it had the name of Juan Mendoza on it. This made me jubilant! I told my companions, "Yes, we are going to win. It is certain!" They were pleased and left for their homes.

This Sunday, June 6, will be happy for the winners; sad for the losers.

It was raining when I arrived at the tribunal at 5:30 A.M. I was the first to get there. Later the representatives of the other parties came as did the electoral committee and the president of the voting table, *profesor* Carlos Cano Arbenz.

When the voters began coming in about 7:00 A.M., the representative of the MLN had to leave the table because he is the military commissioner and the election law does not permit such persons to sit as a party representative at the voting table. Another person was named to sit in his place.

[After all the campaigning] the people of the *aldeas* did not come to vote because of the heavy rain which did not ease until 3:00 P.M. By 6:00 P.M. there were no more voters, and the poll was closed.

As a crowd of people gathered outside, we representatives confined ourselves inside the courthouse to count and pack all of the official votes. When the results were known, there were 333 votes for the MLN and PID and only 88 votes for the PR and PDC. When the opposition saw that they had lost, they raised the issue of Juan's discharge, but by now we had the certificate and this ploy did not work.

Not until 11:00 P.M. did we finish having everything ready to send to Sololá, where the officials would notify Guatemala how it turned out. By the time we emerged from the courthouse, nearly the whole town was waiting outside to hear the results.

When I told the crowd that we had won the election, they were ecstatic! They exploded *bombas* and firecrackers. More than 200 persons went to Juanito's house to celebrate. Because he had also been married on this same day, there was added reason to rejoice.

The townspeople offered me several drinks, but I did not want to drink much in front of them because I wished to show proper deportment before the people who had just voted me into office. They persuaded me, however, to drink a few *tragos*, but I certainly did not drink enough to get drunk—not at all!

Finally, after the festivities, I went to sleep about 2 A.M.

New Municipal Officers
JUNE 7–30, 1976

I was asleep at 9:00 A.M. when some *principales* arrived at my house, followed by my party companions. They had all come to arrange a *marimba* in my house. But first I was obliged to help them move all of my furniture out of my house and temporarily put them in a neighbor's home in order to make sufficient room for a victory fiesta.

A *marimba* showed up and began playing at 11:00 A.M., and several people came to dance. By night my house was full. I was so exhausted, however, that I fell asleep by 9:00 P.M.

When I got up from bed the next morning, they told me what had happened. The *marimba* did not leave until 3:00 A.M. The townspeople paid them $40. Because the owner was my uncle Huberto who lives nearby, he did not charge much for his band, *Alma Joseña* [Soul of San José].

Today [June 9] my body aches all over, and I have an acute headache. But I still sent for my friend Bernardino. He bought a bottle of *aguardiente* and six bottles of Coca Cola. We began to drink. Other friends arrived, and we drank even more. Soon we were very drunk. I was celebrating privately, in the tranquility of my home.

In this campaign I had suffered a lot. I had walked under heavy rain, a strong sun, and against the strong cold winds of the night. As I have said before, I suffered and fought not just for the well-being of myself or my family but for the benefit of my whole town, San José. I want it to prosper a little and to see men in office who will act on behalf of the majority of the people and not mistreat them as the present municipal secretary has.

On this day [June 11] I made a trip to cash a check that my unforgettable friend James Sexton sent me in May. In Sololá there is no Banco Agricola Mercantil [the agency that handled the international money order that I sent Ignacio when he requested help for his indebtedness because of the *cuadrilla* abandoning their work]. But there is a Señor Gayo Peraza who cashes checks and only charges 5 cents for each dollar. Doing business with Señor Peraza was more convenient than traveling to Guatemala to the Banco Agricola especially since I was very sick. I had the flu, a cold and sore throat, and my body ached.

Today [June 21] I went with Señor Juan Mendoza to Guatemala City to inquire about the electoral record. When we arrived at the registry, the director, Señor Arturo Maldonado de la Cerda, received us very well. He told us that the date for assuming office is June 30. Also he told us that credentials were given out in the afternoon. We waited, but he did not show up again.

We stayed in Guatemala for the night at a pension called Mansión Mundial on Sixteenth Street between Sixth and Seventh Avenues of Zone 1. This is a good but cheap lodge which charges only $2 a day including meals. If a person only wishes to eat, each meal is 40 cents. Other *comedores* charge $2 just for a lunch.

We left Guatemala Tuesday [June 22] at 9:00 A.M., arriving in Sololá at noon. Not until we reached Panajachel did we have a good lunch of fried chicken and plenty of tortillas and beer. They charged $5, but I did not pay a cent. Rather, my friend Juan paid it all. This is all right because it has been only a short time since he left the national police [so he has the money]. But not me, I just have been losing time [campaigning and tending to party matters while Mendoza worked].

When I finally arrived home, I ached all over. All I did was go to bed, no place else.

Today [June 29] is the patron fiesta of San Martín, but I am still too ill to celebrate. During the past few days, I have taken a lot of medicine, but no injections.

On this same day those who will assume offices tomorrow in the tribunal arrived to prepare for tomorrow's transferring responsibilities. But I was feeling regretful about my new *cargo*. I am sick and broke, but I have a lot of expenses for my family. I'm not sure what I will do. But God willing, I will have to assume my duties because they are an obligation to the town.

We decided to hire a new secretary named Cornelio Demócrito Savada to replace Señor Marcos Erasmo Ramos Lorenzo. The latter has lost his job, but it is clear that he conducted himself poorly with the people: he did not like to perform marriages for the Catholics; he threatened to send the Protestants to jail in Sololá for preaching with a loudspeaker without a license; he punished many with excessive fines; and he would only work when people paid him [extra]. In short, both Protestants and Catholics had reason to vote for the official candidate [Mendoza] and they did.

On the morning of June 30, I went to the meeting at the house of the new mayor even though I had a cold and fever. At 9:00 A.M. we went to the tribunal accompanied by the *principales* of the town and a large number of neighbors. At 10:00 the ex-mayor began to transfer his many functions to the hands of the new mayor.

The ex-syndic, Antonio Cholotio Canajay, handed over to me my responsibilities—the property of the town. I received titles to the following:

    1. the *sitio* of the municipality;
    2. the *sitio* of San José's School of Rodolfo Juan García;
    3. the *sitio* of the town's general cemetery;

4. the plot of undeveloped land owned by the town;
5. the *sitio* of the school of the *aldea* Tzarayá;
6. the *sitio* of the school of the *aldea* Patzilín;
7. the *sitio* of the general cemetery of Patzilín;
8. the *sitio* of the school of the *aldea* Pachichaj;
9. the *sitio* of the general cemetery of Pachichaj;
10. the *sitio* where a new school will be built in the *aldea* Patzilín.

They also gave me the tools that belong to the town, and each was in good order.

But the town's finances were not properly accounted for. The unseated mayor, syndic and treasurer (secretary) had difficulty handling the town's money. They have not acted according to the rules. That is, the mayor and syndic gave the departing secretary a quantity of $832 as an indemnification but without the authorization of the superiority. We have to investigate what has happened to this money, and it is possible that we will initiate a suit against these señores.

After the responsibilities were turned over to the new officers, the old officials left for their houses. At the same moment Señor Marcos Erasmo Ramos Lorenzo departed from San José. His family had left the day before. When the señor left, most of the townspeople were very content.

❧ The Corporation Initiates a Suit against the Ex-secretary
JULY 23, 1976

The municipal corporation had me authorize an economic suit against the ex-secretary for not having paid the rent for the house he lived in for 60 months. At $15 a month, he owed $900.

I went with the new mayor, Juan Mendoza, and secretary Cornelio Savada to Sololá to initiate a claim against Señor Marcos Ramos. But I don't know if it is possible for this señor to pay the quantity of $900. The señor lawyer with whom we consulted told me that there is no prison for debtors. All that we could do is seize his house or some other property like land that has some value. Because the señor lawyer would be prejudiced, I thought it was better to drop the suit. But my companions are going to oblige me to complete it.

ᘯCelebrating a Municipal Mass Acción de Gracias
AUGUST 1, 1976

On this Sunday the municipality celebrated a mass *Acción de Gracias* [thanksgiving], and the new tribunal had its first corporate lunch. After mass we went to an unoccupied house to prepare lunch. For $6 we bought 15 pounds of beef. We also purchased potatoes, *guisquiles* [a climbing plant whose fruit is the size of an orange], and a little liquor. The fishermen gave us 20 pounds of fish and crabs. In total we spent about $20, but this was for the entire corporation, including the guards and *alguaciles*.

After lunch, the mayor and all the *concejales* left for San Jorge on a special official commission to check on a piece of property belonging to the ex-secretary that they might be able to seize if he neglects to pay the $900 for back rent.

In the afternoon I took a launch to Panajachel to work with Dr. Sexton who had arrived again from the United States. In the evening we ate at *El Cisne* [The Swan Restaurant].

I was sleeping [in the house that Sexton was renting] in Panajachel when I was dreaming at 3:00 A.M. I dreamed that I was swimming in the lake, but the lake was immense with a very blue bottom. But I was not in the middle of the lake. I'm not sure of the meaning of this dream, but some say that dreaming of swimming in a lake means good luck. I don't know if this is true; I will wait and see if it is.

> *When Ignacio wrote about this dream, I asked him to clarify the interpretation, and he replied that dreaming of swimming in dirty water means bad luck or illness.*

At 4:30 A.M. I had another dream. I dreamed that the deceased Señora Ignacia Mendoza, the mayor's mother, who has been dead for 22 days, was walking through a street near her house in San José. She was holding hands with her husband and her son Pablo Mendoza. Then a fast-moving bus appeared, and suddenly the dead woman walked in front of it. Then the bus stopped moving, and it did not go anywhere. I am not sure what this dream means.

We woke up this morning [Friday, August 6] at 3:30 A.M. to catch the launch to San José. I did not sleep at all last night because some señores [who were vacationing from El Salvador] in an adjacent bungalow on the beach made a ruckus.

After a quick breakfast, my friend Jaime Sexton and I arrived at the pier to take the launch, but by the time we got there it had already left. We thought the launch might have been late so we waited until dawn. When it did not show, we went back to the house.

The launch returned to Panajachel at 7:20 A.M. This means it must have left about 3:00 A.M. apparently to beat any competition for passengers. The owner agreed to make an express trip for $20 [the normal fare is 40 cents].

We arrived in San José at 8:30 A.M. Then we went to the school to interview the fifth and sixth grades. The teacher received us well, and after the interviews *profesor* Petrona gave Dr. Sexton some school data [attendance records by grade, sex, age, and ethnicity]. We got the same information from *profesores* Isabel, Guido, and Juana.

At 11:00 A.M. we went together to greet the señor mayor who gave us the keys to the municipal cemetery. My friend Jaime and I visited Felipe's grave, and Jaime took some pictures.

After lunch I went with Señor Jaime to visit the Cujil Cavern where in earlier times the shamans had made ceremonies [like the one for Ignacio when he was a dancer]. They still make ceremonies there but not very often because most of the shamans nowadays are too old to negotiate the rather difficult climb up the hill to the cavern.

In the afternoon the doctor took a picture of my family. Then we went to the pier to wait for the returning launch from Panajachel.

When I arrived at the municipality at 4:00 P.M., after Don Jaime had caught the launch, the tribunal told me about a luncheon planned for Saturday for the mayors of San Martín, San Diego, San Luis, San Jorge, and San Benito. I told them that I would not be able to attend because I had to work. The truth is that I did not want to go because such a luncheon would be a great [unnecessary] expense for San José.

The next day, Saturday, they all went to lunch at Cerro de Chuitinamit [a hill on the bank of the lake], but I did not accompany them. In the afternoon, when I went back to my duties as syndic, the tribunal scolded me for not having lunch with them. But I am not guilty of anything.

☙A Visit to the Cofradía Maximón
AUGUST 8, 1976

This Sunday morning Señor Luciano Manuel Estrada arrived at my house from Santa Rosa la Laguna to offer me a *cuadrilla* for the coast. I told him I did not have the money to advance the people, but I agreed to go if I could borrow enough. For the moment I gave this poor boy $5 because he was in dire need of money. But he signed an IOU for it.

After talking with Luciano, I went to Lucas Mendoza at the meat shop to see if he would lend me money. Señor Lucas responded that he would like to see me make the trip but that he could not lend me any money because I still owed him. This made me sad, and I am not sure whether I will be able to take the crew to the coast.

When I left Señor Mendoza, I met Señor Ruben Flores Tziac. He invited me to a beer so we went into a bar. Other friends arrived and offered more wine and rum. I didn't want anymore to drink so what we did was to take a bottle of aguardiente to the *cofradía* Maximón. We gave a drink to Maximón and to Señor Ruben, the shaman. Señor Ruben said, "You need to offer a drink to the other [image of San Simón]." This is when I realized that there are two images, one seated on a chair and the other in a bed on some boards above the loft of the room.

Señor Flores was communicating with Maximón, and I asked him what kind of luck I had. The shaman responded, "You have an enemy who has bewitched you, and it is for this reason that your business deals are turning out poorly." He continued, "You have political enemies. But if you ask Don Pedro (Maximón) in a ceremony of good faith for a gift [of good luck], no one will be able to harm you." But I don't know if what the señor shaman told me is true. Moreover, I do not have money to pay for a ceremony; I can scarcely sustain my family.

Then we swallowed more drinks of liquor. We were drunk when I realized it was time to catch the launch to Panajachel to go to the house of Señor James Sexton. While Señor Ruben waited at the pier, I ran to my house to get my pages [of the diary].

The strength of the sun made me even drunker by the time I reached Don Jaime's house. I did not feel very well. I only remember that when I asked Jaime for a beer he told me no, that it was better to sleep. And I did. I did not go out again.

When Ignacio arrived at my house, he seemed extremely upset, and he was obviously quite drunk. He wanted to continue drinking, but we had planned a trip to the coast to visit some of the farms where the migrant workers from the lake worked. I wanted him to be sober the next day, so I refused him more liquor.

A Trip to the Western Coast With Señor James Sexton
AUGUST 9, 1976

I woke up at 5:00 A.M. with an extremely strong thirst. I waited for Señor Sexton to get up, and then I asked him for a gift of a Coca Cola. Not until then was my thirst quenched. Then we had coffee and prepared for our trip to the coast.

We left Panajachel at 6:00 A.M. on Rutas Mashenas, passing through Patulul and arriving at Cocales at 8:00 A.M. We only waited briefly at Cocales where we boarded a Galgos [large, streamlined bus from Guatemala City] headed for Santa Elena Río Bravo, but they charged us a lot for passage.

In Santa Elena where my friend Felipe lost his life in an accident that I wrote about earlier in my diary, Dr. Sexton took some photos of the cross we erected for Felipe [unfortunately, these did not turn out]. Afterwards, we entered the homesite of Señor Rosario Sumoza Ixtamer, who owns this place, but he was not at home. Only his two daughters were there.

Señor Sexton asked them if they would like to have their pictures taken, but they denied him. When I asked them why they didn't want their pictures taken, they answered that they did not have any money to pay for them. When I explained that the señor did not charge to take the photos, they agreed. [Ignacío later gave them prints that I sent back.]

Afterwards, we walked until we reached the junction of the roads to Mazatenango, Guatemala City, and Tiquisate. We headed in the direction of Tiquisate. [About a kilometer down the road], where there is a sign that reads 24 kilometers to Tiquisate, 55 kilometers to Semillero (the bank of the ocean [beach]), we caught a bus to Tiquisate.

We arrived about 9:15 A.M., and from Tiquisate we took a bus to the Tolimán Farm. On this farm we walked among the sheds where the *cuadrillas* live. Dr. Sexton took a lot of pictures.

It was very hot so we went to the [company] store to buy some soft drinks. While Dr. Sexton rested, I went to the farm office to ask Don Horacio, the administrator, about a *cuadrilla*. He was in the field with workers, but I was able to talk to him by radio. He told me that he did have work for the people.

We left the Tolimán Farm at noon, and we returned to Tiquisate where we had a good lunch in a nice restaurant. After lunch we waited under a tree for the next bus to Cocales.

We caught one at 2:00 P.M., but when it arrived we were unable to transfer to another bus to Panajachel. A bus was headed to
Chichicastenango, but it was full with a *cuadrilla,* and the driver
would not let us board. What we did was to walk to the junction
of the roads from Guatemala City to Lake Atitlán and wait for
another bus.

As we waited we drank some [by now hot] beers that we had
carried with us from Panajachel. Finally, at 3:30 P.M. we flagged
down a bus, the *Reina Martinera,* and we arrived in San Martín at
7:00 P.M.

From San Martín we walked directly to the house of Señor
Ruben Flores Tziac, the shaman, to ask permission to visit Don
Pedro Alvarado [Maximón]. Señor Ruben got out of bed and took us
to the house where Maximón is located. Dr. Sexton took many
photos, and afterwards he left a gift [of $1 in Maximón's pocket].

Luckily the bus was still in San José before returning to San
Martín. My friend gave me some money, and we said good-bye. He
went back to San Martín on the bus to spend the night in an inn.
[Ignacio arranged this with the owner of the new inn as we were
passing through San Martín on the bus to San José.]

A Mission to Pachichaj to Inspect a Fire
AUGUST 11, 1976

At 1:00 A.M. I was dreaming when the municipal guard arrived
to tell me of a commission to the *aldea* Pachichaj to inspect a fire.
I could not get back to sleep, and I got up at 5:00 A.M. I did not
eat breakfast. Instead, I carried some tortillas with me to eat when
I got hungry.

At 5:15 A.M. the mayor, the second *regidor,* the secretary, a
guard, and two *alguaciles* and I left. When we arrived in Pachichaj,
we went to inspect the house of José Hernández that had burned.

Señor Hernández reported that he does not have a wife
and that he had made a big fire before going to buy some tortillas at
a distant house. While he was waiting for the tortillas, a young boy
came running to tell him that his house was on fire. When the señor
returned, all he was able to save was the clothing he was wearing.

The house was five meters long and eight meters wide. Inside
were two deeds to his land, two *quintales* of corn, three bundles of
mazorca [ears of corn], two *arrobas* [50 pounds] of beans, machetes, hoes, clothing, wine glasses, and eight dozen boards. But

the señor could only blame himself because he had left his fire-place unattended.

After writing down these data, we met with the reconstruction committee and a good crowd of residents. We informed them that a new school will be built valued at 11,000 *quetzales* [equals $11,000]. The municipality of San José will contribute 3,000, CARE will give 3,000; CONACE [El Comite Nacional Pro Construcción Escuelas, The National Committee for School Construction] will provide 3,000; AID will give 11,100; and the *aldea* will only have to contribute 900 in labor. The residents were very content to hear this plan.

❧ A Trip to Panajachel to Finish Working for James Sexton
AUGUST 13–14, 1976

Today is my birthday. I was born at 11:00 P.M. on August 13, 1941. I ask God Almighty to give me more life. I am poor, but what can I do about my destiny?

I went to Panajachel today to finish working for Dr. Sexton. During the day, I took two hours off to make an official visit to the governor's office in Sololá.

On this day, Saturday [August 14], we said good-bye to my unforgettable friend Dr. James D. Sexton who left Panajachel for his country. Before catching the bus *Rutas Lima* for Guatemala City, Dr. Sexton gave me many remembrances [gifts]. He is a good person.

After he had left, I went to eat in the marketplace, and then I went to the pier. By the time I arrived at the beach, the launch had already left for San Luis. But a señor told me that in the afternoon there is another launch for San Martín.

It was raining a lot when I ate lunch in the marketplace of Panajachel. I spent most of the day on the beach thinking of Dr. James D. Sexton.

❧ The Sister of My Deceased Ex-wife Dies
AUGUST 16, 1976

The low ring of bells awoke me this Monday morning. When I got up and went to ask who had died, they told me that Señora

Vicenta Méndez Pascual, the daughter of Mario Méndez Coché and María Pascual, had fallen. This señora is the sister of my deceased ex-wife Julia Méndez.

They told me that Señora Vicenta and her baby had died in childbirth. The midwife Concepción Canajay from San Martín was still there. I stayed for two hours and made a coffin for the baby.

The funeral was at 2:00 P.M. About 50 men and a greater number of women attended. I have only known two women who have died in childbirth, but I have seen many die of common illnesses. Vicenta's mother claims that her daugher had been bewitched by her husband, Tobías Gonzáles.

They say that Señor Tobías spent his life beating his wife. She finally got tired of such abuse and separated from him, but by now she was pregnant. Vicenta's mother was convinced of the bewitching because when the baby was born, a plastic *(nylon)* bag full of dirt came out of Vicenta's womb. They believe this killed her. This is very strange, but they gave me the same account at the cemetery, and the municipal mayor confirmed that when the baby came out, a bag of earth came with it. The birth took place at 9:00 A.M. Sunday, but the señora did not die until 3:00 A.M. this morning.

Domestic Problems
AUGUST 17, 1976

After returning from a commission to measure some disputed land near Santa Ana, I discovered that my wife was crying. When I asked her what was wrong, she answered that our son Ramón Antonio had been hit in the head with a rock. He had been wounded by the son of Señor Jorge Sicay Tuc who had run for mayor and lost.

About 20 minutes later Señor Sicay's wife arrived to find out what her son had done. I spoke to her softly and ceremoniously. What we did was to carry Ramón to the health clinic where the nurse treated him.

Some of my friends told me that I should demand restitution before the mayor, but I did not wish to take any action against the boy's parents. I know very well that little boys will fight for a while, but then they will make up and play again together. We parents should not become enemies over such things. It is better to settle such problems in a peaceful manner.

Señor Jorge Sicay's wife departed very appreciatively. She probably thought I was going to the authorities, but I did not.

This morning at 8:00 A.M. [August 18] a dispute erupted in my house, but not with my wife and me. Rather, my mother claimed she lost a chicken and that it would be found in our house. When I asked her why she thought we were to blame, she answered me with very gross words, reiterating that she thought we had killed her chicken. But as God and Jesus Christ are my witnesses, this is not true. We did not commit this fault. I know that I am honorable and that I don't help myself to things that are not mine. I am poor, but not a thief.

My mother Elena said these things to me because she does not admit that I am her son. In the first place, she abandoned me when I was a baby. Now she is definitely contemptuous of me. So be it. God will support me against such slanders against my character.

∾ Imposing a Harvest Tax and Resisting Military Reserves
AUGUST 19, 1976

A *regidor* and I went to Xesucut to investigate whether Señor Mateo Jiménez of San Martín la Laguna was harvesting beans without paying a municipal tax to San José. San José has a municipal law that *Martineros* must pay San José a tax when they harvest crops in San José's jurisdiction. If *Martineros* do not pay the tax immediately, they are captured for jail, fined, and their products are seized.

It turned out that Señor Mateo had harvested two *cuerdas* of beans that produced about two *quintales* [two hundred pounds]. The señor was called before the tribunal. The mayor sentenced him and warned that if he committed the same faults again that the fine would be doubled.

When I arrived at 11:00 A.M. in the municipality, the señor commander (Brigade General Gregorio Solaves of Quiché), of the military reserves, who meet in Sololá, was in the mayor's office. The señor proposed to organize a company of military reserves (The Voluntary Company) in San José. But in my lifetime that has never been a company of military reserves in my town.

The colonel demanded that San José provide 50 persons for service in the reserves along with 50 each from San Martín, San

Jorge, and San Benito. But I don't know why the colonel needs 200 persons to form a company. I was in the army, and I know very well that a company is composed of only 167 persons including the commander.

The mayor and I explained to the colonel that we do not want to organize a unit in San José. The reason is that *Joseños* do not have the economic means. In November and December many of us *Joseños* migrate to work on the coast picking cotton. We do this to earn a little money. Also in the months of February, March, April and May most *Joseños* work on the coast in the milpa on leased land.

Furthermore, we told the colonel that all the *cargos* were gratuitious. The municipality will need in the month of January (1977) and each subsequent January, 3 *comisarios*, 9 guards, and 21 *alguaciles*. These services are important and honorable.

In addition, we told the colonel that the *cofradías* need members. These *cofrades* work a lot in town, especially during fiestas. And when someone dies, the *cofrades* manage their funerals. Moreover, Catholic Action needs catechists. All of these *cargos*, served without pay, are important to the town. We told the colonel that for these reasons we were opposed to a Voluntary Company.

But the colonel was insistent. He is determined to form a company in San José. We will have to take this problem to the señor president of the Republic.

I believe that if they organize the company in San José, it will be injurious to the town. It will create problems for fulfilling the civil offices, and it may end service in the *cofradías* and the church. It is certain that the fellows serving as reservists will not want to simultaneously serve as an officer like *alguacil* because it will cost them too much time. They will need this time for their personal work.

The colonel left very *bravo* [rude] from the tribunal. But what we told him is the truth. I will continue to write about these things, if they come to pass or not. But I pray that they do not.

❧ Examining Municipal Records Creates Problems
AUGUST 24, 1976

This morning I helped supervise a municipal order to clean the roads to San Jorge and Santa Ana and the rustic roads to the *aldeas* Tzarayá and Patzilín. I was considerate of the people working in their fields. They were appreciative and respectful, and they began to clean the section of the roads on their land.

In the afternoon, I had a little problem with the mayor and the secretary. They signed a receipt stating the municipal expenses for August totaled $239.52. When they gave the receipt to me to sign, I wrote down the totals in my notebook for my diary. But the mayor and secretary thought that I disagreed with the expenditures. This was not true. I was simply taking notes for the pages of my diary. In any case, they were mad at me all afternoon, but I don't know why. Well, that's all right with me because those who are angry want to be angry.

What contributed to their resentment was that I noted that the municipality spent $321.28 in the month of July. In other words in two months the municipality had expenditures totalling $560.80. Furthermore, the municipality sells medicine. The seller collected $161, but a little later an entry of $33 was made which means that in total the amount was $194. But the receipts for the cost of the medicine only amounted to $124, or a discrepancy of $70. Since they were the ones who bought this medicine, the mayor and the secretary had made these entries. The money from the sale of the medicine does not include municipal expenses because the money is not from the municipal treasury. Rather, it is a gift that the Ministry of Public Health provides to combat disease. The municipality is responsible for managing the medicine.

When I told the *concejal*, who guards the money well, and the mayor that in this manner we would soon obtain a complete pharmacy, there was much discussion. Finally, they became very angry with me. But I was not angry with them.

In any case, some of the things they said sounded strange for a municipality. It is my obligation as syndic to monitor municipal matters. I suspect the mayor and secretary are trying to find a way to remove me from office, not because they are my enemies, but because they know I want to do a good job for the town. For this reason, I am keeping track of what happens to the money, checking to see if there are irregularities. But it is all right with me if they remove me from my *cargo* because I realize that there will be nothing lost and nothing gained. If they are thinking this way, so be it. If I am removed, I won't be a problem to them.

Today, August 25, is my wife's birthday, but we did not have a fiesta. Since we are short of money, we only ate lunch by ourselves.

❧ The Municipality Agrees to Pay the Mayor a Salary
AUGUST 26

They summoned me to a municipal meeting at 4:00 P.M. today. We all agreed to spend $150 on a *marimba* and refreshments for students on September 15, Independence Day. We also consented to allocating $50 to help the *aldea* Tzarayá inaugurate their new school, and we concurred on a salary of $30 for the mayor. This salary was for the month of August, and it would be the first time the mayor would be paid. The session went well, and everyone was in agreement. The mayor was very content with the results.

❧ A New Celebration in Honor of the Beheading of Juan el Bautista
AUGUST 28–29, 1976

I received an invitation to participate in a new custom to celebrate the eve of the beheading of Juan el Bautista. The actual beheading is celebrated tomorrow, August 29, and it is also when the Blue and White sports club began to celebrate its anniversary.

In the procession, we first went to the *cofradía* Virgen de Concepción; next we went to the *cofradía* Santo Domingo Guzmán; and finally we went to the *cofradía* San Juan Bautista. At these *cofradías* we drank *atol* [a ritual corn meal drink] with chocolate. It was very pleasant.

On this day Sunday [August 29] I went to the portico of the church at 4:00 A.M. Many sounds filled the air—*bombas*, firecrackers, bells, and the *marimba* Alma Joseña.

At 5:00 A.M. there was Liturgy; at 7:00 A.M. Mass; at 9:00 A.M. a Patronal Mass; and at 10:00 A.M. a procession in the principal streets of the town. Although almost all the town marched in the procession, I did not go because I was a little upset from having drunk so much liquor yesterday. But I watched the procession as it passed my house.

Not many of the members of the corporation took part in the procession, but we had a municipal lunch with some drinks. It was very pleasant.

To celebrate the fifth anniversary of the Blue and White Sports Club, there was a soccer game against the Detectives of the National Police of Guatemala. I did not go to this game, but my wife went. She said that the Blue and White team lost by seven goals to three.

At 3:00 P.M. there was a basketball game among the Daughters of María of Catholic Action.

In the afternoon the mayor and the *comisario* hired a *marimba* for a *baile de convite*, that is, a disguise dance. Many boys danced. For the second time in my life I danced in the clothing of a woman, this time the woman's costume of Samayac. Others arrived in the dress of other towns. The dance was very comical, but I got tired and went home.

We had planned a comedy for the evening, but it was canceled due to insufficient number of actors.

❦ I'm the Municipal Syndic, but the Mayor Fines Me
AUGUST 30–31, 1976

I was in bed sleeping early in the morning when two drunks, Diego Cholotio Méndez and Francisco Coj Ovalle, began fighting near the door of my house that faces the street. For certain the culprit is Señor Francisco Coj O. He is always trying to insult someone. He has insulted me twice, but I paid him no mind.

This time Señor Diego Cholotio did not tolerate his insults. He struck Señor Coj, who was walking with his wife. She immediately ran to the commissariat to file a complaint. Shortly thereafter a guard came to capture Señor Cholotio Méndez, but he had already gone to his house.

When I opened my door, I saw Señor Francisco Coj Ovalle lying down with his mouth agape as if he were dead. The guard then called me to find out whether he was actually dead. But Señor Coj was faking in order to condemn Diego. Finally, he got up. Then his wife told the guard that she had asked me for help but I would not open my door. It was true that she had asked me for help, but I thought it better not to interfere because at times this can be worse [Ignacio was fined previously for getting involved in a similar squabble]. Furthermore, because the scuffle happened in the streets, it did not bother me much.

In the end Señor Francisco got up and went to his house. Since it was 3:00 A.M., I went back to bed.

Tuesday, August 31, they ordered me to the courthouse to clarify what happened early Monday morning. I reported that I could hear what was happening. Then Señora Francisco Coj accused me of not having helped her. Finally, the judge decided to have court on the matter tomorrow, Wednesday, September 1.

When Wednesday came, they summoned me again to the courthouse. When I arrived in the office of the judge (the mayor), Diego Cholotio Méndez, Francisco Coj Ovalle, and Francisco's wife were there. Once more, the señor judge asked me why I did not help when Señor Francisco Coj was attacked. I told the judge, "I do not have to witness disputes in the streets nor do I have to intervene with drunks."

Then the justice of the peace sentenced Señor Francisco Coj Ovalle and Señor Diego Cholotio Méndez each $5. But disgracefully the judge sentenced me $5 for not aiding the one who received the blow. For certain, I was in my house and the damage had been done and it was calm when I was aware of all of this.

The judge sentenced me for not having helped Señor Coj Ovalle because the judge's wife is the aunt of Señor Coj. That is to say, the judged showed much favoritism. I feel that in this case I did not commit a crime, but I did not want to argue much. I simply agreed to pay the fine. I am the municipal syndic, and they sentenced me! I understand why. As I have said earlier in my diary, from the day August 24 there was a problem between myself and the mayor and the secretary. They are trying to find ways to remove me from office. It is all right with me, but it is certain that they are committing irregularities in the municipality.

During this afternoon of the same day, I was very sick at heart for having suffered injustly this disgrace.

All the next day, I did not go anywhere for anything. I was still sick, weak of health, and downhearted.

On Friday, September 3, the mayor and secretary went to Sololá to pursue their case against the ex-secretary in the supreme court of Sololá. Many times they said that I should be the formal accuser against the secretary, but I do not think San José will gain from such a suit, and I refused. For the accuser, they named the second *regidor*. In the afternoon of the same day the people saw that I was not going to Sololá with the delegation, and the rumor got out that I had been removed from office. They claimed that I had been removed from office because I was sentenced on September 1 and because I was not acting as the formal accuser against the ex-secretary.

At 8:00 A.M. I went to the tribunal to find out whether what the people was saying was true. I greeted everyone when I entered the office. I sat in my regular place, but none would tell me anything about these matters. I realized that they did not trust me.

In the afternoon of the same day, a lot of friends came to my house to ask whether it was true that I had been removed from office. I told them that I did not understand the rumor because I had just come from the tribunal and neither the mayor nor the *concejales* mentioned anything of the sort.

❧Tribunal Affairs
SEPTEMBER 6–7, 1976

After working all day in the municipality with other members of the corporation on the coming Independence Day celebration, we had a meeting at 5:00 A.M. with the town council. At this time the council asked me whether I had been removed from office because I did not want to continue the suit against the ex-secretary. I told them:

> For me it would be very well if you dismiss me because I am not earning a salary. I will lose nothing. It would be better to continue with my [private] work. I do not have any enemies. Until now I was unaware what [rumors] the people were spreading.

Then we discussed the daily expense allowance for commissions to Sololá and Guatemala City. We raised the amount from $6 to $8 to cover transportation and lodging to Guatemala City and from $3 to $4 to Sololá.

This Tuesday morning [September 7] at 7:00 A.M. the entire corporation left for the *aldea* Tzarayá to participate in the inauguration of a modern school building. At 11:00 A.M. a representative of the governor of Sololá arrived accompanied by the engineer of CONACE and two other companions. The inauguration began at 11:20 A.M. They had decorated the stage well, and they emphasized the value of education. However, they altered the program. That is, according to the program, Señor Guilleron Putzys Alvarez, the representative of the Ministry of Education, would give the inaugural speech. Instead, Señor Gustavo Espina, the representative of the governor of Sololá, gave it. Señor Guilleron Putzys was not present.

Also, the master of ceremonies was the director of the school of the *aldea*. I don't know what was wrong with this señor, but he did not do a very good job. I'm not sure whether he was nervous or afraid, but he could not speak Spanish very well. For a person like me, not speaking well it does not matter as much, but for a teacher it is a vulgarity. There are Indians who can speak Spanish well! But I realize each man in this world has his faults; no one is perfect.

Finally, the program says that the total amount of the cost was $5,050. That is, the municipality gave $887.49; the residents of the community contributed $328.50; CARE gave $1,414.56; AID provided $752.95; and CONACE gave $1,666.95. But I added these amounts up and they totaled $5,050.45. Anyone else can determine the error when he reads it.

After the ceremonies, they gave us lunch that the committee prepared, including drinks of *cusha,* or clandestine *aguardiente.* After lunch the señores took off in their cars, and we on foot to San José.

ᕈA Vaccination and Bad Dreams
SEPTEMBER 8–9, 1976

On this date the Ministry of Public Health ordered that everyone 40 years of age and older be vaccinated against *gripe* [the flu]. They say that in San Juan Sacatepéquez, Tecpán, and Chimaltenango a lot of people have died of this disease. It is an epidemic that is scourging this region. My wife and I are not yet 40 years old, but I asked them to give us the vaccination anyway. They did. However, there are many people who are 40 and older who do not want to be vaccinated. They are ignorant! Instead of appreciating it they despise it, and not until they are sick in bed will they remember that when they had the opportunity to be vaccinated, they scorned it.

When I got up this morning [September 9], I told my wife about my dreaming. My first dream was that I took my family to the coast to earn money. In my dream, I put all of our belongings on the bus, and then my family boarded. This is when I woke up. It was 3:00 A.M. I went to sleep again, and I had another dream.

In my second dream some guards arrived at my house and began to register everything inside my house. I asked them what they were looking for, and they responded that some of my friends had accused me of having a clandestine still for *aguardiente.* It was this that the guards were searching for. Then they left my house. When I woke up it was 4:15 A.M.

I think my first dream means that I am worried about my poverty and my family needs. It indicates that I will have to suffer more months, but the time will pass, and I will be free of these worries.

My second dream indicates that certain enemies are looking for a way to make me fail, to destroy me or imprison me for slander. My enemies are not unknown. They are my municipal colleagues —the mayor and the first councilor. These señores want an incompetent syndic so that they can do what they want with the municipal treasury for their own gain. This is what my dream indicates. But, God willing, I will not fall into the hands of these men. As God is my witness, I do not want to misbehave. During the political campaign, these were my best friends, and now they are turning their backs on me. But I have a pure and clean conscience. Only if these men find me drunk will they be able to carry out their schemes. I will try to quit drinking to foil them.

My wife told me that she also had a dream. In her dream she saw Dr. James D. Sexton walking on the porch of my house. He carried his briefcase in his hand. My wife greeted him, "Good day," and then the dream ended. I believe this is a very good dream.

❧ Señora Alejandra Pantzay Is Jailed for Adultery
SEPTEMBER 11, 1976

On this day the Señora Alejandra Pantzay was jailed. They say that she went to work on the coast with her husband, Geofredo Sumosa. But this señora got involved with another man. She left Señor Geofredo, and ran off with another man.

It happened that this señora had left one of her daughters with her mother in San José. When Señora Alejandra took off with the other man, she forgot about her daughter. This prompted her mother to file a complaint in the municipality of San José.

The justice of the peace [the mayor] ordered the contractor, Andrés Tale Pérez, to bring her back to trial in San José's courthouse. Señor Andrés obeyed the order, and he brought back not only Señora Alejandra but also the man she had run away with. The judge sentenced these individuals according to the law to 40 days in jail or a $20 fine each.

I found all of this out when I went to the post office at 8:00 P.M. I asked why there were two prisoners in both jails [there are two rooms in the jail], and they told me what had happened.

⚘ Independence Day
SEPTEMBER 15, 1976

Yesterday was the second year of the young athletes' carrying the victory torch to San José. While the school children presented a play, I went to the municipal office to learn a little about using a typewriter since the secretary was not working on this day.

This morning at 8:00 A.M. all of the members of the corporation, the *principales, cofradías,* catechists, an escort of military reserves, and many townspeople, men and women, gathered before beginning the parade commemorating the anniversary of independence.

After we filed through the streets of San José, there were lectures, poems, the national anthem of Guatemala and Central America, refreshments provided by the municipality, and a soccer game. Because there wasn't enough money in the municipality to serve expensive drinks, we served *cusha,* clandestine *aguardiente,* which is cheaper.

At 4:00 P.M. a *marimba* began playing in the municipal saloon. As in times past, the members of the corporation were expected to dance with the *principales.* But it had been some years since this actually happened. The *principales* reminded the municipal mayor that this custom should be renewed, and he ordered us to go and dance with the *principales.* But not all the councilmen had the spirit to dance. Nevertheless, in a great file, with the mayor at the head and myself next and the *principales* following, we danced two tunes very contentedly. For me there was no shame. I calmly danced with the *principales.* I am scarcely a man of 36 years of age, but now I danced with the *principales!*

The *principales* proceeded to get very drunk, and at 6:00 P.M. they left, but I don't know where they went. The mayor and I did not take a single drink. Instead, we only drank Coca Cola. The *marimba* stopped playing at 9:00 P.M., and everyone went home.

⚘ A Forced Wedding and Plans to Pave San José's Streets
SEPTEMBER 24, 1976

At 5:00 A.M. I left to work with my wife's father with the understanding that I would have to leave for the municipality to attend a wedding at 2:00 P.M. We went to Xesucut where I planted 8,000 units of onions. Because we did not finish until 1:30 P.M., I arrived at 2:30 in the municipality, 30 minutes late.

The marriage did not come about because the couple wanted it. Rather, it was a punishment by the father of the girl. What happened is that the girl went too far [sexually] with her boyfriend without the knowledge of her parents. When her father found out, he got angry and filed a suit in the courthouse. He demanded that the officials marry the couple immediately to prevent the boy from abusing his daughter. After the civil marriage, they also contracted marriage in the Catholic Church.

On this same day we held a meeting to discuss stone-paving the central portion of the town. In particular the road leading to San Jorge will be stone-paved. None of the previous municipal officers cared about the welfare of the town, but we are beginning to be concerned about such matters, little by little. The stone paving will cost $900. Only part of it will be hewn stone because if the whole section were hewn stone the cost would be $1,528, which would exhaust the town treasury. The section that will not be hewn [fitted together] will be spread out [to cover more ground with fewer stones]. As the representative of the municipality, it will be my job to deal with the contractor Domingo Mendoza Sánchez.

This morning [September 25] at 5:00 A.M. I woke up after having a dream. I dreamed I was enlisted in the national police, but I don't know where the place was. But the dream was clear. When the police chief called me he said, "When it is 12:00 noon before the shift changes, all the people who are visiting here must be removed. Not a single person must be left." I answered, "At your order, my colonel," giving him a click of my heels as I had done when I was in the army. The chief replied, "I like your astuteness." Then he left, and I did what I was told. I saw in my dream that I had on the uniform and carried the revolver of the police.

I don't know what this dream means. Certainly it means something when a person dreams early in the morning. Maybe it means that perhaps someday I will be able to change my occupation or to have a business so that I may have a better life with my family.

On this Sunday [September 26] I got up feeling healthy. I considered going to clean my tomatoes in Xesucut, but finally I decided not to. Instead, I spent the whole day cleaning [rewriting] pages [of my diary] to send to Dr. Sexton. I stayed in my house all day.

❧ Thinking of My Children's Future
SEPTEMBER 28, 1976

After breakfast I took my little son Ramón Antonio to work with me in Tamalaj where I have a little coffee grove. It is just 200 *matas* [sprigs], but when the trees are big they will help me with my expenses. Because I have not had time to clean the grove, there was a lot of growth.

For the first time my little son Ramón ate lunch while working in the fields. We had tortillas and *chipilín* [wild greens]. My little son is learning about working in the fields. But I want my children to have an education so that when they are grown they will not have to live the kind of life that I have. My life is full of suffering. I am intelligent, but I don't have a sixth-grade diploma. Nowadays with a sixth-grade diploma one can get work. It is possible to get a diploma by conspiring to give the heads of the institutions $100. But I don't have this kind of money to give for a diploma because my family expenses are high.

On this same day, they began paving [the road in] the center of the town. As I said earlier it will cost $900.

❧ How the Old People Divide Their Property
OCTOBER 4, 1976

On this date Señora Julia Sánchez García arrived to talk to the tribunal, asking us to go to the house of Señora Francisca Sánchez Mendosa to help make her will. She is sick and about to die, and her children want a guarantee that no one will be upset [over dividing her property] when she dies.

When we arrived at her house, the secretary began drafting the testament. First, Señora Francisca gave a *cuerda* of land to her son Gregorio Pérez. This land is located in a place called Tzancacay. It has 32 *varas* on one side. Señora Julia Sánchez got a half-*cuerda* of land of coffee and *injertos* [soft brilliant green fruit] and avocados. In addition she will get 19 pieces of *lámina* [corrugated steel sheets for roofing] that are 7 feet long, a chest of drawers, a Navico transistor radio with two bands. Señora Enriqueta Sánchez will get 19 pieces of *lámina* that are 7 feet long, 3 awnings, a wooden bed, a grinding stone, and four chickens. Two daughters, Lucía Sánchez and Rosa Méndez Sánchez, were not present. Each of them was given a half-*cuerda* of land (the homesite land).

The Señora Francisca Sánchez said that she did not have any money to give to her children because she had spent it all to get her grandson out of jail. All she has left is $10 to buy candles (light) when God calls her. She also has $20 to pay the priest for her funeral. The two daughters to whom she gave the *lámina* cannot have them until she dies because they are not new pieces but the old pieces that are on the roof of her house. After her death, the daughters will be able to destroy the house and take the tin and adobe.

Señora Francisca recommended that her three children who were present not make a fuss when she dies and that they avoid all kinds of drunkenness. They all agreed. Before we left, they gave each of us a beer.

❧ Celebrating a Birth and Worrying Over Alcoholism
OCTOBER 7, 1976

At 7:00 P.M. Señor Fernando Jorge Méndez came to my house to ask me to accompany him to San Martín to fetch the midwife Concepción Canajay, who is famous in San Martín and San José. Señor Fernando's wife was in labor so we walked very fast even though the road was slippery from the rain.

When we arrived at the house of the midwife, we discovered that she had gone with other persons. And we had to wait for a half hour.

We did not get back to San José until 9:00 P.M. We didn't wait long. By 9:05 the baby was born. The baby's mother is María Concepción Ramos Yojcom, who is my wife's sister.

The rain continued until midnight. When it let up, we escorted the midwife home to San Martín. When we were returning, we entered a bar. Fernando offered me some drinks. I certainly drank a lot without realizing what was happening to me.

When we arrived in San José we continued to drink. It is the custom of almost all the people to drink until inebriated when a new baby is born. And this is what we did. We drank until morning, and we got good and drunk.

I don't know why, but these days I am drinking a lot of alcohol. I drink regularly and in greater quantities. I think I am an alcoholic. A day after getting drunk, my muscles are calmed. Then I am not able to get to sleep because of nervousness. I feel my health is not as good as it was before. God willing, I am going to search for a cure for myself [from drinking so much].

☙Introduction to Alcoholics Anonymous
OCTOBER 9, 1976

At 8:00 A.M. they called me to the municipality to go measure a piece of land owned by Roberto Jacobo Pantzay. A *Martinero* has been encroaching on his land according to his deed dated in 1924. With my measurement Señor Roberto could identify his land very well, and he was quite satisfied.

After measuring his land, we returned to the municipality. But I was still sick—weak of health and nervous, a little afraid.

At 11:00 A.M. we went to Chuitinamit near the beach where we had invited officials of the supreme court of Sololá for a lunch. Before our lunch of fish broth and beef, they gave me some cups of whiskey. These caused me to lose my fear and calmed my nerves. But after awhile, when the effects of the drink wore off, the fear and nervousness seized me again. I wanted to drink more, but my wife advised me not to, warning that the same thing would happen again tomorrow. I continued to tremble.

At 7:00 P.M. of the same day the corporation received a special invitation from the group of Alcoholics Anonymous of San José la Laguna. This was a public meeting to be held in the parochial saloon.

Because the municipal mayor had to attend a baptism in San Martín, he could not go to the meeting of Alcoholics Anonymous in the Catholic Church. Thus I went in his place. The mayor did not realize I was suffering from alcoholism.

The meeting began at 8:30 P.M. The members related grave experiences that they had suffered because of alcohol. This touched me, but I could not join them because the claws of *aguardiente* had me well in their grip and I would just be defeated. Nevertheless, at this moment I thought that one day I will be a member of this group. In this instance, however, it was certain that what I could think mainly about was just another drink! My throat was parched! Finally, at the end of the meeting they gave us a cup of chocolate with bread. I did not want chocolate, but I certainly wanted liquor.

When I arrived home, my wife told me to sleep. I tried but I could not sleep at all. I suffered all night!

This is how the morning [October 10] dawned. I went to the lake to bathe, but I still was unable to control myself. I have not had a drink yet, but I don't know how I am going to cure myself of this sickness.

At 9:00 A.M. they called me to the municipality to announce the new municipal and religious officers for the year 1977. The new *comisarios, guardias* [guards], *alguaciles, fiscales* [heads, treasurers, of the Catholic church], *mayordomos* and *chajales* [unpaid servants of the Catholic church] were named. This all made the day very pleasant.

A municipal lunch of stew was prepared, and when it was ready we all entered the municipal saloon. Then the *comisarios* took out their bottles of *aguardiente* and began to dispatch cups of liquor to the councilmen. The *marimba* was playing pleasantly, and the mayor bought more liquor for everyone.

I don't remember who gave me a cup of liquor in the late afternoon, but I took it. Afterwards I took another. And then I continued drinking. When the *marimba* stopped playing, my companions and I went to a bar to drink wine because a bottle of wine is cheap. It only cost 50 cents. I didn't return to my house until 2:00 A.M.

I Join Alcoholics Anonymous San José la Laguna
OCTOBER 11, 1976

Because I have dire needs for my family, I worked all day today for another person. But my work as a day-laborer was not peaceful.

In the night of this Monday, I was thinking it would be better to join the great society of Alcoholics Anonymous, and my wife encouraged me.

I went alone to the house where the group San José la Laguna gathered. When I arrived, the boys were already meeting, but they welcomed me to join them.

I believe that if I continue drinking I will one day be lying in the streets. The town has chosen me as municipal syndic, but I have this bad drinking habit. And it [my drinking] is not proper. I have noted in my diary that I continue to drink, but I am drinking more than ever since I have become a member of the municipal corporation. God willing, and with the helping hands of Alcoholics Anonymous, I am going to recover from this illness.

On this day [October 14] Geraldo Ujpán Sánchez had a civil marriage. This brother of mine changed his religion to the Assembly of God church (a Protestant church) because, like me, he had been drinking too much. He was involved in drunkenness before, but now he is not. It was for this reason that he decided to change his religion. God willing, all will go well for him.

~ Caritas of Guatemala
OCTOBER 19, 1976

Today I worked all day with another laborer transporting bundles of avocados for my wife's father. We picked and carried 2,355 avocados. It was heavy and tiring work, but sometimes one has to suffer to earn a little.

In the night a señor from San Luis came to San José. On behalf of Caritas of Guatemala [an aid organization of the Catholic church], he invited us to form small groups of agriculturalists and to organize a small industry of typical woven goods. He told us that the money was solicited from the country of Canada on behalf of Caritas of Guatemala. He had a formula for lending money with interest of three percent anually, which is very favorable for us poor people. He said that the money was only for the departments of Guatemala.

First the women organized a group called Las Tamajales. But I don't know how much money they gave to each member. Then the men, including myself, organized a group called Los San Joseños. Our solicitation for money will be for growing onions. The señor said that he will discuss later how much money he will lend us.

The señor from San Luis is named Domingo. The president of the women is named Señora María Luisa Coché. The president of the men is Señor Marcos Ramos Pop. But the real directors of this organization are the priests of San Luis [who have organized similar cooperatives there].

Today [October 20] there is a notice in the town that a man from San Luis was devoured by a jaguar. Because San Luis is not far from San José, this alarmed some *Joseños*. They worried that the animal might come to San José through the mountains between the two towns perhaps to devour a *Joseño*. I don't know whether the notice is true, but it is posted also in San Martín. And there is fear of this beast in San José.

Because today marks the day of the October Revolution in 1944, there was a fair in the municipality. But it did not bother me to clean tomatoes for someone else instead of celebrating.

In the night of October 23, the municipal corporation held a general town meeting to sign a petition protesting the organization of a voluntary company of military reserves. The document outlined all the [personnel] needs of the municipality [as stated earlier in the diary]. One hundred and fifty *Joseños* signed the petition to present to the señor constitutional president of the Republic of Guatemala. The signatures of the municipal corporation were at the head of the petition.

𝒞 A Visit to the Pangolita Farm
OCTOBER 26, 1976

This morning I caught a bus to the Pangolita Farm. The administrator of the farm, Don Esteban del Aguila, was surprised to see me because it had been seven months since I have been to this farm. He said, "Some of your assistants said that you are not able to continue contracting because you are working in the municipality with a salary of $70 a month."

"It is true that I am in the municipality, but it is gratuitous service," I answered. He wasn't convinced until I showed him my credentials of identification. I told him, furthermore, that my assistants were lying because they wanted to bring *cuadrillas* to this farm themselves. They wanted to get the contracts. Finally, the administrator said that he always had me in mind and that I could bring a *cuadrilla* to begin work on November 5. Immediately afterwards, I went to greet other friends on this farm.

𝒞 A Boy From Santa Bárbara Drowns; Maximón's Celebration
OCTOBER 28, 1976

About noon I was on my way to water my onion seedlings when my friend Jorge Ixtamer Lavarencho interrupted me. "Ignacio," he said, "the mayor and the secretary are running to take a body from the lake. A boy from Santa Bárbara has drowned."

"Let's go see," I replied.

"No," answered Jorge, "they can send me to Sololá to take the body."

But I convinced him, and we went to the place where the boy had fallen. By the time we arrived, they had already pulled him from the water and laid him on the sand until boards could be brought for carrying him to the municipality.

The deceased boy's father, Julián Dionisio Canajay, was shocked, but he gave the following account. They had arrived in this place about 8:00 A.M. with two laborers to pick green *jocotes* [a fruit] to take home to ripen in time for the San Martín Fiesta on November 11. After lunch they began to pick more *jocotes,* but then the laborers asked permission to bathe. He gave them permission, and his son went with them. After the two laborers jumped in the water, one of them began to drown. The boy, Nicolás Maximiliano, saw him drowning and jumped in to try to save him. But the boy did not use good sense, and he suddenly disappeared. The laborer said that when he was drowning a *Joseño* jumped in and saved him. He had wanted to save the boy, too, but by the time the man got back into the water to get him, the boy was already dead. He was not moving! The man was afraid that he would be held responsible for the boy's death so he put his clothes back on and ran off and hid.

This was the information that the father provided. Geraldo Ujpán Sánchez and Ricardo Canajay, two commissaries, pulled the body out of the water. The mayor named eight boys to go to San Martín to rent a large canoe to escort the body to Sololá for an autopsy.

When we arrived at the municipality at 1:00 P.M. with the deceased, the father had completely lost control of himself. He had abandoned the bundles of *jocotes* and his animals. When I asked the name of his wife, he told me Petrona Dionisio Sánchez. Then I sent a telegram asking her and his family to come and accompany the father of the deceased.

Later the father tried to find a coffin to buy in San José, but he could not. I commissioned myself to find a box providing the father would pay for it. For the moment, the señor had no money so the secretary provided some money. Then two friends and I ran to San Martín and bought a box for $15 from the carpenter Pancho Monroy.

By the time we returned at 4:00 P.M., the family of the deceased had arrived. There was a lot of crying. At 5:00 P.M. they left with the body for Sololá even though the *Xocomil* [wind] was very strong.

The name of the place where the boy drowned is Chuachoj. It is the same place where Emilio Lavarenzo died only two years ago.

There was much talk in the town about the drowning. Some believe that the bad hour took him; others claim that the owner [goddess] of the lake called the spirit of Nicolás Maximiliano for service; yet others declared that Maximón drowned him. Those who believe that Maximón took the boy's life do so because today, October 28, is the fiesta of Maximón. Those who are celebrating in Maximón's house are the shamans. But many of us think that it was just the boy's destiny or his carelessness. He did not exercise good sense.

At 6:00 P.M. *profesor* Carlos Cano Arbenz invited the corporation to attend the closure of the school. After the invitation some of us in the corporation decided to hire a *marimba* to enliven the act of the students' receiving their certificates and diplomas.

A lot of people came to witness the school-closing ceremonies. But only the mayor, secretary and myself represented the corporation. The closure was very pleasant.

We were leaving the school at 10:30 P.M. when Señor Eduardo Flores Tziac, owner of the *cofradía* Maximón met us. He led us very contentedly to the *cofradía*. When we arrived at the house, they gave us a bench to sit on. Then Señor Flores opened a bottle of Ron Botran Rum, but the mayor and I did not accept the liquor. When the señor realized that we did not want to drink, he gave us sodas instead. The mayor and I only stayed a half-hour and left. But I decided to return to observe what was happening for my diary.

There were many people in this house. The *cofradía* was well adorned. On the altar of Maximón there were 14 large *veladores* [large containers of wax candles], four large candles about 10 pounds each, and several small candles. Also, there was a lot of incense and myrrh. Each moment Señor Eduardo Flores made reverence, asking for money and riches. He told those who were present that if they would ask Don Pedro, he would give them whatever they wished.

Suddenly a great tremor chased everyone outside, and only Don Pedro remained inside the house. I went running to my house to make sure that my family was okay. Many people scattered from their houses, but the fright finally passed.

Gradually, the people began to return to the *cofradía*. I sat in the corridor of the house, and soon the municipal mayor joined me.

At 1:00 A.M., they brought down the image of Maximón which was in the loft. Señor Ruben Flores told members of the Ajcac brothers' *marimba* to play an hour of *son* [popular music in 6/8 time in which couples dance apart, or unembraced]. This was for Don Pedro to say good-bye to the fiesta. Then Señor Flores put Don Pedro on his back and began to dance on the patio of his house. Then the brother who is called Eduardo began to burn incense and explode *bombas*. After the dance they came back inside and climbed up to the loft to put the smaller image of Maximón on the rafters.

It was very cold, and I was very sleepy. I wanted to see the
finish of the fiesta, but I did not have the stamina. I fell asleep. I left
for my house at 2:00 A.M. without having had a single drink. For this
reason, I .emembered everything that happened before I fell asleep.

There was a lot of drunkenness, and many people made re-
quests of Maximón. One man named Tobías Savala Soto, who is the
first *concejal* of the municipality, made a request. His wife died
about six years ago, and he asked Maximón to provide him with
another wife. Señor Flores answered that yes in six months or later,
this man is going to have another woman.

But I believe that it is not necessary to make a ceremony to
find another woman. Finding a woman depends on one's deportment; if one is a good worker women will notice. But if a man only
drinks, he can't support a family. Or if he is rude in his home or
miserable with his loved ones, it is difficult to find a woman to
marry. This is the case of Señor Tobías Savala Soto. When his
woman was alive, he always was fighting with her. Each time he
drank, he beat her. And the other women realize this. So he has not
been able to find another wife. I am quite certain that Tobías Savala
Soto will not find another woman in six months. What the shaman
told him is a lie. He only did it to get the señor to give him money.
Not until I see Señor Tobías get a wife within six months will I
believe that the shamans have some ability [power].

Also, during the night they made a bewitching against Señor
Erasmo Coché Morales. They say that Erasmo mistreated Señor
Eduardo Flores, saying nasty things to him. Señor Eduardo asked
Maximón to make Erasmo Morales die within six months of an
attack of illness that no one can cure.

But I do not believe Erasmo will die because of this witchcraft. If it is his luck or destiny, he may die before six months are up,
but it will not be because another person is able to change the life
of someone else. These are the things I witnessed during the night.

What happened on the following day, October 29, is that the
second shaman, Ruben Flores Tziac, woke up in jail for having
beaten his woman. They say he struck her very hard. But she did
not just endure it. Rather, she made a complaint to the commissary.
Señor Ruben was sentenced $5 or ten days in jail. When he got
over his violent mood, he immediately paid the fine [rather than
remain in jail].

I do not understand these things about shamans. During the
main part of the fiesta, they claimed that Maximón provides riches
and prevents persecution from others. But because he was negli-

gent, Señor Ruben went to jail. These are the real shamans, and they are the ones who fall first.

Today [October 30] they published in the Catholic Church the names of all the persons who visited the Maximón *cofradía* last night. They say that a lot of people went to look at the list during the day, but I did not go until nighttime. There were a lot of people there then.

During today's sermon of the mass, the priest Jorge Rodríquez read a list of the people who were at the fiesta, including myself, and declared that all those who had gone to this *cofradía* could not rely on the church and did not have the right to receive communion in mass. Furthermore, if someone died in a family of one of these persons, they would have to pay laborers to bury their dead. Now the church would not provide *cofrades* for this service.

There was a lot of uproar in the whole town! A number of my dear Catholics were mistreating me and others. True, I went to this house out of curiosity to see how they perform the ceremonies so that I could write a few pages in my diary about them. But I did not go because I am a shaman or I have a commitment to this association. I feel that I am very free. I can go to the fiestas if I want to. No person is able to constrict my behavior. The priest and the director impose strict orders, but they have their motives.

The whole town realizes that the señor director of the church, Juan Bizarro Gómez, imposes his orders that are not in conformity with the Bible. Since this señor wants to run a town, he should first govern his own family as a model. This is no lie. This señor has two sons, Heberto and Bernardo, who are drunk most of the time. They don't work, and sometimes they carry things too far—they hit their papa with stick and stones. Many times they have landed in jail. For this reason, we have told Don Juan that he cannot be the director of the church because he has two boys who are drunks. The Bible says that he who wants to govern a church first has to govern his own family because in no manner is a person able to govern a church if he is not able to govern his own family. In no way can a blind man guide other blind men.

And there were a lot of other problems. The first *principal* of the town, Señor Gómez Ujpán, was visiting Maximón. Because of this, the priest and the director eliminated his *cargo*. In addition they say that this *anciano* [respected elder] does not have the right to continue in the church. At the same time they decided that when Señor Gómez dies, the *cofradías* and Catholic Action are not going to bury him.

Such actions serve no purpose because those who gave the order may die before he does. Or it may be that Señor Gómez Ujpán will die somewhere else. The proverb is true, *"Uno pone pero Dios dispone"* [one proposes but God disposes]. I don't understand what is happening to those of the church. Rather than loving one's fellow man as the first commandment dictates, they believe they are judges. They are not following God's wishes in every way. They are not doing their duty. Instead, they have conspired to do the contrary. I don't know what they are doing each day in the church, but they are walking in darkness.

It happened, furthermore, that Señor Lucas Ujpán García was named the new secretary of Catholic Action on October 10. He was to assume office on January 1, 1977. But this señor worked as a member of the Ajcac brother's *marimba*. The priest and the director of the church told him that he will not be able to take possession of his office and that he was banned from church for at least six months.

But they did not tell me how long it will be until I will be able to go to church again. To me it makes no difference—to go to church or not to go. One can worship God anywhere. Wherever one chooses to be, God is there too. One can obtain grace but through love. What good is it to be in church daily if I don't love my fellow man? If this were the case, I would be in church only for myself. To me it is fine to go to church but only with faith and with love. This is what a good Christian should do.

❧ The Day of San Andrés
NOVEMBER 30, 1976

Today a mass was celebrated for the municipal corporation by Father Jorge H. Rodríquez. It is the day of San Andrés the Apostle. They say that San Andrés is the chief of the mayors, and for this reason they venerate him on this day.

About 20 years ago, this image had its *cofradía* with its *alcalde* [head]. The municipal mayor was obliged to prepare a *cofradía* of San Andrés. In those times if the mayor did not have his own house, he had to look for a house to rent in order to receive the saint. Also, during those times, they guarded the four staffs [symbols of authority]—the staffs of the mayor, the syndic, the first *regidor,* and the auxiliary mayor. The first *alguacil* had to go every morning at 7:00 A.M. to take the staffs out to the tribunal and return them to the *cofradía* in the afternoons. He had to remain in the *cofradía* all day Sundays.

Also, in those days they had a *secreto seguro* [a sure, secret or occult act]. When the municipality lacked funds to pay the secretary, they fastened the four staffs with a chain and put them at the feet of the image of San Andrés. They did this when there were a lot of family disputes. If they created a big disturbance, they had to go to the courthouse to be sentenced with a fine. They quit using the staffs when the municipality began to get a regular source of money. Because the municipality has a good treasury, they don't use the *secretos* anymore.

But the mayor still venerates the image of San Andrés because he still considers him the superior of the mayors even though the image is fastened to the church. The image does not go to the house of the mayor.

On this day, the señor mayor was not here in the municipality. He had to go to Guatemala City to bring *lámina* for the residents. Nevertheless, everything was done that the mayor ordered to honor San Andrés. At 9:00 A.M. a mass was celebrated in the Catholic Church by the priest Jorge Rodríquez; at noon we had a municipal lunch of meat, crabs and fish. But it happened that the councilmen and *alguaciles* began to drink, and after getting drunk they began to fight one another. A lot of people saw them fighting, and they set a poor example before the town. They continued their drinking and fighting in the bars.

In the night when the mayor returned with four trucks of *lámina,* all of the councilmen and *alguaciles* were drunk. Only I helped the fellows unload the trucks. I did not want to tell the mayor how badly the councilmen had behaved. It gave me much pain. I did not get to sleep until 2:00 A.M.

On this day, December 1, I was very tired from having unloaded the *lámina*. At 8:00 A.M. I arrived again at the municipality to apportion the sheet metal according to the names and the number of sheets each had paid for. In one day we gave out 2,560 sheets of *lámina* to 125 persons, including some persons from San Martín. Although the sheet metal was intended for poor people, we gave out many pieces to rich persons. This is because more of the wealthy had the money to pay for them in advance. Many don't have any *lámina*. There are faults with the program, but that's the way it is.

In this business the señor mayor earned a large profit of about $900 in two days. Those of us in the council helped [with the distribution], but the earnings went only to the mayor and the secretary. But I did not want to operate with the señor mayor. It was enough that I knew about his behavior. I have a list of all the people who took the sheet metal. Some took enough for four or five houses. Because the price of the *lámina* was only $3 each, a lot of it was sold. I am sure that the sheet metal came from the Committee for the Reconstruction of Guatemala. I know very well that the señor mayor requested it from the National Committee of Reconstruction of Guatemala, and now this is a business for them.

୧୬I Fall Into the Lake
DECEMBER 3, 1976

On this date I went to Sololá to certify [send by certified mail] 72 pages for my good friend James D. Sexton. They charged me $2.02 for postage. Also I bought some things for the municipality—two floor mats, two wooden chairs, and some brooms. On the return trip, I had a very pleasant chat with some North Americans who got off in San Martín.

When the launch arrived in San José, all the people began to disembark. Then I tried to step over the place on the launch where they store the cargo. I pulled myself over onto the dock, but the planks were very old and could not support me. Two sheets of the pier broke, and what happened, unfortunately, I fell to the bottom of the lake with all the things I was carrying. The people tried to help me, but they could not. I had to struggle to the bank. All of my papers got wet, and the bread that I was carrying for my children fell into the water.

Many people were shouting when I left. My children were waiting for me at the beach. For them it was good laugh. Many people told me that I should take some medicine for *susto* [a rather serious psychological illness of fear, or fright]. But if I took medicine for *susto*, I would not feel anything. The only thing that I suffered was a blow to the ribs.

I did not think about taking medicine for *susto*, but what I did consider was bad. I thought about putting the finishing touches on the pier—to buy some gallons of gasoline and set it afire and put an end to this [ancient] pier! But eventually I decided not to dirty my hands. And there is a saying, *"El que mal hace mal espera"* [he who commits evil will meet evil]. I do feel ashamed that a lot of people saw it happen.

When I arrived at my house, I changed my clothes and went to the municipality to deliver the things that I had bought. When I told my companions what happened, they ordered *aguardiente* to drink. But I did not want to drink. Everyone else did, however, and they became quite drunk. This is how the afternoon passed.

All night long I slept very peacefully, without any pain. One person told me that now I would not be able to sleep well because of *susto*. It was a lie. I slept well!

❧The Fiesta of Virgen Concepción
DECEMBER 8, 1976

This day is the fiesta of María Concepción. This *cofradía* had a big fiesta. The municipality prepared a lunch of meat, fish and crabs but no *aguardiente*. It was a very nice lunch.

In the afternoon the *cofradía* invited the corporation to accompany the [image of] Virgen Concepción to her new *cofradía* [house]. We did. They gave us a lot of *atol*, ritual corn meal, to drink. Many people were there.

❧A Commission to Identify San José's Boundaries
DECEMBER 9, 1976

At 6:00 A.M. I left with the mayor and other commissioners to investigate the landmarks identifying the boundaries of San José. The señor mayor claims that San José has communal land that has been lost to the Santo Tomás Farm and the Tuc Brothers of the *aldea* Pachichaj. He says that he is going to reclaim this land and redistribute it to the people of San José.

On this trip, two señores left with us as guides. They are Señores Clemente Coché Pantzan and Martín Navichoc. They say that these men know the place well. But the first day before entering the mountains the Señor Clemente Coché P. took sick and had to return to San José. I am not convinced he returned because of illness. Rather, I think this man did not know where the landmarks were, and he became sick in order not be become frustrated.

First we arrived in a place called Panpotix. They say that there are many jaguars in these parts. We searched for the landmark that indicates the boundary between San Martín and San José, but it was impossible to find it.

Then, at a rapid pace, we continued on to a place called Chi-nimayá. After eating lunch there, we worked very hard cleaning the growth with machetes to find a landmark. But it was impossible to locate one here too. At 3:00 P.M. we finally found a stone that some were convinced was a landmark. But I was uncertain. The title of the land indicated that it was farther on. Nevertheless, for the sake of my companions, I said it was okay. We were all trembling with cold, and there was no water to drink.

We decided to return. It was very strenuous until we reached a place called Pachichiyut where there are two *ranchos* [little sheds] for workers. There we made coffee and heated the tortillas we carried with us. The señor mayor sent the *alguaciles* to purchase a liter of clandestine *aguardiente* to chase away the cold. When they returned from the *aldea* Patzilín, which was about five kilo-meters away, my friends and the councilmen drank to keep warm. But instead of drinking, I made more coffee and ate the bread that I carried from home. And the fire that we made helped to chase the cold away a little.

At 5:00 A.M. [December 10] we heated up our tortillas for breakfast, and at 6:00 A.M. we headed for the boundary between San José and the Los Angeles Farm. We walked in the mountains until we reached the Naranjo River where we had lunch. It was too wet to start a fire so we ate cold, two-day-old tortillas. Again, it was impossible to locate a landmark. Finally, we began looking for a negotiable route to return. There were many hills and barrancas.

It is true that there is land in these parts that is unoccupied. But who knows whether it belongs to San José or to the Tuc Broth-ers of Pachichaj who own great expanses of land? The Tuc Brothers say that the title of their land is adjacent to the Naranjo River, and if what they say is true San José does not have any communal land here as some of the old folks claim. For this reason, there is much doubt about the boundaries. It will be necessary for an engineer to make measurements to determine whether the town has communal land in these places.

It is true that Señor Martín Navichoc went with us, but he did not know where the boundaries of the town were located. This man told us that he and other *Joseños* accompanied the engineer Carlos Vela in 1914 when the boundaries of the town were made. According to the government report, it is true that the boundaries were drawn in 1914 for San José, San Luis, part of the department of Totonicapán, Santa Apolonia, Samayac, and San Jorge. But this Señor Martín is a liar because he did not know anything about the boundaries. Furthermore, in the mountains I had the opportunity to examine secretly the *cédula* [government identification card] of

Señor Martín Navichoc. He was born on December 15, 1912. The measurements were made in the year 1914. That is to say, when the boundaries were drawn up, he was only two years old. He is not able to give testimony about such matters. It never pays to lie because lies are always discovered.

It will cost a lot of time and money to fight for these lands. It will be a great problem with the señor farm owners and with the Tuc brothers. I believe the dispute will be in court two or three years. It will not be possible for the mayor to redistribute the land to the people of San José. It is a pity that the mayor does not have the intelligence to think clearly. I will continue to write about how this all turns out.

❧I Am Offered a Bribe Over Land Boundaries
DECEMBER 20, 1976

Together with the third *regidor* and some guards, I went on a commission to Patzilín to investigate a dispute over the boundaries of the land belonging to Señor Ricardo Sicay Hernández and Señor Domingo Có Pérez. The title of Señor Domingo mentions only 20 *cuerdas*, but we measured 23 *cuerdas* in a place called Pustla. Señor Ricardo's title read 20 *cuerdas*, but when we measured it, there were only 17. In other words, Señor Domingo had extended onto the property of Señor Ricardo. As municipal syndic, I convinced them of these facts.

These men were very content with my actions as municipal syndic. First Señor Ricardo invited us to lunch in his house. Before going to eat, he gave many drinks to my companions, but not to me. When we left the house of Señor Ricardo Sicay Hernández, Señor Domingo Có Pérez was waiting to invite us to his house to eat. But we had already eaten. Nevertheless, so that he would not feel slighted, we went to eat a little more at Señor Domingo's house. While we were in his house, he offered me $20 if I would not give my report to the señor municipal mayor about the three extra *cuerdas* that actually were on Señor Ricardo's property. But I did not accept this money.

❧Enjoying the Holidays More without Drinking
DECEMBER 24–31, 1976

On this Christmas Eve, I represented the municipality when the *cofrades* took the images of their *cofradías* to the church. This would be for those celebrating Christmas in the church. The councilmen provided a *marimba* and took part in a comical (masked) dance.

At noon the mayor invited us to his house to have tamales, chocolate and bread. They served a lot of Ron Botran Rum.

Afterwards we returned to the municipality, and then the commissary invited us to his house. We ate more tamales, and my companions drank plenty more drinks.

At 2:00 A.M. my companions and I went to the bar of Señora Rosalia where they threw a great drunken party. They began to talk about sensitive topics, and little by little a fight erupted. They tried to kill the first *regidor* with a kitchen knife. Fortunately, in the bar were three friends of mine—Ruben, Santiago and Domingo. They helped me separate the men who were fighting. I helped Jorge, the third *regidor* home, and then I went home. The others stayed drinking in the bar.

When I arrived at my house, my wife was very happy to see me sober. I also felt good about my not drinking when I realized what had happened between the drunks. The day passed very tranquilly. The only problem was that our baby was sick with vomiting and diarrhea.

All day New Year's Eve I worked in the municipality making arrangements to receive the new year. At 8:00 P.M., while the *marimba* was playing, the *alguaciles* and the commissary began calling on the new *alguaciles*, commissaries, and guards. At 12:00 midnight all of the assigned men will assume their duties. The señor secretary gave the departing officers his customary recommendations. They said good-bye with such affection that they cried with happiness, and they began to drink a lot of liquor. The mayor and the councilmen ended up very drunk. But because I have a problem with liquor, I did not want to drink.

I was invited to eat tamales at the house of my good friend Ruben Flores. I was given chocolate with bread and tamales. It was very pleasant. My friend Ruben and his wife had a beer, and they offered me one, but I still refused to drink. They drank their beers. I did eat a lot.

I am realizing that it is much better not to drink because one is more aware of all the nice things that happen if one is not drunk. But before, when I was not a member of Alcoholics Anonymous, the thing of most importance to me was a drink. Without a drink, I did not feel the spirit of the fiesta. Now I am realizing it is beautiful not to drink. It is certain that the first drink is the key to the rest.

Without the first drink there is no drunkenness. It is not that I am against *aguardiente*. For the persons who are able to drink small quantities, who do not create great drunken parties passing the night away drinking, as I have done in the past, *aguardiente* is okay.

❧ The Mayor Holds a General Town Meeting
JANUARY 7, 1977

At 8:00 P.M. the mayor headed a general town meeting in the municipal saloon. The mayor announced that because the corporation and town had fought against a voluntary company of military reserves in San José, the company would not be formed in the town. But a reserve unit will be organized in San Martín and San Benito. The townspeople were happy to be free of such an obligation.

The second point that the mayor made is that the representative, *profesor* Fernando Tesaquic Toom, is going to give San José a Motorola, transmission radio with which to communicate with other towns. This pleased the townspeople very much. But I'm not sure this señor will carry out his promise because I realize well that señor politicians offer gifts, and then they fail to provide them.

The third point that the mayor brought up was the action of *INCAP* [Nutritional Institute of Central America and Panama]. INCAP wants to work three years in this town. Some residents are for it while others are against it. It is certain that the señor mayor does not want INCAP here. He accuses it of being communistic. Also there is a problem concerning INCAP and the Center for Public Health. INCAP wants to operate alone, and it asked that the small health center be closed. Those who are opposed to INCAP do not want the public health center to be closed because it is important to the poor people. They argue one will have to pay for medical consultations with INCAP, and it will only be here for three years. When INCAP leaves, the town will have the expense of establishing another health center. One group of residents argue that both INCAP and the Center for Public Health should operate. But INCAP does not want this; it wants to work by itself. So these citizens want to notify INCAP that they want it to work in San José but with the condition that the public health post will not be closed.

A fourth point that the mayor made is that in a few days Cáritas of Guatemala will give food to the malnourished children of one to two years of age. The person to ask about these measures is Cristina Mendoza, the nurse at the health center. The citizens were very appreciative.

The last point the mayor brought up was the problem of the boundaries of the communal land adjacent to the Los Angeles Farm. The mayor said that it would be necessary for the citizens to go and check the boundaries. Señor Don Domingo Tuc García said that it is best to check the boundaries, but the farm owners should be notified to prevent a problem. But the corporation has already sent the owners notice. I took a list of 27 citizens who are going to make a trip on January 10. The Señor Principal Don Antonio Ramos Cholotio said that he knows the boundaries, but because he is 70 years old, he is too old to make the trip.

◡Another Trip to Inspect the Boundaries
JANUARY 10, 1977

At 7:00 A.M. eight members of the corporation and 50 citizens more than those on the list, left San José. The mayor rented a horse to mount, but all the rest of us walked.

We arrived at the Santo Tomás Farm at 1:00 P.M., but we did not get to talk to the administrator of the farm until 9:00 P.M. All afternoon I studied the title of the town. I was doubtful whether this trip would be worthwhile.

The administrator received us politely and gave us a house to sleep in. We got up early in the morning and made our breakfast around many fires. After coffee and tortillas, we left for the mountains.

At 9:00 A.M. we arrived at a hillock where the farm guides showed us the point of a landmark of stone. In an opening of more or less 50 meters of a plantation of cinchona bark there was a great marked stone. As we walked to the east, the stone was on our left. About 150 meters more we found another landmark of cement posted as the property of the Patzicía and Santo Tomás Farms.

We rested at 9:00 A.M. because the road is very tiring. At 11:00 A.M. we arrived at the summit. It is a towering point where one can see the great [Pacific] coast. We reached the top but we could not pass. But we were able to see the landmark where we had gone in December.

We began to descend by a different route so that we could search for the landmarks of the Los Angeles Farm. We stopped at 11:45 A.M. to eat a lunch of two-day-old, cold tortillas. There was a lot of firewood, but the mayor forbade us to burn it because the mountains were very dry and we could start a forest fire. Instead of fresh water, we had to drink dirty water from a river. After lunch, we cut a path to a bank of coffee trees on the Santo Tomás Farm. The descent was very difficult.

From the Santo Tomás Farm, we walked two kilometers to a bridge over the Naranjo River. Some of the men were too tired to continue, so they remained behind to guard our packs. It took us an hour to walk from the bridge to the landmark. The stone that the guides showed us was definite. It has two painted crosses. Still doubting the farm owners, the mayor wanted to see other landmarks. However, I understand the title. One can see well the landmarks that we have been shown on the map. But one cannot see the landmarks the mayor is talking about. What the mayor says does not conform to the title to the land.

I felt it was better to remain *colado* [traditional but immodest Indian personality] because to talk more with these men is to waste one's breath. It's very clear that the stones we saw before lunch are not on the map. The real landmarks are about 10 kilometers farther. But the stones that we were shown afterwards are indeed in concert with the map. The señor mayor is foolish. He is trying to obtain a great quantity of land that does not belong to the town. But this is not a good thing. One does not know how it will turn out.

In reality it is a great problem that the municipality is creating with the señor farm owners and with the Tuc Brothers. The citizens are very content to hear the mayor say that he is going to divide the land up and give it to them. More than 200 of them have given him money for this land. I believe the townspeople are foolish to give away their money. It benefits the mayor. I am realizing that the señor mayor is very *mordelón* [an authority who takes bribes to break the law]. What he wants is to have a lot of money. It is not important whether things come out good or bad. I believe the mayor is deceiving. He is not able to give out land. An engineer will have to measure the boundaries, and it will not be easy to do. In any case to get the Tuc Brothers to give up the land will require a suit of three or four years.

I am thinking of resigning from the municipality. I don't want to be enemies of the Tuc Brothers. They are my good friends. I don't want people to think badly of me. It is certain that the mayor's behavior is undesirable.

Also, I am the director of the Partido Institucional Democrático. If I begin to fight over land, many will think the party wants to gain land. They will desert me and go over to the other party. I don't want to blemish the prestige of the PID. It is better to be free of [municipal] politics. It is true that the party does not give me money or anything. But I want to stay in good standing with the higher directors because sometimes they give me good advice. And I want to keep it that way. For these reasons, I no longer wish to remain a member of the municipal corporation.

I will continue to write about the things that are happening in the town.

℘I Resign From the Corporation
JANUARY 24, 1977

During the day at the municipality we had problems with the mayor and the secretary. It made me feel bad. It is better for me to resign from this *cargo* rather than to have problems without gaining a single cent. It is impossible to continue in this post.

At 7:00 P.M. I presented my irrevocable renouncement before the señor mayor. The rest of my friends became very sad. They did not want me to leave the municipality. But as far as I was concerned, it was impossible to continue an hour longer. I said good-bye to the corporation.

Then I went home. It is a pity that my companions on the council went to drink liquor. But I was very happy. With a friend, my wife made dinner, but we did not have liquor.

The townspeople said that I left the municipality because of incapacity or something else. It is certain that I resigned. I am capable of carrying the *cargo* of municipal syndic, but I don't like the behavior of the mayor. In order for one in authority to be respected, he must respect others. It seems that other councilmen may resign. I will see how these things turn out, and I will write about them [in my diary].

℘The Fiesta of San Jorge
JANUARY 25, 1977

My family and I went to watch a little of the fiesta of San Jorge. Before leaving I had to water my tomato patch on the bank of the lake. My wife went ahead with the little ones on the bus. My friend Pablo and I took a bath, and set out afoot.

I arrived at 12:00 noon. When I found my family, we had lunch. We enjoyed the fiesta awhile, and then we went home. My wife and my children and I were very happy without drinking a single beer. Thanks to God I am sober. I used to be a person who thought that a fiesta most of all meant to drink. These days I am thinking a little better than I did before.

I would like to say a little about the fiesta of San Jorge which is celebrated January 25 of each year. It is the titular fiesta of the town. There is a curious thing, although some do not believe it. But it is true. Many people visit San Jorge from other towns like San José and San Martín. But most of the people go to make great drunken parties. This includes men and women—only to drink alcoholic drinks! And when the people from other towns are good and drunk, or, better said, when the people of other towns lose control, they commence to take them prisoner in the jail so that on the second day of the fiesta they have a great fine. This is so that the money that *Jorgeños* spend in the municipality on the fiesta can be recovered. They do this customarily. Each fiesta in San Jorge results in 25 to 30 persons in jail. The prisoners include *Joseños*. In this town it is not necessary that one commit a fault. It is only necessary to be drunk to get carried to jail.

The same thing does not happen in San José or in San Martín. There are fiestas in which not a single person gets put in jail. Each town has its own customs! Nowadays, the boys are very careful not to drink in San Jorge!

A Custom With Candles
FEBRUARY 2, 1977

At 4:00 A.M. the bells and drums commenced to sound which is the custom for the fiesta of the Virgen de Candelaria. It is when Lent begins.

On this date, there is a custom that I don't think I have written about before. All of the people go to church with 5- to 25-cent candles to have them blessed in the church. They save these candles and guard them well. They light them when there is a death in the family or when someone is sick or when there is a persecution in the house. That is what these candles are for. Year after year the people carry these candles to the priest for his blessing. This is certain. One can ask any *Joseño* to confirm it.

❧Remembering the Victims of the February 4 Earthquake
FEBRUARY 3–4, 1977

At 5:00 P.M. a Holy Mass was celebrated in the church by the priest, Jorge. The mass is for the souls of our loved ones who died on the fourth of February of last year. It is to remember them. The sacrifice was intended for tomorrow, but the priest was summoned to Sololá by the bishop so he performed the mass a day early. I went to witness the mass.

During the night I went to San Martín to look for a truck to take a *cuadrilla* to the coast. The owner was returning with a truck from the coast so I had to wait. As I waited I chatted with a contractor named Santiago García Estrada. He showed me a notebook in which he had entered an amount of money that he had become indebted for—$1,500. He had lost this on *cuadrillas*. It certainly costs to be a contractor. Sometimes one loses a lot of money. I have lost money, too, but God willing I will settle my debt so that I will not stand in bad stead with the lender. I told Señor García that I had lost money, too, but to him my debt was small and just a laugh.

On this day [February 4] my family and I thanked God for the year that we have continued to live. It has been a year since many of my Guatemalan sisters and brothers lost their lives. And many have remained without their families. For a year now the rest of us Guatemalans have been sleeping well. But during the earthquake, many did not get up; they left forever. But that is life. It is written that sometimes we go to sleep and we do not wake up. But I ask the Almighty that the souls of all my sisters and brothers rest in peace and that God take care of them forever.

At 11:00 A.M. we left San Martín for Chicacao with a *cuadrilla*. We took a very steep road. It is hardly negotiable, but we had to do it to avoid the police. They are pestering the drivers a lot. They say that Gaspar Vásquez, a truck driver, was thrown in jail in San Diego la Laguna for transporting a *cuadrilla*. This is the reason that we went by another road.

We did not eat lunch until we arrived in Cocales at 5:00 P.M. By 8:00 P.M. we were at the Pangolita Farm. I stayed, checking on the crew, until February 10. Then I returned to San José.

Reference Material

❧Notes

1. Like numerous other Latin American Indians, Ignacio is partially assimilated to an Hispanic culture, but he is not necessarily representative of everyone in his community or culture in every respect in a statistical sense. Unlike central figures of other life histories, Ignacio is neither famous nor psychotic. As an ordinary working man, he is more common than a political figure of high office or a well-known shaman. Abandoned at birth by his parents, his childhood was hard. Despite his third-grade education, Ignacio is exceptionally perceptive, and he gives a keenly insightful account of his eventful life.

In previous research, random samples of *Joseños* and Maya Indians in 13 other towns (919 household heads) were gathered. These data clearly show that Ignacio is both alike and different from his countrymen with regard to socioeconomic and psychological characteristics.

Like his countrymen who are also Indians, Ignacio speaks a Mayan language and shares a cultural tradition that is mixed with both Mayan and Spanish elements. Like numerous other countrymen he is socially and economically oppressed compared with richer Ladinos and Spaniards in Guatemala and compared with citizens of more economically developed countries.

Ignacio has been more exposed to the outside world through formal education, military service and travel than the average *Joseño*. He writes and speaks Spanish fluently, and he is teaching himself to type. Also, he is more exposed to radio, films, and television and to newspapers, magazines and books. His superior literacy and greater political knowledge are due to his greater exposure.

Ignacio seems somewhat more oriented toward change than most other *Joseños*. He appears dissatisfied with his life condition; he has high occupational aspirations for himself and his children. Ignacio would have preferred to have been a teacher rather than a farmer and labor contractor. And he would like his son to become a pharmacist, but believes he will have to be a chauffeur. Whenever financially possible, Ignacio believes in putting off his rewards to a later date, deferring his gratification.

Like other *Joseños* Ignacio believes that a person's life is relatively fixed at birth; that it is better to accept things as they happen because a person is not able to shape his own future; and that whether one has good or bad luck depends on one's heritage. But such fatalism may be the result of realistically assessing his limited environment rather than an inherent mental block to change. Ignacio still believes that one should perform ceremonies before harvesting and planting; that there are spirits who may taunt people during the night; and that some people, particularly shamans, can change into their animal form, or *nagual*. Thus, elements of Ignacio's nonmaterial culture are changing more slowly than aspects of his material culture.

2. I should add that I stayed as close as possible to Ignacio's own words to retain his patterns of speech, but grammatical and stylistic concerns dictated a liberal translation. All but a few of the subtitles in the text were added by me. The exceptions are the episodes about Ignacio's life in the military; an engineer's boat sinking in the lake; San Jose's getting electricity; and a mayor's unwittingly signing his own resignation. I first added the subtitles to help me determine what events were repetitive. Because they tend to give the narrative more structure and serve as mini-themes, I have decided to leave them in the book. Since Ignacio's words usually speak clearly for themselves, even to the nonspecialist, I have avoided lacing the text with unnecessary anthropological jargon and explanations.

3. Certainly such writing is not just retrospection, and to the best of my knowledge is not falsification. I have checked as many historical dates as possible, and they are remarkably accurate. What few distortions there are in Ignacio's story arise from his idiosyncratic way of perceiving his life and the events that shape it. No two people would view the same experience in exactly the same manner, and Ignacio has lived just one life. Not all of that life has been lived, and some of his views may change.

Even in anthropological research, it is somewhat unusual for a native to open up his or her life history to an outsider. While I do not believe Ignacio has been intentionally dishonest in reporting his life, one can raise a legitimate question as to what motivated him to interact with me over such a long period of time. It has been suggested that well-adjusted informants may be motivated primarily for money and thus not give sincere accounts. I have always paid Ignacio more than the going wage in highland Guatemala for the time he expends on his life story, but like other subjects of other life histories, Ignacio seems grateful to the anthropologist who shows friendly interest in him. Considering the rather harsh socioeconomic environment in which Ignacio lives, he is, in my opinion, exceptionally well-adjusted. Like others who keep diaries, he seems to use his personal record keeping as a vehicle to express both his joys and sorrows.

4. These statistics are based on the population three years of age or older who speak an Indian language as their mother tongue. Unfortunately, the 1964 Guatemalan census does not list aboriginal languages or the number of Indian-language speakers. Nevertheless, based on the 1964 census, Stewart (1981:6) reports that there are 520,000 speakers of Quiché; 271,000 speakers of Cakchiquel; and 42,000 speakers of Tzutuhil. The 1973 census did not list the aboriginal languages or the number of Indian-language speakers.

5. In the socialistic regimes of the early 1950s labor organizations were beginning to penetrate beyond the large farms such as the United Fruit Company (now the United Brands Company). Their advances were frozen when President Jacobo Arbenz was overthrown in 1954 with the backing of the United States through the Central Intelligence Agency. The role of the U.S. in this controversy has been debated. Defenders point out that the U.S. was in the midst of a cold war with the Soviet Union in which there was a genuine fear of the spread of Communism in the Free World. Furthermore, they argue that the openly socialistic government was stockpiling military arms from the Soviet Union and was responsible for countless mutilations, tortures, and murders. Opposers claim that the U.S. was simply intervening in the internal affairs of a sovereign Latin American republic for selfish economic interests.

Whatever the motive or ethical implications, the result was the same. Colonel Carlos Castillo Armas directed a force of 300 rebels from Tegucigalpa, Honduras, which succeeded in ousting the Arbenz regime. First Castillo, then Gen. Miguel Ydígoras Fuentes became President. Ydígoras' government proved to be corrupt and bloody and was consequently plagued with many internal disturbances. A favorite tactic he employed to quell dissent was to declare a state of *sitio* (siege) which was a kind of martial law. Such was the case during demonstrations against the Guatemalan government in Guatemala City and other urban centers for allowing the U.S. to train Cuban expatriates at an army base in Retalhuleu for the Bay of Pigs invasion, which turned out to be an embarrassing fiasco.

6. In 1899 several U.S. owned fruit companies merged into the United Fruit Company, making use of the lowlands of Central America for farming. In 1906 they began to develop banana plantations in the lower part of Río Motagua. Puerto Barrios became a a banana port with special banana-loading docks. Since the mosquito had been identified as the carrier of malaria, it was practically exterminated around the plantation.

The company built a railroad from Puerto Barrios to Guatemala City and then to the Pacific port of San José. By the 1930s the plantations in Motagua Valley were fighting the Panama disease which attacks the roots of the banana plant and the Sigatoka disease which attacks the leaves. The company decided to shift plantations to the Pacific side of Guatemala. By 1956 a new plantation at Tiquisate was equipped with an overhead spray system for the control of banana disease. The Tiquisate bananas were shipped by rail to Puerto Barrios from San José. The overhead spray system proved to be expensive. Although crop dusting is cheaper and just as effective, the company managed to develop several varieties of disease-resistant bananas, and the chief area of banana producing once again became the lower valley of the Motagua. The company closed Tiquisate plantation in 1964 and made it available to the government of Guatemala for farm colonization.

Some Guatemalan producers are still in Tiquisate and Retalhuleu, but now mostly cotton is grown in this area. Less than 100 bales were produced in 1950 but by 1964 over a million bales were grown. Eighty percent of the cotton is bought by Japan.

Another important product is meat, which is produced by feeding cattle on planted pastures on the coast. Much of the meat goes to the U.S. (West and Augelli 1966:398; James 1969:139–140).

7. On November 13, 1960, President Ydígoras declared a state of siege when disaffected military officers led an armed rebellion in the Zacapa-Puerto Barrios area. Ydígoras crushed the disturbance with his air force (*New York Times*, November 14, 1960).

After the Bay of Pigs invasion of Cuba failed in April 1961, Ydígoras called a state of siege to quiet the demonstrations by students and workers against his letting the U.S. train Cuban exiles at Retalhuleu for the ill-fated invasion. Some demonstrators no doubt remembered the role of the U.S. in 1954 in toppling the socialist regime, but others feared the Cuban government might retaliate against Guatemala. Ydígoras was able to capitalize on this fear by claiming that social unrest was inspired from Cuban based communists.

The states of siege that Ignacio participated in came on the heels of another state of siege that had been implemented after demonstrations against the Cuban invasion (Rodríquez 1965:32). When the chief of secret police Ranulfo Gonzáles Ovalle was assassinated (Kennedy 1971:163) on January 24, 1962, another state of siege was declared. The assassination came right after students had demonstrated in December 1961 against alleged election frauds (Graham 1960:62). This state of siege was renewed for an additional month in February and another month in March. Thus Ignacio and his company were in a state of siege from January to March while stationed at Retalhuleu.

During this period, on February 6, 1962, a guerilla operation made a raid on the United Fruit Company's installation in Bananera taking an $18,000 payroll, food, arms and ammunition. They attacked a nearby garrison and executed its commanding officer (*New York Times*, February 16, 1962). Such activity must have reinforced the fear of invasion by Cuban Communists which Ydígoras fostered, perhaps to mask deeper economic problems in his presidency (Kennedy 1971:33).

President Ydígoras' last declaration of a state of siege was only three days old when he was forced out of office. The exiled Juan José Arévalo, who had helped engineer the junta that overthrew the dictator General Ubico in 1944 and who had become president from 1945 to 1951, had slipped back into Guatemala. There was rumor that he would run for president in 1963, and, of course, Ydígoras branded him a communist since it was his administration that gave the Communists a foothold in Guatemala. But Arévalo became an idol of Guatemalan university students (Rosenthal

1962:31). When Ydígoras began making wholesale arrests in search of Arévalo, the Guatemalan Army acted by arresting Ydígoras and sending him into exile in Nicaragua with his wife. Col. Enrique Peralta Azurdia, the Minister of Defense, was made the new chief executive.

8. These offices are appropriately called *cargos*, or burdens, since they can be quite expensive both in time lost from working and money spent on food and drink during celebrations. Those who accept the *cargos*, and in the past the penalty for not accepting could have been incarceration, may actually go into debt for several years to pay off the expenses incurred. Often they are not much more than free of their debt when they are asked to serve again. Ignacio estimated that this *cargo* cost him some $40 for the year, which at that time was equivalent to about three and one-half months of full time work.

9. *Traje* (native dress) is brilliantly colored and beautifully embroidered. It is made from cotton thread on a backstrap loom in the home. A tie-and-dye method applied to thread before weaving gives shirts a checkered appearance. The traditional uniform for *Joseños* is a white shirt, white *calzones* (knee-length trousers without a front opening or belt loops), red *banda* (men's wide belts), black top coat, and sandals. The traditional costume for *Joseñas* is red and white vertically striped *huipiles* (blouses) with solid red embroidery around the neck, dark navy blue *cortes* (wraparound, ankle-length skirts), and navy blue and brown *rebozos* (shawls).

　　Today in San José, many men wear *traje* similar to that worn by neighboring *Martineros*. The man's shirt has a design of narrow vertical stripes of green, blue, yellow, and red which have black (tie-and-dye) horizontal stripes giving the shirt a checkered effect. The new *calzones* are white with vertical broken-line blue stripes. Sometimes there are embroidered animals of various colors encircling the bottom of the legs. Many women in San José have adopted a generalized *corte* (standard patterns made on footlooms from Totonicapán). Nearly all men wear cowboy-style hats, usually straw but sometimes felt, and with narrow brims.

10. In 1970 I recorded in my field notes that a key informant stated that during the Presidency of Cabrera, San José was reduced to about 12 families. Although this is not the same number as reported to Ignacio by his old informant, it validates that only a few families were left. My key informant also said that widows who could not work on the *fincas* (farms) were allowed to stay in San José, but that they were forced to pay taxes in the form of corn, eggs, chickens, and beans. The same informant stated that the richer *Martineros* were able to pay bribes to the *alcaldes* (mayors) and department officials to avoid being sent to the coast to work. There are many versions of what actually happened, but most agree that the *Joseños* lost a good portion of their best land to the *Martineros*. *Martineros* accuse the *Joseños* of squandering their money on their traditional celebrations with little foresight to their future economic needs. Furthermore, the *Martineros* claim to have bought the land from the *Joseños* legitimately. Nevertheless, in 1925 an *alcalde*, Domingo Yojcom, of San José was suspected of irregularities on behalf of the *Martineros*, and he was assassinated with a knife by one of his enemies (thought to be a *Joseño*). The end

result is that *Joseños* feel as if they have been economic victims of the encroaching *Martineros.*

11. Because this was a time when there was quite a campaign led by the national government against drugs and hippies, Ignacio's friends were understandably concerned that his gringo friends might have given him marijuana, which, of course, had not been the case. In the summer of 1975, police raided a new nightclub in Panajachel named *Tio Pepe's* (Uncle Pepe's) and confiscated drugs. Both patrons and owners were jailed, and the event was recorded in the national newspaper, *El Gráfico,* with a headline, *"Drogas en Panajachel"* (Drugs in Panajachel).

12. Ignacio reported that there are various ways that sorcerers bewitch others including the following: performing magic over hair or clothing; placing a photograph between two boards, weighing it down with rocks and throwing it into the lake to sink; and burning black candles to send death to a victim.

13. According to key informants, in 1958 there was only a narrow footpath the two kilometers from San José to San Martín. A crew of *Joseños* working each day for three years cut out manually a dirt road wide enough for motor vehicles to pass. As of 1980 it was still bumpy and unpaved, and periodically the town officials order *Joseños* to help clear it of debris and weeds.
    In 1970 I recorded in my field notes that a key informant stated that about 70 years ago petty infractions of the law such as not cleaning the streets when ordered (and fighting and stealing) could be punished by public whippings. Twelve lashes would be delivered by the *mayor* (which used to be the *alguacil,* or policeman) for each infraction. Second offenders could receive 24 lashes, third offenders 36 lashes and so on. The severity of the blows, I was told, depended on the *mayor* and the *alcalde,* the latter able to order the blows harder. The jail was used for only serious crimes such as murder or drunkenness or refusing to pay a fine.

14. The Center for Public Health was established by the government in 1972. Before this date there was only an eye clinic staffed by a medic. In 1980 there still was no resident doctor in San José.

15. At this time the director of the church was Juan Bizarro Gómez, the brother of Ignacio's grandmother. He was higher in the church hierarchy than the president, being only below the priest from San Martín. According to Ignacio, he knew a lot about the church, and he was about 70 years old at this time. When he gives classes, even the catechists attend, but it is the catechists who teach the doctrine of the Catholic Church including such prayers as *El Padre Nuestro* (Our Father, Lord's Prayer), *El Ave María* (the Ave María), *El Cree en Dios Padre* (He Believes in God the Father), and *La Confesión General* (the General Confession). Mainly they teach the children these prayers.

16. In the summer of 1975 I discussed with Ignacio the earthquakes around Lake Atitlán (six months before the February 4 earthquake).

Ignacio stated that the people of San José do not feel the earthquakes caused by the San Luis volcano. He said that the people on the coast feel them. But when there is an eruption in Antigua by the volcano *El Fuego* (The Fire), *Joseños* feel the tremors caused by it. He said that he didn't know why this phenomenon exists, only that when there is a quake caused by the volcano San Martín or the volcano San Luis, the people on the coast feel it, but the people right next to it say they do not. Ignacio continued to report correctly that only the volcano San Luis is active and that the volcanoes Martín and San Diego are inactive. Furthermore, *Joseños are able* to see smoke coming out of the San Luis Volcano when it erupts. Ignacio said that the tremors are felt periodically but that he could not remember the exact date of the last one.

17. There are four species of small fish in Lake Atitlán in addition to crabs. Black bass were introduced into the lake, but they fed on the crabs and small fish to the extent that the latter have practically disappeared (Orellana 1975).

18. Unlike San José, some homes in San Martín already had electricity at this time. The inauguration in San Martín was for the new electrical outlets.

19. In San Luis *Maximón's* image is supposed to be able to drink liquor and smoke cigars.

20. A new monthly newspaper in Panajachel, *El Xocomil* (February 1976:1, March 1976:1), reported that the vehicle was a Rébuli bus that had been parked over the concrete boating ramp at the public beach in Panajachel. The driver and three passengers were drowned when the earthquake caused the bus to plunge into 18 meters of water. A crane that was being used by construction workers to build a new hotel, *Hotel Camino Real*, pulled it out on February 11.

21. *Time* magazine (February 23, 1976:26) reported that 19,000 were dead; 66,000 wounded; and at least 1,000,000 homeless. After the first major quake, which lasted 39 seconds, over 800 smaller after-shocks were recorded. Considering Guatemala's relatively small population (about 6 million), *Time* estimated that comparable damage in the U.S. would have been 672,000 killed and 37 million homeless. By August of 1976 the number of dead had climbed to 22,915, and the number of wounded reached 77,310 (Dirección General de Estadísticas 1976).

22. The old public pier was severely damaged by the quake, and the launch might not have been able to dock there because of it.

23. The four political parties are not always aligned in the same manner as in the local 1976 elections. For example, in June of 1979 President Laugerud was succeeded by General Romeo Lucas García who was the candidate for the ruling PID and its ally the PR. The other candidates were General Enrique Peralta Azurdia for the MLN and General Ricardo Peralta Méndez for the PDC (Crawley 1979:154).

✒Appendix: Discussion of Major Themes

In the Background to the Story, I outlined five major themes abstracted from Ignacio's life history that help us better understand a different people in a different environment. These include: (1) family and community solidarity; (2) grinding poverty; (3) reliance on drink during moods of elation and depression; (4) recurrent illness; and (5) sensitivity to agents of change. What follows is an expansion of these significant themes.

Family and Community Solidarity

One example of the way in which Ignacio and the people of San José demonstrate family and community solidarity is that they teach their children to speak Tzutuhil Maya as their mother tongue. Spanish is learned as a second language, usually beginning in primary school. For these people, who share a common heritage and subculture, the Mayan language serves to reinforce a strong sense of identity among them. Ignacio and other *Joseños* are flattered when outsiders attempt to speak a few words in Tzutuhil, and they are impressed when someone is fluent.

Many men and some women have adopted Ladino, or Western, clothing styles because wearing machine-made clothing is cheaper and more comfortable and it helps them avoid ethnic discrimination. But Ignacio and many other *Joseños* believe that their typical clothing is prettier. Although Ignacio and his sons tend to wear Ladino clothing, his wife and daughters mix store-bought blouses with hand-woven, wraparound, ankle-length skirts. Ignacio's wife, Josefa, like other *Joseños*, weaves beautiful cloth on the indigenous backstrap loom. Some *Joseños* also weave wool rugs in strikingly intricate, Mayan motifs similar to those woven by women of neighboring towns. Typical cloth and rugs may either be used in the home or sold to passers-by or owners of shops in more developed towns like Panajachel that cater to tourism.

Communal participation reinforces pride in their religious heritage and gives a sense of security in belonging to common institutions. For Ignacio and other *Joseños*, religion provides some universal functions such as explaining unfortunate events; accounting for natural disasters such as drought and earthquakes; allaying anxiety over daily concerns such as not having enough money to provide sufficiently for one's family; giving hope for a future life that will be better than the present one; and binding people together through sharing fundamentally similar supernatural beliefs.

Besides private mass and rituals, Ignacio and his fellow *Joseños* participate in the annual, public ceremonies. These include the major fiestas of the *cofradías* San José, San Juan Bautista, Virgen Concepción, and Santo Domingo Guzmán. Some also participate, either as spectators or actors, in the celebrations of the unofficial *cofradía* Maximón. In addition to these religious holidays, Ignacio and his townspeople celebrate Christmas, All Saint's Day, Lent, Holy Week, and the beheading of John the Baptist.

In local *tiendas* (small stores) a number of processed foods are appearing and in neighboring towns restaurants offer Chinese dishes and North American hamburgers. Ignacio and most other *Joseños*, however, prefer indigenous foods such as fish from the lake, wild greens, tomatoes, avocados, chicken, and especially corn, beans, and squash because they are cheaper, readily available, yet still nutritious. In fact these three common foods form a fairly well-balanced diet, with corn providing carbohydrates, oil and protein; beans providing protein; and squash providing a variety of essential viamins. But even Ignacio and other *Joseños* will consider a steady diet of just tortillas and beans monotonous.

Not only do Ignacio and other *Joseños* take pride in their language, typical arts, religion, and indigenous foods, but they tend to be exceptionally hardworking. Ignacio and other *Joseños* spend long, tiring days farming corn, beans, tomatoes, onions, and coffee with a hoe and machete. Good weather, irrigation, fertilizers and insecticides may produce bumper cash crops of onions and tomatoes which must be carried on their backs to distant markets. Such effort may be so exhausting that alcohol is needed just to kill the resulting aches and pains.

Periodically, Ignacio journeys with other *Joseños* to the coastal plantations to weed and pick cotton. Whether he goes as a picker or overseer, Ignacio must endure arduous labor in a hot, humid climate while barely subsisting on a continuous diet of tortillas and beans. There are inadequate sanitation facilities and dilapidated, overcrowded barracks for housing. Farm hands are subjected to poisonous insects and snakes and malaria-carrying mosquitos. It takes considerable grit to endure a month of contracted work. Furthermore, while the men are off working on the coast, their wives suffer more at home. Ignacio's wife, Josefa, for example, may be left in charge of tending the crops in addition to her time-consuming domestic chores. She and other *Joseños* do not enjoy the conveniences of gas or electric stoves, clothes washers and dryers, dishwashers, or even piped water inside their homes.

Just as Ignacio was enculturated to hard work as a youth, he is teaching his own children the value of industriousness so that they may survive in a rather harsh economic environment. Considering that some outsiders,

especially nonlocal Ladinos and foreigners, have stereotyped peasants to
the extremes of either taking extended midday naps under a giant cactus or
having the inhuman durability of a burro, Ignacio's account of his continuous but exhausting work is insightful. Moreover, it is noteworthy that
Indians like Ignacio, do reinforce the idea that only Indians, not Ladinos,
can do back-breaking work.

Not only are Ignacio and other *Joseños* hard-workers, but they also
tend to be generous. They help both relatives and friends with labor,
materials, or money whenever they can. Although Ignacio is honorable,
he is not sanctimonious. He has his share of both moral and physical
shortcomings. He quarrels and fights, but he shows remorse when he fails
to use proper deportment. His troubled conscience is reflected in some
disturbing dreams. More often, however, Ignacio's moral behavior is
guided by a few local proverbs and native wisdom that sometimes have
biblical bases.

Joseños like Ignacio, who exercise proper deportment, enjoy the support of large families that are bound together by blood and marriage ties.
Ignacio's grandmother was especially concerned about the childrearing
practices of Ignacio's foster parents, his aunt and uncle. Despite Ignacio's
harboring negative feelings toward his blood mother for rejecting him
as an infant and being contemptuous of him as an adult, Ignacio dutifully
helps her in time of need. The only close relative whom Ignacio deeply
resents is his real father, and for that reason he has very little to do
with him. Ignacio also helps more distant members of his family when
necessary, even when it means he may get into trouble himself for doing
so. And Ignacio does not hesitate to appeal to his relatives when he is
in need himself.

In contrast to blood and marriage relations, godparents play a much
more minor role. Ignacio rarely mentions ritual kin like the coparent of his
son José. But it is very obvious that blood and marital ties are crucial in a
small town like San José where institutions such as welfare, social security,
and insurance are absent.

Even without modern social benefit systems, Ignacio and other
Joseños are quite proud of their town. They unite against outside threats or
competition; they collectively participate in both civil and religious ceremonies. Pride and solidarity go beyond the family and immediate community. Ignacio and his townspeople not only identify strongly as Indians
and *Joseños* but also as Guatemalans. Ignacio and his friends seem ob-
sessed with international sports in which Guatemala participates. They
take part in the Independence Day celebrations either by making
patriotic speeches, reciting nationalistic poems, carrying the liberty
torch, marching in parades, playing athletic games, or just watching
all the special events.

Like Ignacio, a rather large number of men in San José have served in
the military. Such service encourages identification as Guatemalans. Some
former soldiers may consider military training a vehicle to resist unpopular
officials and governments, but others may be more tolerant of military
regimes that run the national government. In any case, patriotic, con-
scientious persons like Ignacio often find themselves struggling against

corruption in politics. Considering the successive number of dishonest, prejudiced, or incompetent persons who gain political office, it is a wonder that the sense of patriotism remains as strong as it is in San José.

Interminable, Grinding Poverty

Poverty is one of the most glaring themes to surface from Ignacio's life history. Ignacio worries over having to introduce his sons to hard work when they are still toddlers. He feels that one of the reasons he is poor is that he lacks a formal education, and he even considers bribing the officials for a counterfeit diploma. He wants his children to get a better education so that they may not be so poor. Ignacio longs for a change in his luck so that he can enjoy a better life with his family. With a growing family, he often finds himself destitute. His employment history mirrors his extreme impoverishment, and the resulting agony he feels is reflected in some of his bad dreams and sleepless nights.

As a contractor of crews for coastal *fincas,* Ignacio sometimes gains and sometimes loses. He has earned enough money to build a new house with a sheet metal roof, cement floor, and white plastered adobe walls. Although this is above average housing for San José, compared with more developed towns and more developed countries, it is rather simple. It is meagerly furnished, has no indoor plumbing, and consists of one room.

When Ignacio loses money on a bad trip to the coast due to inclement weather, mechanical failure of trucks, or a crew's simply taking his advance money and leaving before fulfilling its contact, he usually goes deeply into debt. He has owed as much as $350 to the money lenders, and these debts often must be paid with exorbitant interest. The end result is that in some years Ignacio makes a handsome profit by San José's standards, but in other years he owes an enormous amount of money. Nevertheless, because Ignacio often is desperate for cash and because he is reinforced when some trips are profitable, he continues to gamble that journeys to the coast will yield financial rewards.

Reliance on Drink

Reliance on alcohol during moods both of elation and depression is a recurrent theme. Special occasions such as births, marriages, and holidays may traditionally prompt drinking, but very often drinking becomes a mechanism to escape certain aspects of hopelessness. Quite often, when frustrated over social and economic failures, which may be attributed to witchcraft, inclement weather, bad luck, or corrupt officials, Ignacio and other *Joseños* turn to alcohol and get good and drunk. They also drink to blot out grief over sudden death of friends or loved ones.

Some alcoholics may find a cure by joining a Protestant church or a new branch of Alcoholics Anonymous. Refusing to serve in offices of the civil and religious brotherhoods eliminates some of the pressure to drink at public and private rituals. For those who are able to refrain from drinking, their physical and mental health improves; less time is lost due to hangovers; no money is squandered on alcohol; and celebrations may be more enjoyable because they are more cognizant of what is going on around them in both the good and bad sense. But, in an environment where temptation is great to drink for joy and despair, one has to exercise considerable willpower to stay sober.

Recurring Illness

Too often Ignacio and other *Joseños* face constantly recurring illness that turns out to be serious; however, many times the sickness is minor and seemingly psychosomatically induced. Because of the potential for serious illness which might under less impoverished living conditions be relatively routine, parents may become alarmed over simple illness and give sick children effusive affection and attention. When children become adults, they may regress to the behavior in childhood that brought consideration and love and that allows them to escape briefly from punishingly hard work for very little pay. A throbbing headache from hard work on hot coastal *fincas* may provide an excuse not to return to the cotton fields for just a day. A little rest may even bring refreshing sleep and satisfying dreams of more pleasant conditions.

Better work with higher pay might cure some of the seemingly psychosomatically induced illness, but in towns such as San José with inadequate medical facilities even adults may die of illness that would seem trivial in more medically advanced communities. For example, complications in childbirth are more likely to be fatal than in more developed towns. Although some families fear physicians and hospitals, many can neither afford to pay for a doctor nor the medicine he prescribes.

Sensitivity to Agents of Change

San José and other lakeside towns are experiencing rather rapid change in the form of community development. The national government is providing more government salaried positions for nurses, policemen, and teachers. Roads are being constructed, water is being piped into homes, electric outlets are being installed in houses and other buildings, and new stores and businesses are being established. Also, since the 1944 Revolution, increased religious freedom has encouraged the growth in Protestant sects and reformed Catholicism.

Ignacio is responding sensitively to shamans, military officers, farm owners, electric workers, anthropologists, priests, teachers, doctors, and politicians as well as to fellow townspeople. Depending on the conditions, he may either be critical or receptive to those who wish to preserve and those who wish to change his world. Like many other Indians, Ignacio's material culture is changing faster than his nonmaterial culture. If change agents are to be effective in promoting solutions to social and economic problems of developing communities, it is crucial to identify and understand the role of influential individuals such as Ignacio Bizarro Ujpán.

❧References Cited

Aguirre, P. Geraldo G.
    1972   *La Cruz de Nimajuyú: Historia de la Parroquia de San Pedro la Laguna*. Guatemala City: Litoguat Ltda.

Crawley, Eduardo
    1979   *Latin American Annual Review and the Caribbean*. Essex, England: World Information, Rand McNally.

De Borhegyi, Stephan F.
    1965   "Archaeological Synthesis of the Guatemalan Highlands." In *Handbook of Middle American Indians*, vol. 2, pt. 1. Robert Wauchope, general editor; Gordon R. Willey, volume editor of Archeaology of Southern Mesoamerica. Austin: University of Texas Press.

Díaz, Bernal
    1972   "Appendix II." In *An Account of the Conquest of Guatemala*. Sedley J. Mackie, ed. Boston: Milford House.

Dirección General de Estadísticas
    1973   Guatemala City, Guatemala.
    1976   Guatemala City, Guatemala.

El Gráfico
    1975   "Drogas en Panajachel," July 13:3.

El Xocomil
    1976   "Causa del Terremoto en Panajachel," February 1976:1.
    1976   "Activa Labor Desplegaron Bomberos Voluntarios Durante la Emergencia que Vive Nuestro País," March 1976:1.

Graham, David L.
    1962   "Guatemala's Shrine of Blood," Nation 2:496–97.

Hinshaw, Robert E.
   1975   *Panajachel: A Guatemalan Town in Thirty-year Perspective.*
          Pittsburgh: University of Pittsburgh Press.

James, Preston E.
   1969   *Latin America.* Fourth Edition. New York: Odyssey Press.

Kennedy, Paul P.
   1971   *The Middle Beat: A Correspondent's View of Mexico, Guate-
          mala, and El Salvador.* New York: Teacher's College Press.

Lane, Hana Umlauf
   1981   *The World Almanac of Facts 1981.* New York: Newspaper En-
          terprise Association, Inc.

McBryde, Felix C.
   1933   *Sololá: A Guatemala Town and Cakchiquel Market Center.*
          Middle American Research Institute. New Orleans: Tulane
          University.

Mendelson, E. Michael
   1967   "Ritual and Mythology." In *Handbook of Middle American
          Indians,* vol. 6. Robert Wauchope, general editor; Manning
          Nash, volume editor of Social Anthropology. Austin: Univer-
          sity of Texas Press.

Miles, S. W.
   1965   "Summary of Preconquest Ethnology of the Guatemala-
          Chiapas Highlands and Pacific Slope." In *Handbook of Middle
          American Indians,* vol. 2. Robert Wauchope, general editor;
          Gordon Willey, volume editor of Archaeology of Southern
          Mesoamerica, Part One.

Muños, Joaquín and Anna Bell Ward
   1940   *Guatemala: Ancient and Modern.* New York: The Pyramid
          Press Publishers.

Nash, Manning
   1969   "Guatemala Highlands." In *Handbook of Middle American
          Indians,* vol. 7. Robert Wauchope, general editor; Evon Z. Vogt,
          volume editor of Ethnology, Part One.

New York Times
   1960   "Guatemala Fights Revolt; State of Siege Is Imposed."
          November 14:1.

   1962   "Guatemala's President Reports Crushing of Bananera Rebels:
          Arms and Some Guerillas Captured, Statement Says—Curfew
          Eased." February 16:7.

Orellana, Sandra L.
   1975   "Folk Literature of the Tzutuhil Maya." *Anthropos* 70:840–76.

Ravicz, Robert
   1967   "Compadrinazgo." In *Handbook of Middle American Indians,*
          vol. 6. Robert Wauchope, general editor; Manning Nash, vol-
          ume editor of Social Anthropology. Austin: University of Texas
          Press.

Recinos, Adrían, Delia Goetz and Dionisio José Chonay
1953 *The Annals of the Cakchiquels and Title of the Lords of To-tonicapán.* Norman: University of Oklahoma Press.

Rodríquez, Mario
1965 *Central America.* Englewood Cliffs: Prentice-Hall, Inc.

Rosenthal, Mario
1962 *Guatemala: The Story of an Emergent Latin-American Democracy.* New York: Twayne Publishers, Inc.

Ruddle, Kenneth and Kathleen Barrows
1974 *Statistical Abstract of Latin America: 1972.* Los Angeles: Latin American Center, UCLA.

Serrano, Manuel
1970 *El Lago de Atitlán.* Colección de la Casa de la Cultura de Occidente. vol. 3. Quezaltenango, Guatemala: Tipografía Nacional.

Sexton, James D.
1978 "Protestantism and Modernization in Two Guatemalan Towns." *American Ethnologist* 5:280–302.

1979a Modernization among Cakchiquel Maya: An Analysis of Responses to Line Drawings." *Journal of Cross-Cultural Psychology* 10:173–190.

1979b "Education and Acculturation in Highland Guatemala." *Anthropology and Education Quarterly* 10:80–95.

Sexton, James D. and Clyde M. Woods
1977 "Development and Modernization among Highland Maya: A Comparative Analysis of Ten Guatemalan Towns." *Human Organization* 36:156–172.

1982 "Demography, Development and Modernization in Fourteen Highland Guatemalan Towns." In *Highland Guatemalan Historical Demography.* Christopher Lutz, Robert Carmack, and John D. Early, editors. Institute for Mesoamerican Studies, SUNY at Albany, Pub. 6, pp. 189 –202.

Stephens, John L.
1969 *Incidents of Travel in Central America, Chiapas and Yucatan,* vol. 2. New York: Dover Publications, Inc. First published in 1841 by Harper and Brothers.

Stewart, Stephen O.
1981 "Language in Guatemala: Planning and Prospects." *The Linguistic Reporter* 23:6–7.

Tax, Sol
1941 "World View and Social Relations." *American Anthropologist* 43:27–43.

Thompson, J. Eric S.
1970 *Maya History and Religion.* Norman: University of Oklahoma Press.

Time Magazine
  1976 "Guatemala: Death in the Tragic Triangle." February 23,
        Volume 107:26–27.

West, Robert C. and John P. Augelli
  1966 *Middle America: Its Lands and Peoples*. Englewood Cliffs: Pren-
        tice-Hall, Inc.

Whetten, Nathan L.
  1961 *Guatemala: The Land and People*. New Haven: Yale University
        Press.

❧Acknowledgments

I should like to express my appreciation to Ignacio and the people of Guatemala, who welcomed me as a guest in their country. Also, I should like to thank my departmental chairman, William B. Griffen, for providing me with an able Spanish translator, Teresa Kelleher, during the 1975–76 academic year at Northern Arizona University. Teresa's aid in translating a good portion of Ignacio's handwritten pages and our taped conversations was invaluable. In addition I should like to express my gratitude to my wife, Marilyn, and to the readers and editors of the University of Arizona Press, especially Patricia Shelton, for editorial suggestions.

My first two trips to Guatemala were under the auspices of the Cora Black Fund for ethnological research at the University of California at Los Angeles. During my second trip, I was a teaching assistant for a UCLA field school directed by Clyde M. Woods. Another trip was made possible by a grant from the Agency for International Development through the Latin American Center at UCLA. Trips in 1975 and 1976 were supported by Northern Arizona University. The university also funded manuscript revision and a final trip to Guatemala in 1980 to consult with Ignacio after the book had been accepted for publication.

J.D.S.

❧ Index

guaro, 26
Guatemala, 5–7, city of, 8, 10, 51,
75, 126, 131, 147, 163, 165, 167,
180–193; demography of, 5; departments of, 8
guisquiles, 186

horno, 161
Hospedaje Esquipulas, 133

identity, ethnic, 7; Ladino
culture/Indian identity, 13
incarceration, 93, 106–108, 155–
156, 162, 201, 212
indígena, 7
indio, 7
injertos, 204

jocotes, 209
jornalero, 54
juez, 14
juntos, 16, 148

Ladino, 9, 21, 84, 107, 123, 129
lámina, 204
lengua, 71
licenciado, 152
Los Pueblos del Lago de Atitlán,
70, 83, 87, 100

Mam (people), 5
mandamientos, 10, 60
marijuana, 69, 234 n. 11
marimba, 52
markets, 10, 158–159
marriage customs, 17, 33, 34, 122–
123, 142–144, 146–147, 157, 176,
179, 180, 203, 207
mayordomo, 14, 47
max, 15
mazorca, 175
Mexico: Aztecs, 6, 13; Montezuma,
6; route of Spanish invasion of
Guatemala, 6; Tenochtitlán,
6, 14

military: recruiting, 35, 93; reserves, 193–194, 208–209, 221;
service, 35–46
misterio, 167
mordelón, 223
*Movimiento de Liberación Na-
cional* (MLN), 144, 173–176,
182, 235 n. 23
mozo, 161
municipios, 8

nagual, 14
Nash, Manning, 8
national police, 143, 180–181
natural, 7
nichos, 169
Nutritional Institute of Central
America and Panama (INCAP),
221
nylon, 148, 192

papeletas, 173
Partido Democrático Cristiano
(PDC), 175–179, 182, 235 n. 23
*Partido Institucional Demo-
crático* (PID), 108, 142, 144, 169,
173–178, 182, 223, 235 n. 23
Partido Revolucionario (PR),
175–176, 179, 182, 235 n. 23
paxte del lago, 103
pilas, 63
Pipil-Nicarao, 5
Pipils, 6
pírricos, 42
Pokomam, 5
politics: boundaries, 217–219;
bribe offered, 219; conflict:
59–63, 106–107, 109–110, 115–
116, 122, 130, 192, 197–198, 206,
234 n. 13; civil offices, 207; election 1976, 144–145, 152, 156,
169, 173–188; speeches, 175,
177–179; fined by mayor, 197–
199; inauguration, 111, 235 n. 18;
mayor resigns, 114; municipal
employees records, 194–195;
secreto seguro, 215; socialism
27–28; town secretary, 156,
170–171, 179, 184–185, 198; tribunal affairs, 199–200

250 INDEX